Praise for the Book

❝ Miss Aida has written a compelling and deeply personal guide to figural candle magick that challenges assumptions and reintroduces the sacred relationship between practitioner, fire, and form. In Figural Candle Spells, she doesn't just offer techniques, she invites you into a worldview where each candle is a living conduit for transformation, healing, and communication with the spiritual realms. Her initial skepticism, turned reverence, for figural candles is a story many rootworkers can relate to, and her journey offers an honest and relatable entry point into the practice. From skull candles that activate the spiritual power of the brain to careful instructions for syncing behavior with spellwork, this book is rooted in experience, not just theory.

What sets this book apart is Miss Aida's insistence on integrity, discretion, and alignment between intention and action. She does not coddle the reader—she teaches with clarity and directness, offering a set of *"Golden Rules"* that every conjurer would do well to memorize. The integration of candle history, elemental fire wisdom, and magical mechanics is handled with precision and reverence. This book is a practical manual, a history lesson, and a spiritual awakening all in one. Whether you're new to figural candles or a seasoned worker, Miss Aida's work will make you rethink how you engage with the flame."

Denise Alvarado, author of *The Magic of Marie Laveau* and *The Marie Laveau Voodoo Grimoire*

❝ From the basics to the delightfully unusual, Miss Aida expertly guides the reader on a luscious magickal journey in the embrace of fire magic! With commonsense prose, inspiring stories, and easy-to-follow techniques, the author gives you an amazing gift—empowerment through knowledge! Light the way to your dreams with Miss Aida's genuine understanding and sage advice. Don't just watch life pass you by—make the magic happen with this book as your guide! Ignite your potential and transform your life as you set your lights for love, luck, good fortune, healing, compassion, and more. Are you ready to focus your inner fire and watch the universe respond? Figural Candle Spells is a go-to for all your candle magic needs from set-up to completion. Don't let this book slip through your fingers! It's a library staple!"

Silver RavenWolf, author of *Poppet Magick, Solitary Witch, To Ride a Silver Broomstick,* and *Teen Witch*

❝ The candle is surely synonymous with any imagery one imagines in regards to spell work, yet until reading Figural Candle Spells; Conjuring Magic with the Power of Fire, I had not realized how few books there were on the subject, let alone a book that explains how to work with figural candles in the first place. Miss Aida's seminal book shares encyclopedic levels of history and formula for candle magic, and uniquely delves into the relationship humans have had with the element of fire since time immemorial. Miss Aida's attention to detail, preparation and intention is also valuable and applicable to just about any form of spell work, truly an inspiring effort that taught me a lot. Figural Candle Spells; Conjuring Magic with the Power of Fire, without a doubt Sets the standard for all future books on candle magic."

Witchdoctor Utu, founder of the Dragon Ritual Drummers and Author of *Conjuring Harriet "Mama Moses" Tubman and the Spirits of the Underground Railroad*

❝ Figural Candle Spells: Conjuring Magic with the Power of Fire by Miss Aida stands as the definitive guide to candle magic in hoodoo practice. Miss Aida has crafted an exceptionally comprehensive resource that transforms both novice and experienced practitioners into confident candle workers. Miss Aida' masterfully guides readers through every aspect of figural candle work from initial selection and preparation to the final moments of your magical working. Her coverage of fire safety protocols is not just thorough but essential, ensuring practitioners can work with confidence and security.

Miss Aida's expertise shines through her exploration of advanced candle topics rarely addressed in other texts. She doesn't simply tell you what figural candles are; she demonstrates precisely how to integrate them meaningfully into your spiritual practice. Her clear, accessible writing style makes complex concepts immediately actionable, regardless of your experience level. Miss Aida provides the knowledge and techniques that transform uncertainty into mastery, making sophisticated candle work accessible to everyone. Whether you're taking your first steps in hoodoo or deepening an established practice, Miss Aida's guidance will elevate your craft.

We are proud to carry and consistently recommend this exceptional work at 3 Crows Conjure. Miss Aida has created an indispensable resource that belongs in every serious practitioner's library.

Amanda Keith & TJ Vancil, Owners of 3 Crows Conjure (3crowsconjure.com)

" Figural Candle Spells: Conjuring Magic with the Power of Fire" is yet another outstanding contribution from Miss Aida. She truly knocks it out of the park with this one! Not only is the book an engaging and powerful read, but it also serves as a rich educational resource. The depth of research is impressive, making it an essential guide for both beginners and seasoned practitioners interested in candle magic. Miss Aida's wisdom and clarity shine through on every page."

Lelia Marino (MH/CD), Proprietress, The Sacral Healing Garden (thesacralhealinggarden.com)

" In the art of candle magick, there is absolutely no stone left unturned in Miss Aida's book Figural Candle Spells Conjuring Magic With The Power Of Fire. Miss Aida has written a very powerful book filled with a wealth of intimate knowledge regarding the use of candles in magickal practice. This is one of the most comprehensive books ever written on the subject of Figural Candles. It will not only aid and advance your magickal skills, it will also help you to form a closer relationship with the essence of fire itself. This book is a definite MUST for anyone wishing to learn and further their candle magick skills."

Toni Rotonda, The Buckland Museum of Witchcraft and Magick

" This isn't just a book, it's a fire-lit guide into the world of candle magic. Figural candles are more than just wax; they're tools of transformation. And in this book, Miss Aida doesn't just teach you how to use them… she hands you the fire itself. Her spells are honest, strong, relatable, and come from real experience. Reading it feels like learning from a wise, no-nonsense Witch who actually gets it. If you want to step up your candle magic, this book deserves a spot in your Witch's lair. Because like I always say, knowledge is power, Witches. Stay wicked!"

WhiteRaven,
www.youtube.com/@WHITERAVENandWitchsLair

" If you think that figural candles are just simple novelties, Miss Aida will set you straight. From ancient times when candle magic had its roots, to our magical, mystical era, this enlightening comprehensive grimoire introduces us to the wonderful world of figural candles and its role in spellwork."

Marla Brooks, author of *Magic for All Seasons* and host of Stirring the Cauldron radio

"As the Love Witch of Salem, I've lit more figural candles for my clients than I can count—and I sell a whole wall of them at Crow Haven Corner, Salem's oldest Witchcraft shop. But I've never seen anyone break down how they work the way Miss Aida does in Figural Candle Spells! She really gets how the spirit of Fire speaks through the candle and how to make that candle work for your intentions. This isn't just another candle magic book. It's the real deal, and if you're serious about your magic, this book is exactly the kind of firepower you need!"

Lorelei, Salem's Love Witch, proprietress of Crow Haven Corner, and author of Mob Witch: A Magical Memoir (Warlock Press, 2025)

FIGURAL CANDLE SPELLS
Conjuring Magic with the Power of Fire

Miss Aida
Foreword by Tamara Von Forslun

Warlock Press

Figural Candle Spells: Conjuring Magic with the Power of Fire

© 2025, Kerrjie Aida Severini, MS, BSN, RN

All rights reserved. No part of this publication may be reproduced, stored in a retrieval system or transmitted in any form or by any means, electronic, mechanical, photocopying, recording or otherwise without the prior permission of the publisher or in accordance with the provisions of the Copyright, Designs and Patents Act 1988 or under the terms of any license permitting limited copying issued by the Copyright Licensing Agency.

Published by:
Warlock Press
1219 Decatur Street
New Orleans, 70116 LA, USA

Typesetting and Cover Design: Christian Day
Cover Illustration: Parkash Joshi
Interior Illustrations: John Rey B. Ramos

ISBN-13: 978-1-7332466-9-9

Acknowledgements

Having seen numerous candle book titles throughout the years, it occurred to me that not one book has ever addressed figural candles in depth. For years, it had been my plan to propose the idea of such a book to a publisher. After discussing the matter with Christian Day, not only was he impressed, but encouraging. He tolerated my annoying, perpetual progress reports and immediately provided forms when needed. So, Christian has been my inspiration for this project.

Next, wanting to learn more about the element of Fire through firefighters, I interviewed Captain Robert Anglin, who did an amazing job by providing us with treasured information. So, I was rescued by a firefighter!

My German Shepherd Dogs (GSDs) must also be acknowledged for having patience with the endless hours of writing. They willingly sacrificed playtime as their contribution to this project. Thank you, Junior and Jakob! Good Boys!

Most importantly, thank you to my dear friend and sister, Tamara Von Forslun, who wrote the phenomenal foreword to this book. What an honor to have such a glowing review by an elder of her immeasurable magnitude!

DEDICATION

This book is dedicated in loving memory to all of the firefighters who have perished in the line of duty.

Contents

Acknowledgements VII
Dedication VIII
Foreword XV

Introduction 1

CHAPTER ONE
The Magical Candlelit Journey 3
▶ The Paleolithic Period 4
▶ Fire: The Gift-Giver 5
▶ Fire Worship 5
▶ Oil Lamps 6
▶ Conventional Candles 7
▶ Fairy Lamps 10
▶ The End of the 19th Century to the Beginning of the 20th 10
▶ Figural Candles 11

CHAPTER TWO
Making Yourself a Magical Instrument 12
▶ The Golden Rules 12
▶ Magic And Energy Output 16
▶ Where To Obtain Extra Energy 18
▶ Spiritual Cleansing 19
▶ Spiritual Protection 24
▶ My Madrina: A Success Story 25

CHAPTER THREE
Preparing Your Tools & Strategy 29
▶ The Role of Figural Candles in Spellwork 29
▶ Ten Steps for Preparing Your Figural Candles . . . 30
▶ Preparing Your Petition Paper 36
▶ Your Altar 37
▶ Personal Concerns 39
▶ Your Strategy 40
▶ Getting Assistance from Your Spiritual Court . . . 44

CHAPTER FOUR
THE IMMEASURABLE POWER OF FIRE 46
- ▶ The Fostering Nature of Fire 47
- ▶ Let Fire Teach You Spirituality Through Your Candle Flame 48
- ▶ The Formidable Nature of Fire 50
- ▶ Asking the Big Guns 51
- ▶ Candle Fire Statistics 54
- ▶ Always Be Conscientious of Fire Safety 55
- ▶ What To Do If There's a Fire 57
- ▶ Homage To Firefighters 57

CHAPTER FIVE
THE SECRET LANGUAGE OF FIRE 59
- ▶ The Cardinal Directions 59
- ▶ Considerations Prior To Lighting the Candle 63
- ▶ Once The Candle Is Lit 64
- ▶ Pyromancy: Interpreting Fire Talk 65
- ▶ Defining The Language of Fire 66
- ▶ Capnomancy: Interpreting the Smoke of Fire 70
- ▶ Ceromancy: Interpreting the Shapes of Wax Left Behind 73

CHAPTER SIX
A FIGURAL CANDLE MAGICAL GRIMOIRE 78
- ▶ Deciphering The Format 78
- ▶ Angel Candle *(Large)*: For Veneration, Guidance, or Protection 79
- ▶ Angel Candle *(Small)*: For Health or Reconciliation 82
- ▶ Animal Candle: For Healing 84
- ▶ Ankh Candle: For Long Life 85
- ▶ Bride & Groom Candle *(Heterosexual)*: For Marital Matters 86
- ▶ Bear Candle: For Courage And Emotional Strength 92
- ▶ Butterfly Candle: For Freedom 93
- ▶ Cat Candle *(Black)*: For Protection From Negative Spiritual Forces 94
- ▶ Coffin Candle: For Justifiable Revenge 95
- ▶ Cross Candle *(Red)*: For Saint Michael's Protection 97
- ▶ Dog Candle: For Loyalty 99
- ▶ Double-Action Candle: To Reverse Bad Luck In Various Matters 100
- ▶ Dove Candle: Invoking The Holy Spirit For Favors 109
- ▶ Egg Candle: For Fertility 111
- ▶ Four-Leaf Clover Candle: For Good Luck 112

- Gargoyle Candle: For Home Protection 113
- Ghost Candle: To Banish Haunting Memories 114
- Heart candle *(large and small)*: For love. 116
- Human Candle: For Attraction, Cursing, Healing, Mastery, & Money 119
- Jack-o'-Lantern Candle: To Scare Away Malicious Spirits. 124
- Lip Candle: For Communication, Eloquent Speech, or to Stop Gossip 125
- Lovers Candle: To Incite a Lover or to Break Up an Affair 128
- Mouse Candle: To Assert Your Dominance Over Bullies 132
- Owl Candle: For Wisdom & Passing Exams 134
- Penis Candle: For Lust, Sexual Virility, Or Impotence 135
- Praying Hands Candle: To Petition God 139
- Pyramid Candle: For Money 140
- Rose Candle *(Large and Small)*: To Attract Love 141
- Same Gender Marriage Candle: *(Bride/Bride, Groom/Groom)* 143
- Seven Knob Wishing Candle: For Blessings or To Send Someone Away . . . 145
- Skull Candle: For Reconciliation 149
- Snake Candle: To Bind an Enemy 152
- Star Candle: For Connecting to the Metaphysical 154
- Sun Candle: For Empowerment and Strength. 156
- Venus Candle: For Beauty And Grace 157
- Vulva/Vagina Candle: For Healing, Lust in A Woman, or Cursing 159
- Witch Candle *(Black)*: To Increase Your Powers As A Magician 163

CHAPTER SEVEN

ADDING MOTION TO THE MAGIC 164

- How Long Does It Take to Perform This Spell? 164
- Come To Me: 5-Day Moving Candle Spell 166
- Send away *(move out of town)*: 5-day moving candle spell 168
- Separating a Heterosexual Relationship: 5-Day Moving Candle Spell 170
- Sex Worker's Better Business: 3-Day Moving Candle Spell 173

CHAPTER EIGHT

TENDING TO WAX & OTHER REMAINS 177

- How to Deploy Your Remains 178
- Locations For Deployment of the Remains 178
- A Deployment Cheat Sheet 180

CHAPTER NINE
PRAYERS & PSALMS FOR YOUR SPELLWORK 183

- ▶ Archangel Gabriel Prayer: for Clear Communication 184
- ▶ Archangels Michael, Gabriel, and Rafael Prayer: 3-Day Wishing Spell 184
- ▶ Beauty And Grace Prayer to Venus 185
- ▶ Break Up Relationship Prayer 185
- ▶ Fertility Prayer: For Conception 186
- ▶ Communication Prayer 186
- ▶ Connecting To the Metaphysical Prayer 187
- ▶ Courage & Strength Prayer 187
- ▶ Divine Power Prayer 187
- ▶ Gargoyle Prayer: For Protection 188
- ▶ Guardian Angel Prayer: For Guidance and/or Protection 188
- ▶ Holy Spirit Prayer: For A Favor 189
- ▶ Interfaith Wedding Vows 189
- ▶ Intimacy With Spouse Prayer 189
- ▶ Just Judge Prayer: For Court Cases 190
- ▶ Loyalty and Faithfulness Prayer 190
- ▶ Money Prayer 191
- ▶ Novena To God The Father 191
- ▶ Reconciliation Prayer 192
- ▶ Restore Sexuality Prayer 192
- ▶ St. Francis of Assisi Prayer: For All Animals 193
- ▶ St. Gertrude Prayer: For Cats 193
- ▶ St. Joan Of Arc Prayer: For Victory 193
- ▶ St. Josephine Prayer: To Escape Physical or Spiritual Slavery 194
- ▶ St. Michael Prayer: For Protection 194
- ▶ St. Roch Prayer: For Dogs 195
- ▶ St. Peter Prayer: To Open the Roads 195
- ▶ Sex Worker's Prayer To Venus 196
- ▶ Sun Prayer: For Empowerment And Strength 196
- ▶ Test-Taking Prayer 196
- ▶ Traditional Irish Blessing 197
- ▶ Venus Prayer: For Lust 197
- ▶ Wisdom Prayer 198
- ▶ Wisdom In Relationships Prayer 198
- ▶ Psalm 1: To Bind Enemies 199
- ▶ Psalm 12: To Stop Gossip 200
- ▶ Psalm 23: To Bless An Item and For General Good Luck 200

- Psalm 37: For Uncrossing and To Bring Money 201
- Psalm 41: For Emotional and Physical Health 203
- Psalm 45: To Obtain Love 204
- Psalm 51: Forgiveness of Sins. 205
- Psalm 61: For A Long Life 206
- Psalm 91: For Protection. 207
- Psalm 94: To Stop Gossip 208
- Psalm 105: To Drive Enemies Away 209
- Psalm 109: For Cursing and Crossing .211
- Psalm 121: To Repel Evil Entities 212
- Psalm 133: For Friendship 213
- Psalm 145: For Blessings. 213

Conclusion 215
Appendix A: Recommended Shops 216
Bibliography. 217
Index 219
About Miss Aida 226

FOREWORD

What an exciting opportunity to write the foreword for my dear friend and sister, the amazing Miss Aida. When we spoke of her new book, I did not have a clue what it was going to be about. When I saw the title, *"Figural Candle Spells: Conjuring Magic with the Power of Fire,"* and that it was dedicated to Fire and all the Firemen, I thought to myself being a magical creature; do I place the manuscript on my Altar and ask the Ancestors to speak to me of this great knowledge; and to send me the Elementals of Fire and guide me to feel the magic of this book?

But turning just the first few pages excited me to read more, and more I read until I reached the end of the book. It kept me wanting to know more about the detail and history of fire and the power of Candles and Lamp Magic throughout history, which was a lesson indeed. This book is written with such dedication to detail and filled with information and facts to guide the reader into the in-depth knowledge behind true Candle Magic, and working with the Element of Fire. Which, in fact, is the most dangerous and involved Element to work with, and yet the most Magical.

The great part is that I am a Fire sign, a true Sagittarian, and have always loved working with Fire, the Red Serpent of our tradition that takes us betwixt the Realms. I also live in a town named by Australian aboriginals as Murtoa (meaning lizard, goanna, salamander, or dragon) also I am not only a fire sign but endure in the bale fires of old and the traditions of magic and flame. So I was instantly drawn to this magical book and the journey it took me on.

This incredible book is a journey to take you through every aspect of Fire, through the physical, mental, astral, psychic, and spiritual. After fifty years in the world of magic, I have learnt so much, and yet through reading this easy-to-read and understand book, I found this very in-depth and detailed book so interesting and instructional on Fire and Candle Spells.

I felt that in the past the two best books about Candle Magic were by Raymond Buckland, my Mentor and friend, and Scott Cunningham, and have to say that they were watching over her when she wrote these sacred pages, guided her and also blessed her. I feel this book is up here with theirs and is now among my top three books on candle magic.

As you read this book, you will follow the journey through the historical and then end up with the knowledge to gain your practical experience within the Magical Realm; it is an instructional manual that guides you through all the stages to the final achievement in the world of REAL Candle and Fire Magic.

My blessings to Miss Aida and I hope that each reader of this book finds it not only well informed and instructional but also leads you to a greater spiritual understanding of Fire and the power of the Spirit Flame both within and without, above and below.

May this book serve as a beacon and bring more light into our world.

Love and Blessings,

Tamara Von Forslun
The Witch of Oz
Matriarch of the Clan of Boskednan Church of the Old Religion Inc.

INTRODUCTION

Welcome to the world of figural candles! As you can see from the illustration below, these precious magical tools have emerged in an array of shapes and forms. Figural candles provide the magical practitioner with tools that visually relate to the magic they're practicing.

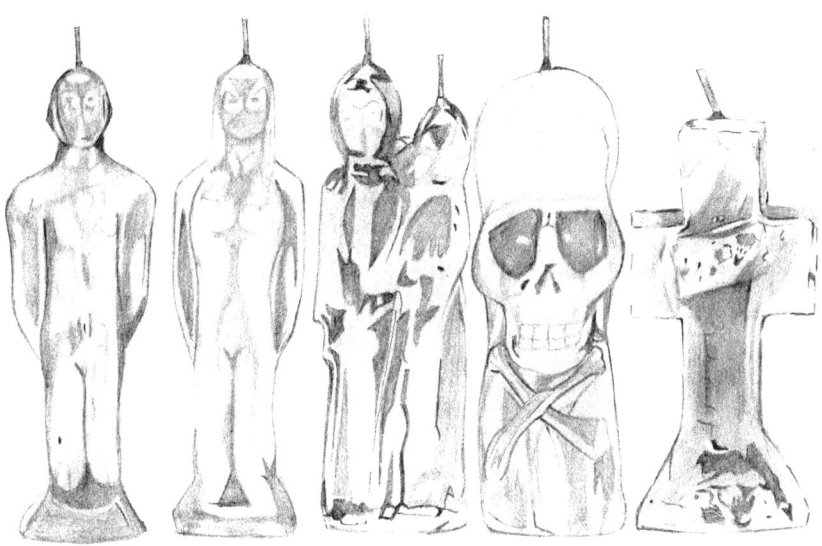

After successfully working exclusively with taper and vigil candles for many years, I had no interest in figural candles, the type of candle molded into the shapes of people, animals, and objects. My initial and erroneous assumption was that they were created solely for decorative purposes.

Then, about thirty years ago, during a visit to a metaphysical store that sold skull candles, my initial encounter with them shocked me. They appeared to be ugly, scary, and intimidating. I hurriedly stepped away and thought to myself: *"It's not even Halloween season, so what's the purpose of these candles? Whomever invented this candle mold was crazy!"*

But after that initial fright, my curiosity was aroused so I returned to that display and began to examine the exquisite craftsmanship in greater detail. As a Registered Nurse (R.N.), it occurred to me that the skull candle represented the human brain. Additionally, each lobe of the human brain has a different function that can be manipulated through magical work. My initial fear of the candle quickly transformed into great admiration, and my thoughts about the inventor quickly changed to: *"Whomever invented this candle mold was a genius!"*

From that day forward, working with skull candles has been a part of my practice and the results have been astonishing. My practice also includes various other figural candle types that have produced fantastic results. This is because, as you will learn by reading on, figural candles have certain advantages over conventional taper and vigil (glass-encased) candles.

The goal of this book is not only about how to perform spellwork with figural candles, but how to have a special relationship with them. Think of a candle as being your child. The more you know about the youngster, the better you are able to understand his or her every move.

But, to know candles intimately is to also know their history. So, join me on a journey beginning in the Stone Age period, when portable lights were first developed. Then, we'll travel together, throughout time, to learn the fascinating history of candles and how they developed into what they are today.

You'll even share several intimate moments with the element of Fire and familiarize yourself with his nurturing, fostering, and formidable nature. After all, how can we know a candle without knowing its flame?

So let's get started on this journey. Enjoy!

CHAPTER ONE
THE MAGICAL CANDLELIT JOURNEY
From Sacred Fires to Figural Candles

In many cultures around the world, candles are used as tools to assist us toward achieving success when seeking miracles, communicating with deities and/or spirits, and performing magical spells. But it is the fiery flame of the candle that actually connects us to the spiritual realm in order to help us accomplish our goals. Seasoned metaphysical practitioners know this and do not simply light a candle without acknowledging and embracing that very flame.

The element of Fire has always been a sacred and extremely powerful symbol throughout the world. Fire represents purity, purification, and renewal. In some cultures and religions, revered deities even appear to their people as fire. As a matter of fact, it is believed that the element of Fire was responsible for teaching spirituality, spiritual practices, and religion to mankind. Even highly acclaimed academic scholars, such as John H. Morgan, PhD, speculate that the use of fire, as well as the size of the human brain, are the foundations of religious and spiritual consciousness.

The candle flame also maintains a two-way communication with the spellcaster, as you will see in subsequent chapters, to assist us with our magic. But, to have that intimate relationship with the element of Fire, we must first acknowledge and appreciate his historical contribution to mankind. Most importantly, always remember that Fire is a powerful entity, and we are obliged to display respect in his presence. When we are kind to this element, he is kind to us in return.

In order to better understand candle magic, it is important to familiarize ourselves with its historical, as well as present-day, magical tools.

In doing so, it makes us more knowledgeable metaphysical practitioners, and knowledge is power! So, we will briefly explore the progression from stone lamps to oil lamps, taper candles, vigil (glass-encased) candles, and finally figural candles.

Now, let's start from the beginning and take a brief look at the evolution of mankind with the help of Fire…

THE PALEOLITHIC PERIOD

Honestly, it isn't as complicated as it looks to be! The term *"paleolithic"* simply means the stone age period ranging from about 550,000 to 20,000 years ago. It is divided into three segments:

- **Lower Paleolithic/Old Stone Age:** This period started around 550,000 years ago. No archaeological proof has been found to suggest that mankind worked with fire. Because the brain sizes of these people were much smaller, religious and/or spiritual awareness may not have existed.

- **Middle Paleolithic/Middle Old Stone Age:** Also called *"The Caveman"* era, this period started around 125,000 years ago and gave rise to the Neanderthals. With an increase in brain size, there was some sort of spiritual awareness. They had an affinity toward certain crystals and ritualistically buried their dead. The archaeological findings of people being buried with cooked food, working tools, and weapons highly suggest that the Neanderthals believed in the afterlife. They also worked with fire, but to a lesser degree. All these scientific findings imply that spiritual and religious consciousness began in this era.

- **Upper Paleolithic/Stone Age:** This is where the action really begins! Starting around 70,000 years ago, the Cro-Magnon people were prevalent. Because there was a significant increase in brain size, these people learned not only how to create fire, but to manipulate it in order to engineer the physical environment to satisfy their needs and desires. They invented the first portable lamps, using concave stones filled with moss wicks. They also domesticated their animals and, with the help of fire, produced art such as jewelry, paintings, sculptures, and even nude female figurines that are believed to have honored the divine feminine and were perhaps evidence of matrifocal societies. This flourish of artistic expression clearly conveys one part of a whole in terms of their psychological, sociological, and emotional integration.

FIRE
The Gift-Giver

Groups of people would gather in caves while the fires within provided them with warmth, cooked food, and protection. This ambiance, provided by the element of Fire, gave birth to the components that distinguish mankind from other life forms: development of languages, a sense of community, and most importantly, culture.

Culture is a complexity of behaviors, consisting of myths and rituals, which define a group's belief system, values, and conduct. It is the foundation of spiritual and religious consciousness.

Additionally, when a system of religious veneration and devotion is directed toward a particular object or figure, a cult ensues. Archaeological discoveries of cave art have revealed that the Cro-Magnon not only practiced fertility magic and shamanistic rituals, but also engaged in cult behaviors. The two most predominant cult practices were the veneration of bears and, you guessed it … Fire!

FIRE WORSHIP

Pyrolatry, originating from the Greek words *"pyro,"* meaning fire, and *"latry,"* meaning worship, is defined as the worship, reverence, or deification of fire. It can also refer to the religious rituals that center around fire. This practice is alternatively known as either *"pyro-dulia"* or *"pyro-latria."*

As we already know, pyrolatry began in the Paleolithic period of history. This is because, aside from its practical uses, these people understood that fire held both symbolic and mystical significance. While time passed and societies progressed, cultures from around the world were also intrigued by fire's transformative and seemingly magical powers. Accordingly, they too engaged in the practice of pyrolatry for various reasons.

Fire was seen by some as the manifestation of divine presence. For example, in the Holy Hebrew and Christian Bibles, God first appeared to Moses as a burning bush. To other societies, fire represents purification, knowledge, spiritual protection, and a cyclical nature, representing destruction followed by rebirth. Others deified fire and believed it was a God. We magical practitioners believe that fire acts as an intermediary between our world and the spiritual world because it pierces the veil between both in order for our petitions to be heard by entities. Fire is also seen as a source of energy consumption for spirits and entities.

To this day, pyrolatry is practiced in various styles such as conducting fire-temples, bonfires, maintaining perpetual flames, or engaging in fire dances. Others simply use portable fire sources, such as oil lamps or candles.

Oil Lamps

This type of lamp is a device that holds and burns fuel, typically oil, as a means of producing light. Although oil lamps have taken on a variety of shapes and sizes throughout history, the basic required components are a wick, fuel, a reservoir to hold the fuel, and an air supply.

The mechanics are easy. The wick is partially immersed in the fuel. The fuel is drawn up the wick and continuously does so once the wick is ignited. With the help of the air supply, the fuel is vaporized to maintain a constant flame.

Archaeologists believe that the Cro-Magnon people entered into caves alone to engage in either private artistic work, spiritual and magical practices, or private fire worship. For their light source, we already know that they had invented the first portable oil lamps using concave stones with moss as wicks and, most likely, animal fat for fuel. Shells, such as conch or oyster, were also employed as fuel reservoirs, which may have served as the prototypes for early lamp forms.

As the millenniums passed, clay oil lamps appeared throughout the world in a plethora of breathtaking designs. They were single-unit reservoirs with floating wicks. Animal fats, fish oil, or plant and seed extracts were commonly used for fuel. As civilization advanced, single-unit reservoirs were also made from metals while their designs became even more elaborate.

In modern times, we typically see much larger oil lamps with metal bases and glass chimneys. They are known as kerosene or paraffin lamps. With a little ingenuity and a natural-based fuel, they are sometimes used by metaphysical practitioners, in lieu of candles, for prayers, veneration, and spellwork.

Yet, other magical practitioners prefer the one-unit reservoirs. For example, in some magico-religious practices, such as the African Diaspora Religion (ADR) of Santería, a *"jicara"* (pronounced he-cah-rah), is used as the fuel reservoir. The bowl, made from the dried shell of a calabash gourd, is filled with fuel such as vegetable oil, or most commonly, olive oil, and finally, a floating wick is placed atop the fuel. Implementing oil lamps in worship, prayer, or spellwork is usually performed by traditionalists. From my personal perspective, there are both advantages and disadvantages of working with oil lamps.

The advantages are that the practitioner can add several items into the reservoir, such as personal concerns, symbolic curios, etc., in order to reinforce their magical intentions. Similarly, more fuel can be added to the reservoir to prolong the energy output of the flame.

On the other hand, one always has to worry about spillage from a single-unit reservoir. With the slightest of movement, this frequent event can lead to a sloppy mess. Modern kerosene lamps have fragile glass chimneys that can easily shatter when handled. Another common problem with all of the lamp types is wick nuisances. In most spellwork, it is important to maintain a continuous flame. Yet, one never knows when a floating wick of a single-unit reservoir may drown itself in the oil. While working with the modern lamps, continuous attention to manual wick extension is necessary; otherwise, the flame will perish. Along with other hindrances, my preference is to instead work with candles.

Conventional Candles

Today, a candle is defined as an ignitable wick embedded into a molded or dipped mass of either paraffin, beeswax, soy wax, palm wax, gels, or other combustible solid substances. They are available as either freestanding or glass-encased units that are either scented or unscented.

Aside from their uses in metaphysical practices, candles are frequently employed by the general population to honor ceremonies or celebrations. Many believe that they symbolize romance because they're pleasing and soothing to the senses. But, back in history, the combustible materials used for candles were not so appealing.

The First Primitive Freestanding Candles

Around 3,000 to 5,000 years ago, the ancient Egyptians invented unwicked candles called *"rushlights."* They were the dried cores of rush plants dipped in melted animal fat, called *"tallow."*

Later, around 2,700 years ago, candles with wicks appeared. The Ancient Romans wrapped rolls of papyrus around twine, then repeatedly dipped them into the tallow of either beef or mutton. The fat acted as the combustible material while the twines inside, slightly extended over the tallow, were the wicks.

While the Romans had this style, various cultures around the world created other versions. For example, the early Chinese molded insects and seeds into paper tubes while using rolled rice paper for the wicks. In some parts of the world, dried oily fish was used. Needless to say, the sound and odor of burning insects, fish, or animal fat couldn't have been soothing to the senses! Nevertheless, after mankind learned how to mold the fat while inserting wicks into what resembled the standard taper candles of today, the tallow candles prevailed in popularity.

The Beeswax Revolution

During the Middle Ages, around the years 500 to 1500 A.D., the quality of freestanding candles took a turn for the better. Beeswax candles were created as an alternative to the pungent-smelling tallow ones. Derived from melted honeycomb, this was a much more humane method of acquiring wax rather than killing animals or insects. Additionally, these candles have a cleaner burn, a pleasant odor, and are virtually smokeless. Thus, they quickly became the new fad.

Unfortunately, because beeswax candles were also costly, many couldn't afford them. So, the tallows remained on the market for those who were financially underprivileged.

From Ancient Paganism to the Catholic Church

Paganism is an umbrella term used to describe a variety of religious traditions, mostly based on a polytheistic and/or nature-based belief system. These religions were initially practiced in Europe, the Mediterranean region, and parts of Asia and Africa.

As with various natural elements, Fire was revered across most, if not all, of these continents. Along with the many previously mentioned attributes of Fire, Pagans also believed that through invocations, this element assists in the pursuits of inspiration, passion, and even divine connections.

Together with the several types of sacred fires employed for worship, ignited candles were frequently utilized to facilitate these quests. In many cases, they replaced the use of oil lamps because candles are solid materials that can be transported without creating spillage. They can also be cleansed, blessed, anointed, and inscribed for use in the diverse pagan rituals and ceremonies. Additionally, as time progressed, the Pagans determined that the number of candles used must correlate to the type of ritual or ceremony being performed.

Even though candles are often mentioned in the Hebrew and Christian bibles, the early Christian churches, both Catholic and Eastern Orthodox, resisted the use of candles in liturgical rituals because they were associated with Pagan practices. Then, around the third century, the Christian church leaders had a change of heart. In their hypocrisy, they proclaimed that employing candles during liturgy is not specifically Pagan. They decreed that candles will therefore be utilized in their own rituals because the tradition is being *"rightly rescued"* from the evil associations of false religions. Then, they concluded by declaring that this practice would now be consecrated into the service of the *"True Religion."*

Because the Christian church had plenty of money, they were easily able to purchase beeswax candles for their rituals. But to offset any complaints associated with their high costs, the church leaders claimed that because bees are virgins, the purity of their wax is essential while in the presence of God. Later in time, unbleached candles were also used.

After numerous Pagans converted to Christianity, either by brutal force, threats, or of their own volition, they introduced a few of their own customs to the church. Thereafter, as with the pagan practices, the Catholics and Eastern Orthodox first bless the candles prior to any rite. Then, the number of candles lit had to correlate with the type of ritual or ceremony that was being performed. Thanks to the Pagans, these procedures remain in place to this very day.

Freestanding Candles in the Modern Era

As the centuries passed, the conventional freestanding candles endured many changes in both their composition and mode of manufacturing.

- 🕯 **The 17th Century:** Colonial women discovered that after boiling large quantities of bayberries, a residual waxy substance would float to the top of their pots. This substance was used to make candles in lieu of the expensive beeswax or foul-smelling tallow. However, the process of making the wax was both time-consuming and tedious.

- 🕯 **The 18th Century:** Sadly, this century had a booming growth in the whaling industry. The whalers discovered that within the cavity of the sperm whale's head, a waxy substance, called spermaceti, existed. Candle-makers started using this wax to replace previous candle fuels. Although the candles were sturdier, they were also foul-smelling.

- **The 19th Century:** Most of the major developments in candle-making occurred in this century. Amongst many innovations, a machine was developed that allowed for the continuous production of molded candles. Other candles were devised to keep time. Thankfully, paraffin wax, derived from petroleum, coal, or oil shales (sedimentary rocks containing oils), was invented to replace tallow and the spermaceti obtained from needlessly slaughtered whales. Today, it is the most commonly used candle wax. Plus, the first glass-encased candle, called a *"Fairy Lamp,"* was created.

FAIRY LAMPS

These lamps, also called *"fairy lights,"* were molded squat lights, resembling the votive candles of today, that were wrapped in paper. The candle was placed inside a glass container that held a small amount of water in its base. Then, the unit was covered with a glass dome.

Patented in 1885 by Samuel Clarke, they were called fairy lamps/lights because he used the image of a fairy when registering the trademark: *"Clarke Fairy Lamps."* Within a short time, the glass containers became available in many shapes, colors, sizes, and designs. Although there isn't much information regarding exactly when wax was first poured directly into glass vessels, these fairy lights were the forerunners of the vigil candles that we see today.

THE END OF THE 19TH CENTURY TO THE BEGINNING OF THE 20TH

When Thomas Edison patented the light bulb in January 1880, the popularity of candles began to dwindle. But they later enjoyed renewed popularity during the first half of the twentieth century with the growth of the U.S. oil and meatpacking industries. This is because both industries produced an increase in the byproducts that had become the basic ingredients of candles.

With an abundance of these byproducts, candles were being mass-produced in a broad array of sizes, colors, and most importantly, shapes. The initial assortment of shapes included objects like stars, hearts, and simple holiday representations such as ghosts for Halloween. But the metaphysical community saw the potential in these candles. So, they developed candle molds to increase the spellcasters' chances of successful manifestation through the concept of correspondence.

Correspondence is based on the idea that one can influence a target, such as a person, body part, animal, or even an event, based on an object's resemblance to it. Thus, candles were created in various mystical, magical, and uncanny shapes to represent the practitioners' targets. In the metaphysical community, they are referred to as figural, or image candles.

Figural Candles

Initially, figural candles were obtainable largely through mail order. As a matter of fact, skull candles, one of my favorites, were being sold in metaphysical catalogs as early as the World War II era.

Figural candles were mainly available as human male and female forms, human body parts, entities, animals, and various objects. But, as the success rates of magical manifestation increased by working with these shapes, so did the demand for a wider variety of choices.

Shortly thereafter, innovative candle creations emerged representing events that could also be manipulated through spellwork. They included candles that symbolized occasions such as divorce, same sex marriages, sexual relations, etc., which can be magically influenced or affected.

Why Are Figural Candles Effective in Spells?

Major components of successful spell manifestation include conviction in your beliefs and actions, and energy output. When handling a tangible object that represents a goal or outcome, one can see and feel what is actually being manipulated. Additionally, just as is in role-playing, we can pour out our emotions and commands. These acts not only enhance one's convictions, but they allow us to disperse greater energy output. The common term used to describe these actions is sympathetic magic. Other applicable terms include similarity magic, imitation magic, and of course, correspondence magic.

In the next chapter, we will discuss the use of sympathetic magic in greater detail. We will also explore energy output and other maneuvers that can make any spellcaster a formidable one!

CHAPTER TWO
MAKING YOURSELF A MAGICAL INSTRUMENT
Honing Your Spirit to Be Ready for the Work

Before discussing the mechanisms of magic, it is essential to first modify our behaviors and attitudes. As mundane as it sounds, hundreds of people perform their spells impeccably, sometimes taking many months to complete, but ultimately ruin everything by thinking or acting in a manner contradictory to their spellwork. As a matter of fact, many more have instead hired spellcasters to perform the work, but nevertheless managed to ruin the practitioners' spellwork for the same reasons.

So let's explore the necessary key elements that can either *"make or break"* any magical spell. Think of them as being the *"Golden Rules."*

THE GOLDEN RULES

Rule #1: Sync Your Magic With Your Actions

Remember that magic is not the complete answer to every pursuit; it acts solely as a facilitator toward your goal. So, if behaviors or words oppose the type of magic being performed, then the spell will cease to work. The target, or the person for whom the spell is directed, can unknowingly annul the magic.

This is because everyone has free will, and if enraged, repulsed by, or afraid of another person, the target will feel threatened. Next, the target will subconsciously convert to high alert status regarding any visible, invisible, real, or imagined threats pertaining to the inappropriate person. When this happens, their protective aura becomes stronger and will shield the practitioner's magic. Did you ever hear someone say, *"I don't even want to hear his/her name"*? When this happens, it's a clear example of the person's protective aura at work. That shield becomes so strong that it will not even allow the person's name to enter the ear canals. Amazing!

The most common problems in this category are commitment and reconciliation spells. Whether straight or LGBT, most of my clients tell me the same stories. In other words, same game, different players. The target is affected by the magic and becomes sweet to the client. Because the target doesn't move fast enough to satisfy all of the client's desires, the impatient client gets angry, and an argument ensues. Nasty, threatening, and/or degrading words are exchanged. Then, the target leaves, infuriated and vowing never to return.

Next, the client feels remorse. He/she either performs more spellwork or pays a practitioner to do so. The cycle of inappropriate behaviors repeats itself. When the third or fourth attempt at spellwork occurs, the magic just doesn't work. Why? Because the target's aura created a stronger shield to protect him/her from any association with the client.

Remember that one can attract more flies with honey than with vinegar. If these clients had used just a little bit of psychology, their goals would have manifested. Instead, the lack of confidence and patience with the spellwork turned into disasters. Which brings me to the next golden rule...

Golden Rule #2: Adjust Your Attitudes

Thought processes emit vibrational energies that must conform with the spellwork. Below are the four essential attitudes necessary to maintain that collaboration:

DETERMINATION

The fortitude of the need or desire to accomplish your goals must be an overpowering emotion that will not falter. When this happens, those intense emotions will outpour blasts of energy into the universe to assist us in our spellwork. If obstacles are consistently present, do not surrender. Keep reminding yourself that failure is not an option.

Sometimes targets can be extremely difficult to manipulate. This is because they either have a resilient aura, they're strongly protected by entities, or they have placed you into a docile position by their endeavors to weaken you.

My own encounter with such a person, who possessed all three advantages, created a lot of work for me. Thirty years ago, there was a neighbor who, I believe with all of my heart and soul, had demons for spirit guides and guardians. She hated my nationality and perpetually harassed me. Once, she even called the police when my *"ferocious"* seven-week-old puppy barked outside. Later, she enlisted both of her children's schoolmates to join in her quest to drive me out of the neighborhood.

Then, she eventually poisoned and killed my precious dog. It broke my heart and pierced my soul. So that's when I became determined to seek revenge…

PERSISTENCE

Almost every spell performed on that evil woman had a drawback. For example, a doll in her image was frozen between two blocks of ice. But the head and torso of the doll broke through the ice and sat up in the container. Just seeing that type of resistance was obviously intimidating, but nothing could stop me. Although it took around twenty different spells in a two-year period, my persistence finally prevailed, and that healthy, vibrant woman was stricken with a debilitating illness.

Never be intimidated by, or surrender to, blockages. If obstacles are presented before, during, or after performing spellwork, perform a variety of other spells until your goals are accomplished. Unless you are seeking the impossible, don't cease performing magical spells until the target submits to your will.

PATIENCE

This is a virtue that most people lack. Being an Aries, impatience is one of my greatest weaknesses, and an ongoing struggle to control. But I also know, from decades of experience, that impatience is crucial to constrain when it pertains to spellwork.

Although it's easier said than done, patience is a behavior that complements your magic.

Additionally, as we will see later, patience assists in the flow of energy output which accelerates your spellwork. On the other hand, impatience, as discussed earlier, can lead to inappropriate thoughts and behaviors that can easily ruin your spellwork.

Always remember that, unlike in the movies, magic does not manifest within minutes or overnight. In fact, although atypical, spellwork can sometimes take up to two years to manifest.

CONFIDENCE

Even before initiating spellwork, it is imperative to believe that the magic is going to manifest. Do not begin second-guessing yourself or the work. A distrust of yourself or the entities assisting you with your spellwork is a recipe for failure. Despite seeing or hearing anything that conflicts with your goals, just think of them as snags, minor hurdles, or bumps in the road.

Sometimes, it might be necessary to readjust your petition or prayer, but only if the problem is new, or something that was unanticipated when your spellwork began. But don't fret over the ongoing work. Think of the process as making a long-simmering beef stew. If it's missing an ingredient, we don't proclaim that the stew is ruined and then discard it. Instead, we simply add the missing ingredient and continue cooking, knowing that when it's ready to eat, it will be a chef's delight!

Golden Rule #3: Be Discreet

Never tell anyone that you plan to perform spellwork. Most importantly, never reveal, allude to, or insinuate the fact that you are in the process of doing so. No matter how well-trusted the other person might be, the channels of communication might inadvertently lead right back to your target.

If a target learns of your activities, it allows that person an opportunity to amplify and strengthen his/her protective aura. The target might also petition an entity for protection, and/or wear spiritual protection gear such as amulets or blessed oils, etc. All of these measures will weaken, or even negate, your magic.

Bragging about spellwork on the internet is a very common occurrence. People use screennames but in an overwhelming number of cases, their true identities are ultimately disclosed. Additionally, even if your identity remains inconspicuous to living people, this conduct demonstrates superiority over the entity who is assisting you. Any behaviors or words viewed as being condescending toward that entity may lead to abandonment. Always remember the old saying: *"Loose lips sink ships."*

Also keep in mind that taking pictures of spellwork to display on the internet is the same as bragging about spellwork. Additionally, my family had always emphasized their beliefs that taking pictures of work in progress is absolutely forbidden. This is because the entities assisting with the spellwork do not want to take the chance of having their true images revealed. Although this conviction has been incorporated into my belief system, it is only my personal viewpoint.

Try to keep your spellwork hidden at all times. Aside from compromising safety measures, which will be discussed in a subsequent chapter, there are additional consequences. A trusted person might become curious or intrigued and unintentionally insert their unwanted energies into the spellwork. If the person is a skeptic and believes the work is nonsense, those thoughts could also interrupt the energy flow. Last but not least, gossip may follow, spread by those who are not as trustworthy as they were believed to be.

Although pets cannot ruin spellwork by simple observation, they can do so by other means. My German Shepherd Dogs (GSDs) obey my commands, but they are still untrustworthy when it comes to curiosity. The minute that my back is turned to them, they begin snooping around by smelling, tasting, and chewing. These actions can easily dismantle or break anything that has been set on my altar. While my dogs are *"nosey,"* cats love to slap things around, and pet birds sometimes have clumsy landings. So please keep an eye out for playful pets.

Magic And Energy Output

Energy is the force that causes movement, as it travels through waves, from one location to another. The intention of spellwork is to communicate a precise request into the spiritual world, the universe, and/or to a specific person or location. We do this by pouring out as much energy as possible because the more energy surges involved, the better the chances of manifesting your desires.

It is important to keep the flow of energy output smooth and consistent. Thus, this is another reason to do everything necessary to control our thoughts, attitudes, and behaviors. Think of a water gun as being the energy output. As the trigger is being squeezed, water is released in a steady flow. Any disruptions in that flow, such as inconsistencies in behaviors, thoughts, and attitudes, are akin to placing a barrier between the snout of the water gun and the target.

Keeping this in mind, energy can be smoothly distributed through an array of techniques. The more methods applied in spellwork, the greater the chances of successful manifestation. Listed below are some of the most common modes of energy transmission:

- **The Candle:** The flame of the candle is a source of energy output, as is its smoke. If the candle is dressed with herbs, plants, or minerals, their spirits also provide supplementary energy.

- **Smoke:** Incense distributes energy, as well as the smoke of cigars. Additionally, both the odor and the smoke are pleasing to the entities assisting you.

- **Sound:** One of the most important modes of energy transmission is sound. Prayers and petitions ought to be transmitted vocally to output our desires as well as call upon entities. As of twelve years ago, the last of my elders had passed on. But, having spent over fifty years with Santeros, Babalawos, Brujas, and Paleros, they never once engaged in silent prayer, nor did they silently plead their petitions. They always repeated their petitions three times per session, and did so many times a day. Some of the elders would even stomp their feet while calling out their prayers and/or petitions.

- **Symbols, Sigils, and Written Words:** Although symbols and sigils emit a higher amount of energetic strength, written words are also power sources. It is one of the reasons practitioners inscribe candles and craft petition papers. Since consistency in energy output is important, ensure that the written petitions are consistent with the verbal ones.

- **Vibrations:** According to many parapsychologists, even thoughts can transfer from one person or entity to another through vibrations. They believe this is because all thoughts have substance, and the substance of thought is vibration, which is emitted through energy transferences in the air.

Precise Communication

Most people falter in manifesting their desires due to faulty communication practices. Whether using verbal and/or written petitions, the communication must be brief, clear, direct, concise, and, of utmost importance, consistent.

Changing the petition will weaken the spell or the prayer. Do not ask for something and then change the verbiage. Be consistent to ensure that all the energy is reaching the mark. Think of it this way: if your favorite song suddenly had a change of words, what would you do? If it were me, I would stop listening to it.

WHERE TO OBTAIN EXTRA ENERGY

Unless there are extenuating circumstances, my clients are encouraged to cast their own spells prior to hiring me to do so. This is because their own spellwork may work, which will boost their self-confidence, plus save them a lot of money. However, the virtually perpetual response is: *"But I don't have the power to perform magic!"* Well, in my metaphysical belief systems of Christianity and African Magico-Religious Diasporas, God gave everyone the power. The only requirements to manifest your goals are knowledge, self-confidence, and practice.

However, if my clients are just not feeling the power, they are encouraged to obtain it from outside sources or to extract their hidden reserves. These techniques ought to be performed after your spiritual cleansing has been completed, which will be discussed shortly. Here are a few suggestions:

The Sun

Go outside and face the most powerful source of energy, the sun., being careful to avoid direct blinding eye contact. Stand with your feet at least twelve inches apart and raise your arms. If you believe that the blessed sun is a God, address him by his name. Otherwise, just call him *"Sacred Sun."*

Humbly ask him to share a little of his energy with you. Feel his energies entering you and imagine that your entire body is a glowing yellow color. Since his number is six, bask in his rays for at least six minutes. Then, verbalize gratitude. In most cases, not only will you feel power, but you will also feel empowered by his energy.

Uplifting Music

Play the type of music that makes you feel like dancing. Music can release endorphins, your hidden reserves, which are hormones that make a person feel good. Sometimes endorphins will give us a rush of energy, vim, vigor, self-confidence, and happiness.

However, when the music begins to make you feel better, do not sing or dance because you will be dispensing the energy needed for your magic. But do try performing your spell work shortly after receiving your endorphin rush. Two of my favorite songs that satiate me with energy include:

- *"Girls Just Want to Have Fun"* by Cyndi Lauper.

- *"Beat It"* by Michael Jackson.

Just writing out the song titles makes me want to get up and dance. Oh boy, those endorphins!

Crystals

My Facebook page at *www.facebook.com/MissAidaPsychic* has hundreds of seasoned metaphysical practitioners in the group. I posed the following question to these experts: *"What crystals do you believe provide you with the most energy?"*

The three most popular answers were moldavite, citrine, and clear quartz. However, moldavite is becoming rare, very expensive, and counterfeits are frequently sold.

- **Citrine:** In her book, *Love is in the Earth: A Kaleidoscope of Crystals,* Melody said that this crystal, along with its many other wonderful properties, never holds negative energy. It also emits an elevated energy level, which provides one with supplemental initiative.

- **Clear Quartz:** Melody shared a plethora of information regarding clear quartz. Of interest to us is that this crystal *"…brings the energy of the stars into the soul,"* amplifies both body energy and thoughts, and can assist in the creation of power.

It was recently brought to my attention that, just as with talismans and other paraphernalia holding the essence of spirits, there are crystals that conflict with one another.

For example, citrine is said to be incompatible with amethyst, while clear quartz and malachite are also an unharmonious combination. Whether due to mismatched energy frequencies or for various other reasons, be prudent. When combining crystals, research them thoroughly, trust your intuition, or consult an expert.

Now that we have explored how aspects of magic work, it's time to clean the aura.

Spiritual Cleansing

We've all seen paintings of God, saints, or revered deities with depictions of glowing light forms around their heads. They are actually light energy fields called *auras,* something that all matter and that living beings possess.

The radiance of the aura can emit different degrees of brightness or dim luminosity, as well as being able to emanate different colors.

Auras are shields that protect us from outside negative influences that might affect our psychological, physiological, and spiritual well-being. The healthier we are, both emotionally and physically, the more vitalized our auras become, thus producing a greater radiance and sturdier armor. All of these attributes promote enhanced energy output.

Simple attacks on the aura, such as arguments or having a bad day at work, can leave us feeling invaded. This is because the negative energies dispersed from these events will attach themselves to the aura and suppress it.

When our auras are attacked, we are either consciously or subconsciously aware of the fact that something is wrong. We may feel uncomfortable, irritable, fatigued, or lack motivation. Any of these feelings can overpower your spellwork and weaken the energy output needed for successful manifestation.

Therefore, immediate cleansing of the aura after any disruptive stimuli is imperative. Otherwise, we can invite further assaults to the shield and suppress it even more so. Cleansing the aura will repair most injuries brought on by minor attacks, while protecting it will provide us with optimal spiritual immunity from further assaults.

Cleansing the Aura of Minor Attacks

There are numerous ways of cleansing the aura. With the utmost respect to the practitioners of diverse faiths, the techniques listed in this book are those that are applied in my own magical practices.

Remember that sound is a form of energy output. So, while cleaning yourself, your petition, plea, or command ought to be stated aloud with confidence. As an example, you might state: *"All dirt on my aura is being washed away."* Doing so alerts your brain, as well as the entities surrounding you, to your intentions.

While cleansing and verbalizing your objective, imagine the cleansing agent dissipating any spiritual dirt resting upon your aura. Then, envision that shield expanding in radiance.

Florida Water

Florida Water, a cologne named after the alleged Fountain of Youth located in the state of Florida, was introduced to the United States in the 1800s. It is now available in other continents, including South America, Central America, and Asia. It has an appealing fragrance that can be worn by both men and women.

Spiritual practitioners of many faiths found that it also has amazing metaphysical properties. To this day, Florida Water is utilized in ritual offerings, blessing rites, purification ceremonies, and the cleansing of negative energies from people, objects, or areas.

To rid oneself of minor negative energies, the process begins by either splashing yourself with the water or using a spray bottle. To perform the latter, simply pour the Florida Water into a previously unused spray bottle. Then, spray yourself starting from the crown of your head and working downward toward your feet, which is a symbolic gesture of making something go away. In most cases, people feel an immediate sense of revitalization. If this doesn't occur, then repeat the ritual.

You may also spray your surrounding area if negative energies have attached themselves to something in your dwelling. However, be mindful that Florida Water has an alcohol base. Do not spray the cologne onto wood, leather, or other materials that can be damaged by alcohol. Instead, spray it up into the air, while avoiding these sensitive articles.

Holy Water

Mainly used as a spiritual cleansing agent, this water is also utilized in blessing and protection rites. The water becomes Holy after having been blessed by a religious or spiritual leader or consecrated by a revered deity. Oftentimes, experienced practitioners can bless the water themselves. People often ask me: *"What makes the water Holy?"* The answer is that once blessed, its molecular structure changes.

Throughout the world, many believe that the first rainwater of the month of May is also sacred. To this day, numerous metaphysical practitioners place their buckets outside in the late evening of April 30. The buckets are kept in place until the first rainwater of May is collected. Once obtained, my recommendation is to pour the water into new, unused bottles and store them in the refrigerator for future use.

Holy Water can be obtained, free of charge, from Roman Catholic, Anglican, or Eastern Orthodox churches. Just bring a brand new, unused bottle, for collection. Many Eastern Orthodox churches also offer Holy Oil.

My preference for Holy Water is that which has been consecrated by a revered deity. In Lourdes, France, around 1858 A.D., a young girl had visions of the Virgin Mary at the Basilica, which is located directly atop the grotto's underground spring. The infirm began flocking to the site and, even to this day, many were cured by the healing waters. In 1862, the Catholic Pope declared the grotto's spring to have miraculous properties.

After having personally witnessed the miracles that this water has performed for close friends and relatives, my only source of Holy Water is purchased directly from Lourdes, France. It's a little costly, but well worth the price.

Please do not buy Holy Water from questionable sources. So many people have told me that they had made their purchases from popular, and even unpopular, online suppliers. There is no proof whatsoever that the water was either blessed by a spiritual leader or came directly from Lourdes, France. It is much safer to obtain it from the types of reputable sources mentioned here.

Just as with the Florida Water, either splash it on or simply pour the Holy Water into a previously unused, clean, spray bottle. Starting from the crown of your head and working downward to your feet, spray yourself from top to bottom—a symbolic gesture of making something go away—while stating aloud with each spray that negativity will leave you and your aura is cleansed and protected. Repeating the process at any time is never harmful. It can only help.

Unlike Florida Water, Holy Water will not damage wood, leather, or other materials. Therefore, it is safe to lightly spray it in your dwelling or places where negative energies may have attached themselves. Do this while demanding that all negativity leave the area at once.

Similarly, spaying your beloved pets with Holy Water is also beneficial. My dogs are sprayed once a week as a precautionary measure. Additionally, if one of them hurts a limb or other body part, special attention is given to that area by directly spraying over the injured area. However, never spray any prepared or altered waters directly into an open wound.

Herbal Waters

While some practitioners prefer moistening themselves with either Florida or Holy Water, others favor herbal waters. This is because many, if not all of us, believe that plants and minerals have spirits that will assist with our endeavors. A tea is made from the herb and, just as with the other waters, is either directly splashed on a person or poured into a spray bottle.

Preparation of Herbal Teas

To make a tea, place a tablespoon of the selected herb in your hand. Then, place your hand close to your mouth and slowly recite a blessing prayer or just state that by your own power, you bless the herb. A common prayer recited over most herbs is Psalm 23.

My personal ritual involves asking God to awaken, bless, and thank the herb for sacrificing its life for me. Then, the request is made for the herb to remove negativity. After the prayer and request to God is completed, the appeal is finalized with the word *Amen* (meaning: *"So be it"* or *"The Truth"*). Then, tell the herb exactly what will happen. After all, its spirit is entitled to know the procedure without any surprises.

Next, a pot is filled with enough water to fill a spray bottle. Boil the water and, as soon as it reaches the boiling point, the herb is added, and the pot is immediately removed from the heat. The herb is allowed to steep in the water for thirteen minutes. Then, the herb is immediately strained and set aside, while the tea water is left to cool off.

As with the other waters mentioned earlier, pour the tea into a previously unused spray bottle. Starting from the crown of your head and working downward to your feet, spray yourself from top to bottom. While doing so, it is stated aloud, with each spray, that negativity will leave, and the aura is now cleansed and protected. Finally, the herb is taken outside, humbly thanked, and respectfully placed on the ground from whence it came.

Although there are numerous herbs that will aid in cleansing and protecting the aura, the most popular ones are as follows:

- Agrimony (Agrimonia eupatoria)

- Eucalyptus (Eucalyptus globulus, Eucalyptus spp.)

- Rosemary (Rosmarinus officinalis)

- Rue (Ruta graveolens)

> **A note about rue:** Although one of the most ancient, effective, and commonly used herbs, rue is also abortifacient, meaning that it can cause miscarriages. If you are pregnant or trying to conceive, avoid this herb.

Other Means of Cleansing the Aura

Another simple spiritual cleansing mode is to shower using either sulfur or rue soap. However, sulfur soap is abrasive to sensitive skin so perform a *"trial test"* by just washing your hands and lower arms with the soap and wait a day to see how your skin reacts to it. If there are signs of a rash, such as burning, itching, blisters, bumps, or stinging, do not bathe with sulfur soap.

A more detailed cleansing involves filling a bathtub with warm water, adding either a tablespoon of sea salt or a tablespoon of ammonia (no more than a tablespoon). Then sit in the bathtub for at least thirteen minutes while reciting Psalm 37 aloud. This is an uncrossing prayer that has a wonderful side effect in that it also attracts money!

Spiritual Cleansing After Baneful Magic

When performing a spell that involves inflicting adverse effects upon another, whether justified or not, it is highly recommended to perform a *"forgiveness of sins"* bath afterward. Hyssop is a popular spiritual cleansing agent, and it helps to acquire spiritual forgiveness.

The ingredients required for this bath are:

🔥 1 Teaspoon of extra virgin olive oil

🔥 2 Tablespoon dried Hyssop (*Hyssopus officinalis*)

Prepare the herbal tea as previously instructed. Fill a bathtub with warm water, then pour the olive oil and the tea into the water. Then sit in the bathtub for at least thirteen minutes while reciting Psalm 51 aloud. This Psalm actually mentions the hyssop herb.

SPIRITUAL PROTECTION

As we already know, spellwork emits particles of energy. In almost every case, without spiritual protection, many of these stray particles will attach themselves to the spellcaster. Thus, the reason numerous neophyte practitioners will complain that the love spells aimed toward their intended targets also affected them.

Spiritual protection helps to shield the aura from everyday negative energies as well as exposure to other types of excessive particles. Think of it as a spiritual raincoat. Although crystals, sigils, magical bags, and other modes of protection are employed by spiritual practitioners, the most common modes of armor include amulets, oils, and waters. Listed below are several examples:

Protection Amulets

- Anti-Evil Eye/All Seeing Eye/Nazar
- Cross
- Hamsa Hand
- Pentacles
- Pentagrams
- Religious Deities

Protection Oils

- Eucalyptus oil
- Holy oil
- Protection oil
- Rosemary oil
- Rue oil

Protection Waters

- Herbal teas
- Holy water
- Florida water

Some people will also pray Psalm 91 aloud prior to and after performing spellwork. It is believed to be one of the most powerful protection prayers in both the Jewish and Christian faiths. Psalm 121 is especially helpful in protecting against and warding off untoward entities.

Now that we have reviewed the many ways of turning ourselves into magical tools, let's briefly take a look at an actual event that happened, while utilizing many of the techniques we have learned. This is the true story of my Godmother's revenge.

MY MADRINA
A Success Story

Many are familiar with the story of my Godmother (*Madrina* in Spanish) in Santería. It's been told on podcasts, radio shows, in-person presentations, on my website, and even in one of my books. This is because it is essential to once again repeat the story to demonstrate how my Godmother, a master spellcaster, performed her magic, flawlessly, to accomplish the impossible. Then, we will review the mechanisms she implemented to achieve success.

Decades ago, there was a happily married man named Tony, who was also a successful spiritual practitioner and owner of a flourishing botanica. He was a *Babalawo*, a powerful high-ranking priest in the religion of Santería. His thriving house of Santería, called an *ile*, had numerous members who loved and admired him. He was a highly gifted and approachable practitioner. Along with these traits, his humor and charm made him near famous and people traveled long distances to seek his services, or to just be with him.

Both my Godmother and I adored Tony. A priestess herself (called a *Santera*), she had won a lottery to leave communist Cuba. So, without money, she left her homeland hoping to find a better life in the U.S.A. Hoping to make enough money to deport her children and grandchildren from Cuba, she would always say, in Spanish, *"I want to bring my family to this country of freedom."*

Tony offered her a paying job to assist him with his numerous, intricate, and tedious ceremonies. She happily complied with his requests and practically worked her fingers to the bones, while contributing her vast years of acquired wisdom and knowledge to his services.

But ultimately, he kept all her profits for himself and never paid my Madrina one single dime for her months of services. In the end, he cheated her out of thousands of dollars while creating rumors about her in order to ruin her credibility and any respect she had earned within the *ile*.

Fortunately, my Madrina wasn't an idiot. Upon every single visit to Tony's home or store, she collected anything that contained his DNA (deoxyribonucleic acid—the blueprint of life), such as hair and other personal concerns. She had always professed that these items might be needed for a *"rainy day."* Unfortunately, that *"rainy day"* arrived when she came to the realization that Tony had no intention of ever paying her. So with these personal concerns, she made a doll in his image.

Madrina was adamant about cleanliness and negative energies. When performing negative spellwork, she bathed every morning and every night. Her negative spellwork was always performed outside and her positive spellwork was performed inside her home. So, in her backyard, she hung the doll-baby, by its neck to a tree branch. When I asked who the doll-baby represented, she replied: *"It's Tony. When I am finished with him, he will lose his wife, his house, his business, and his money. I will destroy him!"* Truthfully, I thought to myself that the old lady was crazy to think that she, a mere *Santera*, could ruin such a powerful spiritual practitioner. But she was confident that she could indeed do it.

So, every single day, at least three times a day, she would forcefully and repeatedly strike that doll with a heavy stick, repetitiously screaming while striking the doll, that he would lose his wife, house, business, and money. After finishing each round of battering the doll, she would douse herself with Florida Water \before entering her home.

Two months later, she was still working that doll. Honestly, it was exhausting just to watch her constantly beating and yelling at it! Being impetuously outspoken and becoming convinced that she was just a crazy old woman, I had the audacity to question her actions. I said: *"Madrina, you're wasting your time. The spell is not working. Nothing is going to happen to Tony. As a matter of fact, his business is flourishing and he's thinking of expanding his store."* With disgust and contempt toward my confrontation, she replied: *"You have no faith! You have no patience! That lack of patience will destroy your spells and your life!"* Several weeks later, she was still beating that doll with that heavy stick while screaming her demands. Even though Tony was becoming wealthier and more popular than ever, it meant absolutely nothing to her. She didn't fret over his triumphs, nor did she care.

Shortly after my Godmother had scolded me, I received a phone call from Maria, the Babalawo's wife. Inflamed and infuriated, Maria said that she had caught Tony making love to another woman in her very own bed! She then proclaimed that if he wants that woman, he'll have nothing to offer her.

I immediately informed my Madrina of the phone call. Her cool, calm, and collected response was: *"Good. Now, sit back and enjoy the show because it's just beginning."* From that moment forward, Tony's life plummeted.

Because the Santería community holds Babalawos to a higher ethical and moral standard, adultery is not tolerated. So as retaliation for the hurt that Maria suffered, she had called all of his clients, friends, and followers, exposing his disregard for the religious standards.

Next, Maria withdrew all the money from their joint bank accounts, moved away, and then filed for divorce. The courts awarded her a large sum of money in lieu of the physical home and business. After Maria ruined Tony's reputation as a virtuous man, he was left with a failed business and no money to pay the mortgage. He ultimately lost his home, followers, and business.

The manifestation of Madrina's spellwork resulted in a fast deterioration of everything that Tony had worked so hard to attain. As a matter of fact, it took less than a year to destroy what Tony had worked decades to build. Shortly thereafter, he disappeared.

My Madrina's actions were clearly justified. Tony's greed and lack of payments kept her children and grandchildren destitute. So she did the same to him. The punishment was clearly commensurate with the offense. It was justified revenge, and he paid the price!

The Moral of the Story

First of all, my Madrina didn't care that Tony's business kept flourishing even after months of performing her spellwork. That's because she was self-confident, patient, and determined that she would prevail. She knew this for two good reasons. She once told me that she was confident that her Orishas, the deities of Santería, would indeed help her. But if they didn't move quickly enough, her persistent behaviors would continue until they did. This is akin to the popular American analogy: *"Squeaky wheels get oiled."*

Madrina also poured tons of energy into the work via her screaming, actions, thoughts, behaviors, and convictions. People, such as myself, tried to avert her from continuing the spellwork. As much as she loved me, my words meant nothing to her. She ignored any and all deterrents.

Most importantly? When I asked her who the doll *"represented,"* she didn't acknowledge my verbiage. She instead replied, *"This is Tony,"* implying that the doll was actually Tony and not just a representation of him.

This is the same attitude that is needed when manipulating figural candles. While working with candles that symbolize a body, or body part, it is imperative to believe that we are actually working with the authentic corporeal element.

CHAPTER THREE
PREPARING YOUR TOOLS & STRATEGY
Getting All Your Magical Ducks in a Row

Now that you've prepared yourself for the work, it's important to gather the proper tools for the magic at hand. It's also crucial that you learn how to utilize them effectively for the goals you're hoping to accomplish.

THE ROLE OF FIGURAL CANDLES IN SPELLWORK

About twenty years ago, a lady bought a lottery ticket and won around fifty million dollars. She was *"media-friendly"* and eagerly shared her wisdom regarding how she was able to win In her opinion, it wasn't a matter of luck. Instead, she vehemently professed that she manifested the winnings through creative visualization.

The lady said that for six months prior to buying a lottery ticket, she spent fifteen minutes a day, every single day, in meditation. While doing so, she envisioned herself winning millions of dollars. Thereafter, she bought lottery tickets, consistently playing the same numbers, while continuing her meditation. Although it took her around a year altogether, she visualized herself as a multi-millionaire and ultimately manifested her goal.

Creative visualization is a technique that involves producing a detailed mental image of a desired outcome and believing that image to be true. This technique has been practiced for millenniums.

In fact, the Stone Age people went a step further. They practiced sympathetic magic, which assumes that a person, object, or event can be magically affected through an object representing it. Our ancient ancestors drew pictures on cave walls with great skill and accuracy of animals in general, and those they wished to hunt down. Archaeologists recognized the latter because these specific drawings had real or molded spears hurled into them, or included in the drawings themselves.

Figural candles provide us with the ability to practice both creative visualization and sympathetic magic more effectively. Unlike cave paintings, we can feel, hold, smell, taste, maneuver, and manipulate the person, object, or event, which better enables us to magically overshadow the current situation. Moreover, sometimes spell work may require role playing, and these candles facilitate the gestures by providing the practitioner with a focal point.

We can also use unlit figural candles as *effigies*, which are objects that represent a specific person, or people if the candle is made up of two individuals, side by side. Candles shaped as a man or woman are frequently used in lieu of cloth, clay, or other types of dolls.

How does one make a figural candle spell effective? You MUST believe! After preparing a candle, apply your knowledge of creative visualization and sympathetic magic. You must believe that it is no longer a mere candle, but an existing life force. If the figural is that of a person, imagine and feel their negative and positive attributes. An angel candle or a beloved deity will emit vibrations of love. Hear the sounds coming from an animal candle, and feel the pulsating heartbeat of a heart candle. Talk to it and wait for responses either through vibrations or, if it's ignited, through fire and candle communication. If you believe, it will happen.

Now that we know about visualization and sympathetic magic, let's get started on the work!

Ten Steps for Preparing Your Figural Candles

Step One: Choose the Color For Your Intention

First, ensure that the correct candle color has been selected. White is a neutral color and can be used in lieu of any other color. However, if white is not available, or if you wish to strengthen the spell by coordinating the color to the condition of the spellwork, here are the most common colors for any array of conditions:

- **Black:** Banishing any unwanted condition, such as a bad habit, negativity, weight gain, etc. Also employed for banishing people. Black is also used for negative spellwork, such as cursing, crossing, hexing, jinxing, breakup spells.

- **Blue:** Peaceful home, harmony, health, emotional and physiological healing, forgiveness. Although any shade of blue is acceptable, my preference for health and healing conditions is light blue.

- **Brown:** Court case spells and other legal matters, grounding, stability.

- **Gold:** Honoring the God, masculine power, wealth.

- **Green:** Business spells, fertility of crops, general good luck and luck in gambling, money spells, nature spells, steady work.

- **Orange:** Blockbuster, energy, road opener.

- **Pink:** Attraction, friendship, romantic love.

- **Purple:** Authority, control, domination, mastery, power.

- **Red:** Anger, lust, passionate love, sexual attraction.

- **Silver:** Dream magic, honoring the Goddess, feminine power, intuition, moon magic, psychism.

- **White:** A neutral color that can effectively replace any other color. But it is used for worship and spells of attunement with the higher self, blessings, harmony, purity, and spirituality.

- **Yellow:** Communication, intelligence, learning, memory enhancement, success.

Please keep in mind that certain revered deities are partial to particular candle colors.

However, if you are unaware of their preferences or are unable to obtain a particular candle color, it is acceptable to offer white as a substitute.

Step Two: Have the Basic Tools on Hand

Candles ought to be inscribed to identify who or what they represent, as well as with your command. Although some practitioners go to great lengths to do so with different instruments, the easiest route is to simply use a sharp pencil.

If you employ a spell that requires boring a hole into a candle, a soldering iron is an essential item for this purpose. Keep in mind that this device must be operated outside, as it emits toxic fumes.

Next, you will need tools to refill the hole. My method is to place a small candle, of the same color, into a metal cup. The cup is placed into an old pot and set on the stove. The heat is turned on to the lowest setting, which allows the candle to melt in a safe and uniform manner. Refill the hole of the figural candle with the melted wax using a syringe or a spoon.

Holy water is used to baptize and name the candle. To anoint the candle, use either olive oil or a prepared oil that complements the condition of the spell. Crushed plants and/or minerals are often used for dressing a candle.

Most importantly, be conscientious of fire safety. Since conventional candle holders are not designed to accommodate figural candles, you will need a sturdy aluminum pie plate, cake pan, or cookie sheet. Disperse sand over your altar. Place a few coasters over the sand and set the pan directly upon the coasters.

Step Three: Prime The Candle

We all know that fast, sloppy, and inattentive spellwork yields poor results. A common error is the lack of attention given to any tool utilized in magical practices. Because they aid us with spellwork, each tool must be given proper care and respect. Although Paganism is not my area of expertise, I have witnessed dozens of High Priests and Priestesses investing great efforts in consecrating their wands, chalices, blades, and other tools, prior to commencing a ceremony.

The same principles apply to candles. They are to be given proper attention and respect. Likewise, the more we interact with the tool, the greater our energy output. That same energy, released from our preparatory efforts, is absorbed by the candle wax, then later released during spellwork. This is the reason to prime a candle.

> **Note:** Please be aware that if a spell requires boring holes into the candle and stuffing it, do so before you prime the candle.

Step Four: Trim The Wick

Almost all candles are sold with extra-long wicks. Not only are long wicks a fire hazard, but they also produce high flames, excessive smoke, and wick knotting. In my experience, once a wick begins knotting, it will continue to do so, even with continued trimming thereafter. To prevent these complications, ensure that the wick is no longer than a quarter of an inch.

Step Five: Cleanse The Candle

Particles of energy attach themselves to objects in a swift and efficient manner. To make matters worse, candle wax is particularly suited to absorb these particles. Even if the candles are prewrapped by a factory machine, we just don't know where the wax, or the candles, have been. Additionally, we don't know who may have handled the candles prior to wrapping.

Aside from any negative or conflicting energy particles on the wax, dormant germs may also be resting upon them. Although factory-produced and wrapped candles may not have been directly handled by anybody, it's better to be safe than sorry. Thus, it is important to cleanse them prior to performing spellwork.

For cleansing, simply spray the candle with either Holy Water, Florida Water, or a mixture of one teaspoon of sea salt to one cup of water. Then wipe off the moisture with either a clean white towel or a paper towel. Better yet, set the candles directly on the towel and allow them to air-dry.

Step Six: Inscribe The Candle

The rationale behind inscribing a candle is that as the candle wax is being consumed, the energy of the command will be released into the spirit world.

Inscribing onto a figural candle can be a little tricky, as there are usually not enough smooth surface areas for engraving. There are usually many bumps, knobs, and bulges creating obstacles for a smooth, steady inscription. But there's a way to override the problem.

Try to find three smooth surface areas on the candle. Over each area, inscribe the target's birth name and birthdate in a horizontal fashion. If it represents an object or location, identify it in the same manner. Try not to lift your pencil or inscribing tool.

Cross over that identity with your command. For positive spellwork, the command is inscribed starting from the bottom of the candle and continuing toward the top, representing attracting something to you, such as love, success, money, and all favorable things. Conversely, inscribing the command starting from the top of the candle and continuing toward the bottom represents removal, banishing, or menacing requests.

On taper candles, it is usually traditional to inscribe both the identification and the command a certain number of times. But, due to all of the different shapes of figural candles, three times will suffice. However, you can also continue to write the command, independently, all over the candle to enhance your intentions. Just ensure that the command is consistent with your verbal and/or written commands.

Step Seven: Bless and Baptize the Candle

All candles, whether they represent a person or object, can be charged or blessed to infuse more of your energy into them. To charge a candle, visualize volts of electricity running down your arms and into your hands. Once these volts are in your hands, clutch the candle and visualize it absorbing the electricity. If you have performed this procedure correctly, you will feel the energy within the candle.

Blessing a candle is to use your own god or goddess–given power to do so. Hold the candle in one hand, and make the sign of the cross with the index and middle fingers of your other hand while stating aloud: *"By the power invested in me, I bless you in the name of the Father, the Son, and the Holy Spirit. Amen."* If your spiritual beliefs differ from Christianity, bless the candle according to your own faith.

A figural candle in the form of an effigy, such as a man, woman, animal, or body parts, ought to be named and baptized, just as one would name and baptize a doll. The acts of baptism and naming summon an essence of the target's spirit into the candle. This ensures a magical connection to the target.

To do so, anoint your right index and middle fingers with either Holy Water, Holy Oil, Florida Water, or whiskey while holding the effigy in your left hand. If you are a Christian, make the sign of the cross directly on the crown of the effigy's head with your anointed fingers while saying aloud: *"I baptize you in the name of the Father, the Son, and the Holy Spirit. Amen."* If you are of another religion or spiritual faith, baptize the effigy in the name of your deity.

If the candle represents a body part, baptize it anywhere on the image. If the candle represents two people, baptize them independently.

Step Eight: Name the Candle

To name the effigy, hold it in both of your hands and raise it up as high as possible. Envision electrical volts arising from your shoulders, traveling into your arms and hands, and finally into the effigy. While doing so, name the doll by screaming its name a total of nine times.

If the candle represents two people, such as a bride and groom, lovers, or a married couple, the naming ritual differs. Rather than holding it up to ceiling or sky and screaming the target's-- name into the tool, instead place the face of the first image in front of your lips and state: *"I name you [target's name],"* for a total of nine times, then repeat the steps with the other image's face.

Step Nine: Infuse Candle with the Breath of Life

Finally, breathe life into the candle by saying: *"I now give you the breath of life."* Then place your mouth directly over the effigy's mouth, and blow air into it. If it's a body part without a mouth, blow onto it slowly and rhythmically for a total of three times.

Step Ten: Anoint and Dress the Candle

The Holy Bible often mentions olive oil and it's my preference for anointing purposes. However, condition oils, also known as dressing, ritual, Hoodoo, or conjure oils, are mass-produced and readily available. They are created to complement the condition of your spellwork.

No matter what they are called, if you opt to purchase a prepared oil, in lieu of using olive oil, ensure that you are getting a quality product that contains herbs and/or an essential oil that relates to your spellwork. Also avoid purchasing scented candles in lieu of a prepared oil. In most cases, they are either artificially or improperly scented, which could ruin your spellwork.

Anointing a candle typically follows the same directions as inscribing it. To draw someone or something to you, anoint the candle starting from its base and continuing up to the wick. Conversely, if performing banishing, or negative spellwork, you would anoint the candle in the opposite direction.

This is just a symbolic gesture. If you make an error in the anointing process, don't panic. It is seriously doubtful that Spirit would deny a request just because the candle wasn't anointed per symbolic protocol.

Dressing the candle predominantly involves rolling the candle onto crushed plants, minerals, or incense immediately following the anointing process. But, because figural candles are irregularly shaped, it's easier just to sprinkle the dressing ingredients onto the candle.

Do not dress your candles with sachet powders as they will obstruct both the burning and communication processes. This includes powders that begin with the word *"precipitado."* They are designed to expedite manifestation, but not as a candle dressing.

Oftentimes, people are overzealously generous in dressing their candles with gunpowder, which is an explosive as well as a serious fire hazard. Gunpowder ought to be used sparingly and only by seasoned practitioners.

Now that you've been told what not to use, you might be asking yourself, *"Well then, what the heck do I use?"* Don't worry! Suggested dressing ingredients will be provided in the spellwork chapter.

If you have prepared your candle as directed, there is no doubt in my mind that it is loaded with energy. You will be able to feel the energetic vibrations emanating from the candle. To do so, without touching the candle, simply surround it with your cupped hands.

Preparing Your Petition Paper

Petition papers contain either requests, commands, prayers, or glyphs. Although they can be written on an array of materials, my preference is to use a torn piece of brown paper bag. This is because it is a traditional custom in the African magical diaspora practices. While many practitioners simply write out the entire petition and place the unfolded paper underneath their candles, my preference is the Hoodoo method as described below.

Simply tear off a piece of the paper bag while avoiding the manufacturer's designs, letterings, cuts, or folds. Then, without using scissors, attempt shaping it into a uniform square.

The petition is then inscribed with either a pencil or a fine-point marker. Avoid using ink pens as they tend to skid on this type of paper, thus losing letters, or even entire words.

For positive outcomes, write the target's name, or the identity of the place or object, on the first line. Then, underneath that line, repeat the technique. For money, success, and similar outcomes, there ought to be a total of five lines. If your pursuit is that of a romantic nature, such as attraction, commitment, love, lust, marriage, then write out seven lines of names

Turn the paper ninety degrees to the right and write a brief command, usually one to five words, directly over the names, superimposing them. This symbolically asserts your domination over the person or situation. Do this in the same fashion, writing one line below the other, either five or seven times, respectively. Each line must have the identical command as the line above it. Upon completion, it ought to resemble a square.

For banishing or negative spellwork, as with the positive work, write the target's name, or the identity of the place, or object, on the first line. Then, underneath that line, repeat the technique, But, this time, it is instead written either nine or thirteen times, once on each line. Turn the paper ninety degrees to the left and write a brief command, usually one to five words, directly over the names, superimposing them. This symbolically asserts your domination over the person or situation. This is again written nine or thirteen times, with the command on each line being identical to the one above it. Again, upon completion, it ought to resemble a square.

Next anoint the petition paper with either a condition oil that correlates with your spell or either olive oil or almond oil mixed with the appropriate herb that correlates to the condition of the spell.

Anoint your petition paper with the oil in five areas, commonly called the *5-Spot pattern*. To do this, moisten your index finger with the oil, then proceed to lightly dab each of the five spots with the oil, in this order: upper left-hand corner, upper right-hand corner, lower right-hand corner, lower left-hand corner, and finally, the middle of the paper.

For positive spellwork, fold the paper, only once, toward you. For banishing or negative spellwork, fold the paper, only once, away from you. Set the petition paper on the base of the candle holder. Then, place your figural candle directly over the petition paper.

If a petition paper is being stuffed into a candle, the process is completely different. A very tiny piece of brown paper, no larger than ½ inch by ½ inch, will contain your command, written only once, on both sides. A piece of paper any larger can become a serious fire hazard. My skull candle was once stuffed with a larger piece of paper. When the paper was ignited, the flame almost reached the ceiling. It was an intimidating, as well as a humbling, event. So, please be careful.

YOUR ALTAR

An altar is a table or place that serves as a center of worship or ritual. Many spiritual practitioners have stunning, if not breathtaking, altars. Sometimes, neophytes will feel either intimidated or overwhelmed by the sophisticated structures of these elegant altars. But the altars are easily explainable.

Most seasoned metaphysical practitioners adorn their altars with items representing the four elements of air, fire, water, and earth. They may have statues on it representing the deities assisting the spellcaster. The altar might also be adorned with items representing the condition of the spellwork, such as hearts for love, coins for money, skeletons for cursing, or keys for opening roads, which prompts the practitioners to engage in creative visualization. The color of the altar cloth may correlate to the condition of the spell.

Although stunning, the truth is that as long as the workplace is treated with reverence and respect, a simple altar will suffice. As a matter of fact, my altars are simple wooden fold-up tables. Sometimes other items are placed on my altars and sometimes it's just the candle.

Your altar can be ornate, or like mine, plain and unassuming. The choice is yours. Just avoid cluttering your altar with unnecessary items.

There was once a fraudulent woman who taught metaphysical practices. Upon personally visiting her domain, it was devastating to see her money altar, which was treated with utter disrespect. Not only was it in plain sight for all to see and handle, but it was also literally cluttered with *"junk,"* which collects dust and other unwanted particles. All these obstructive energies resulted in ineffective spellwork. Additionally, a cluttered altar is a potential fire hazard. If you wish to keep it simple, for indoor altars, you could use:

- A table or desk
- A workbench
- A bureau
- A bathtub*
- A sink
- A shower*

* Remove the shower curtains first.

Please do not place your candle in areas such as closets, or near combustible items such as curtains. Keep the altar at least twelve inches away from walls, too.

With the exception of moving candle spells or 7-knob wishing candle spells, my candles are rarely extinguished. If it's a skull candle spell, I'm awake until the wax is completely consumed. Otherwise, by the end of the night, the work is moved into the bathtub until the next day, when it is carefully returned to the altar.

For outdoor altars, which are strongly recommended for performing negative spellwork, you could use:

- The ground
- A porch or deck
- A backyard
- A graveyard*
- A barbecue pit*
- A secluded area

* for negative spellwork

Never perform positive magic concurrently with negative magic, on the same altar. Most spiritual practitioners have distinctly separate areas. They use one room or one side of a room for positive magical spells and another room or another side of the room for negative magical spells. My positive spellwork is performed in a room upstairs while my negative spellwork is performed either downstairs or outside.

Additionally, with the exception of emergency spellwork, positive magic ought to be performed during a waxing moon phase, whereas banishing and negative magic ought to be performed when the moon is waning.

Personal Concerns

Once in a while, you may wish to add one or more of your target's personal concerns, or *taglocks*, into the candle. Because most personal concerns contain DNA (deoxyribonucleic acid), which is a person's personal blueprint for life, you are adding an essence of that person's very being into the candle. Although not mandatory, having a personal concern allows the spellcaster to assert their domination over the target. Here is a list of bodily discharges containing DNA:

- Blood
- Feces
- Mucus
- Semen
- Tears
- Urine
- Dandruff
- Fingernails
- Saliva
- Skin cells
- Teeth
- Vaginal secretions
- Earwax
- Hair
- Scabs
- Sweat
- Toenails

Although fingerprints do not contain DNA, they are also considered personal concerns because they are each individual's personal identification mark. If the target is walking barefoot, those prints are also considered personal concerns.

Adjuncts to personal concerns are items that have been in contact with, or represent, your target. Although they have a weaker connection, these have sufficed in thousands of spells. They are items such as the target's photograph, his or her full birth name and birthdate, or the person's signature.

YOUR STRATEGY

It is always helpful to have a strategy prior to performing spellwork. This includes finding and learning as many facts as possible about the person, place, or object that you wish to manipulate. For example, performing a *"come to me spell"* spell on someone who just recently moved to another country will most likely have been performed in vain. One of my clients placed an employment spell on a company that had just filed for bankruptcy. She wasted money on supplies, time, and lots of energy. So, always get the facts first!

Another important factor in spellwork is timing. In numerous metaphysical practices, it is traditional to perform spells during specific moon phases and days of the week. This is because of the assistance provided by the energies emitted during specific times. Additionally, by waiting for the ideal timing, it also provides the practitioner with a window for optimal preparation.

Although it is beneficial to comply with spell timing guidelines in order to enhance your magic, there is an exception. If an emergency arises, such as a devastating health dilemma, or preventing someone or something from doing harm, perform the spell despite the moon phase. However, there are two distinct times when all spellwork ought to be avoided:

- ☽ **A Lunar or Solar Eclipse:** While some people profess that these events are times of gathering great power, it couldn't be further from the truth. During an eclipse, the energies of both the sun and the moon are blocked. Additionally, in ancient times, witches refused to cast spells during an eclipse because they believed that these events created great discord, and sometimes, even chaos. To this day, their beliefs still ring true.

- ℞ **When Mercury is in Retrograde:** Mercury is the planet that fosters communication. Three or four times a year, for a three-week period, the planet will appear to be moving backwards in the sky, as viewed from Earth. During these events, there are interferences in communication, resulting in confusion. We will find that others either don't understand the verbal or spiritual messages being conveyed, or there are misunderstandings. Since magic depends upon delivering messages into the universe, avoid this time to perform spellwork.

The good news is that the aforementioned events to avoid are infrequent. There are at least two hundred and seventy-five solar days during which spellwork will not be obstructed by celestial occurrences. During this *"free time,"* try to perform your spellwork under the following guidelines:

Moon Phases

A complete lunar cycle, or lunar month, lasts about 29 days. It consists of the waxing and waning moon phases, each lasting around fourteen to fifteen days. There are thirteen lunar months in a calendar year.

If you wish to start your spellwork on the day when the desired lunar phase appears, please check your calendar, your phone, or the internet for the exact time that it begins. This ensures that your spellwork is not being performed during an incorrect moon phase.

- **The Waxing Moon Phase:** This phase begins on the new moon and ends with the full moon. It is the time when the moon visibly increases in size, on a daily basis, from complete darkness to the brilliance of the full moon. Therefore, it is the ideal time to perform spells for growth. It is also a great time to draw something, or someone, to you, such as a job, money, and love. The waxing moon phase is also an ideal time for spellwork involving the improvement of situations, self, and others.

- **The Waning Moon Phase:** This phase begins two to three days after the full moon and lasts until the day before the new moon. As the moon wanes, or decreases in size, it emits banishing energies that eliminate or remove unwanted people or situations. It is also a great time for performing negative spellwork.

- **The Full Moon:** While scientists proclaim that the full moon immediately begins to wane minutes after it appears, its intense energy lasts for about two days after it first appears. It is a great time to perform any type of spellwork. But there are two specific nights, occurring yearly, of full moon activity that optimally enhance your chances of successful manifesting:

- **The Full Moon Closest to Halloween:** As both Samhain and All Saints' Day approach, the veil between our mundane world and the spiritual world begins to weaken, which facilitates our ability to communicate with entities. On the first night of the full moon closest to October 31, the veil completely disappears, and entities roam freely amongst us. This is a great day to cast a spell and will result in a heightened chance of success..

- **The Full Moon in Your Moon Sign:** Once, or sometimes twice a year, the full moon will fall on the astrological house of your moon sign. It is believed that on this day, if Mercury is not in retrograde and there are no lunar or solar eclipses, your chances of successful manifestation are optimal. This is your day, and you can perform any spell you wish. The sky is the limit!

Days of The Week

Each day of the week carries different magical energies. This is because the sun, moon, and planets are governed by the energies emitted by the sacred deity who rules over the individual celestial body.

SUNDAY

Ruled by the Sun, it is a day of masculine energy, strength, prayers, and God rituals. Sunday is also a good day to perform spellwork on conditions pertaining to:

🔥 Blessings   🔥 Boys   🔥 Energy

🔥 Fatherhood   🔥 Healing   🔥 Heath

🔥 Masculine issues 🔥 Strength

MONDAY

Ruled by the Moon, it is a day of feminine and Goddess energy, emotions, intuition, and mysticism. Monday is also a good day to perform spellwork on conditions pertaining to:

🔥 Divination   🔥 Feminine issues   🔥 Fertility

- Girls
- Motherhood
- Psychic vision

TUESDAY

Ruled by the planet Mars, the Roman God of war and courage. It is a day of both physical and emotional strength, dynamic energy, revenge, courage, and power. Tuesday is also a good day to perform spellwork on conditions pertaining to:

- Athleticism
- Competition
- Conflict and War
- Confrontation
- Courage
- Cursing
- Military matters
- Strength
- Victory

WEDNESDAY

Ruled by the planet Mercury, the God of trade, communication, and messages. It is a day for orators, public speakers, and entertainers. Perform spellwork on conditions pertaining to:

- Communication
- Conflict resolution
- Deal-Making
- Eloquent Speech
- Gambling
- Haggling
- Stage fright
- Throat ailments
- Travel

THURSDAY

Ruled by the planet Jupiter, the God of the sky and thunder. He is also called the King of Kings. Thursday is associated with abundance, prosperity, strength, and wealth. It is a great day to perform spellwork on conditions pertaining to:

- Court Cases
- Leadership
- Money
- Success
- Power
- Wealth

FRIDAY

Ruled by the planet Venus, the Goddess of erotic passion, beauty, fertility, and love. This is an excellent day to perform spellwork pertaining to:

- Attraction
- Beauty
- Charm
- Fertility
- Love
- Lust
- Romance
- Seduction
- Pregnancy

SATURN

Ruled by the planet Saturn, the God of agriculture and abundance. But he is also known as a malefic entity who rules over the domains of death, destruction, dissolution, and war. Saturday is associated with matters surrounding farming, including the cultivation of the soil for the growing of crops. It's also a good time for banishing situations, such as health problems or curses, or even people. It is also a good day for warfare against magical enemies as well as spellwork for the following conditions:

- Agriculture
- Banishing
- Break up
- Discipline
- Enemies
- Hunger
- Imprisonment
- Stability
- Uncrossing

Getting Assistance from Your Spiritual Court

Now that we have prepared our tools in order to generate as much energy as possible, we can also petition entities for help. Adhere to the old saying *"There is power in numbers"* because their assistance provides even more energy output. Additionally, they see and know things that we don't, so they can also battle unforeseen obstacles.

When petitioning for assistance or aid, always remember that each of us has a spiritual court we can call upon for assistance in both our lives and in our spellwork. They are readily available to us, and they are safe to petition because they are only looking out for our best interests. You must simply have faith in them. Who to call? Here are some suggestions:

- 🔥 The god or gods of your religion or spiritual practice

- 🔥 The archangels in heaven

- 🔥 A beatified person

- 🔥 Ascended spirits

- 🔥 Your ancestors who you know to have loved you

- 🔥 Your spirit guides

- 🔥 The god or goddesses of your religion or spiritual practice

- 🔥 The canonized saints

- 🔥 Folk saints

- 🔥 The deities of your religion or spiritual practice

- 🔥 Deceased friends who had loved you

- 🔥 Your guardian angels*

* for protection only

Getting acquainted with one, or perhaps even a few, of the members of your spiritual court prior to initiating spellwork is important because you will then have had an established rapport. Set up a little private area in your home to offer white candles and fresh water. Call upon the ones who make you feel comfortable. Address them by their proper names or titles. Introduce yourself and speak aloud with humility and respect, as if you were speaking to your own parents.

Do not request anything. Just continue talking to them and offering fresh water on a daily basis. Once the familiarization process is completed, they will most likely be readily available when help is needed.

While performing candle work, and the flame is ignited, there is one entity who is constantly present and also engages in communication. Most neophytes are usually unaware of his spiritual presence, his splendor, and his astounding powers. He is the element of Fire.

In the subsequent chapters, we'll explore his nurturing, loving, magnificent, and intensely formidable authorities. Then, we will discuss how he communicates with us in candle magic, through the behaviors of both his flames and his smoke.

CHAPTER FOUR
THE IMMEASURABLE POWER OF FIRE
Its Fostering and Formidable Nature

> *O Sacred Fire, radiant and transformative, I humbly bow before your power. You are the spark of life, the warmth of the sun, the burning passion within my heart. May your flames illuminate my mind, ignite my courage, and purify my intentions. Guide me with your fiery wisdom and grant me the strength to overcome challenges with unwavering determination. As I tend to your sacred flame, I will be ever mindful of your potential for both creation and destruction. I ask for your blessings of light, energy, and renewal. Amen.*

The deep-rooted bond between Fire and mankind has existed since prerecorded history. Throughout the millenniums, Fire has treated humankind as any loving parent would treat their own children. He has provided us with warmth, comfort, protection, safety, and security. Fire was, and always will be, our companion, guardian, and teacher. And just as parents raise their children from infancy to adulthood, Fire has done the same for mankind. He has enabled us to evolve from simple cave dwellers to impressively intelligent members of a highly advanced human race.

As mentioned earlier, there are different types of fire rituals conducted around the world, including Native American practices, Zoroastrianism, Hinduism, and modern Witchcraft. The ancient Babylonians held a fire ritual called the Maqlû which was employed to banish harmful magic. Some rituals include feeding Fire in return for safety or protection. In ancient Rome, it was believed that by feeding Fire huge quantities of food on an annual basis, he would not burn down the entire city if he enters a state of ravenousness.

Fire has also taught us spirituality on numerous levels. The Druids used to conduct fire ceremonies in sacred groves. They believed that spirits roamed there, and the flames of fire would connect the Druids to that world. To this day, metaphysical practitioners still believe that fire acts as a bond between our mundane world and the spirit world. When lighting a candle, we believe that the flame also pierces the veil between these two worlds, thus making it easier to convey our messages.

After reading of his contributions worldwide, you might be asking yourself: *"If Fire is a single entity, how can he be in a multitude of places simultaneously?"* The answer is simple. An essence of his immeasurable spirit accompanies each individual fire, and that includes candle flames.

THE FOSTERING NATURE OF FIRE

I once had a profound spiritual experience with the element of Fire. If you hadn't noticed (or maybe you have?), in my vocabulary, Fire is referred to as *"he."* Fire is of a masculine nature but my once-in-a-lifetime experience with him only fortifies my need to refer to the element of Fire as such.

While temporarily living in Florida, a Pagan coven conducted an outside ceremony that was open to the public. Not knowing anybody, I attended out of curiosity, as did about two hundred other people. Upon my arrival, the High Priestess immediately approached me and said that she was *"told"* that I must be the fire keeper. This baffled me but I complied. She led me to a huge bonfire, relieved the person who was attending to it, gave me negligible instructions, then walked away.

Alone and worried about making mistakes, I heard a very deep, monotone, and emotionless voice say: *"Don't worry, I'll tell you what to do."* My first reaction was to search for the man talking but nobody was around. Thinking that my imagination was working overtime, I placed one log into the fire and the voice told me that it wasn't enough, and to add another. Realizing that the element of Fire was actually having a conversation with me was dumbfounding! Amazingly, he didn't scare me. In fact, it was comforting to know that he wouldn't allow me to make mistakes.

Feeding the fire became physically and emotionally challenging. It was hotter than hell, the logs were heavy, and he was hungry. It became a laborious task, but he kept my mind occupied. Later, he said: *"Look up at* the woman, straight ahead, with the dark hair. She's talking to the Priestess. She needs help. Her husband beat her and put her in the hospital. She wants to tell somebody but she's afraid. Go tell the Priestess. NOW! Go! Go!"

I ran to the Priestess and whispered in her ear that this woman is being severely abused and needs her help. The Priestess acknowledged by nodding, so I immediately returned to the bonfire.

After telling him what was said, he replied: *"She will help her. Just watch."* Minutes later, the Priestess was holding the lady in her arms while she wailed like a baby. Then he said, *"I have to go now."* I begged him not to leave and gave him another log. It was untouched. He said *"Goodbye"* and abruptly left. The fire quickly extinguished itself. Shortly following his departure, the event came to an end.

Realizing that I never saw any aspect of the ceremony left me feeling a little miffed. But when the High Priestess arrived and vehemently thanked me for my contribution, it felt sincere. She also told me that the lady confessed to enduring ongoing abuse and asked for help. So, my negative feelings dissipated because my experience with the element of Fire, as well as helping the battered woman, was well worth my attendance.

Interestingly, the Priestess never asked me how I knew about the lady, nor did she tell me why I was *"chosen"* to be the firekeeper. My only suspicion is that my sun sign is Aries, a fire sign, and I was born on a Tuesday, ruled by Mars and associated with the element of Fire. But we were complete strangers to one another, so how would she know that?

Nevertheless, I have never since had such an intense experience with the element of Fire. However, to this day, the flame of a candle always stirs feelings of a deep bond forged between the two of us.

LET FIRE TEACH YOU SPIRITUALITY THROUGH YOUR CANDLE FLAME

Throughout the ages, Fire has represented a diversity of magical symbolism, as well as a divine presence. Because of these beliefs, complex systems of rituals and ceremonies developed around the flames. Many believed, and still do, that the dance of the flames reveals mysteries of truth, secrets, and fate. Others believe that the element of Fire will grant favors.

But engaging in fire magic does not require complex ceremonies or great gatherings of people. The truth is that once you light a candle for spellwork, you are automatically engaging in a form of fire magic. Nonetheless, just as with firewalkers, fire eaters, and the experienced practitioners of the various fire rituals and ceremonies, a bond with this element ought to be established. Moreover, whether he's a God, a lesser divine deity, or an essence of the element of Fire, he is an existing entity. Approaching him with immense humbleness and respect will gain his approval.

While vacationing in the Caribbean, a professional fire-eater and dancer befriended me. We dined together on a few occasions, and he once carried me through the flames of his fire during one of his shows.

His attitude about fire was awe-inspiring and he regarded the element as being his partner. During his shows, he would calmly speak to the flames. His interaction with fire ought to be an example for all magical practitioners to follow.

Many people just light a candle, completely ignoring the majestic presence of Fire, and continue on with their spellwork. If the person extinguishes the flame, they simply blow it out, which is not only disrespectful, but this act also ridiculously insinuates the person's dominance over the element.

Below is a quick exercise toward establishing a 2-way familiarization process. The responsible and prudent approach ought to follow these guidelines:

1. Engage in fire safety practices (to be discussed later in this chapter).

2. Light the candle and wait five minutes, allowing the flame to pierce the veil between the mundane and spiritual worlds.

3. Introduce yourself to the element of Fire.

4. Spend about five minutes completely focused on the flame.

5. Look to the flame and its smoke on an ongoing basis to check for his communicative feedback.

6. Talk to the element on a frequent basis while focusing on its flame.

7. If you must extinguish the flame, tell him what you plan to do and when the candle will be reignited.

8. Thank the element of Fire.

9. Use a candle snuffer to extinguish it.

10. Repeat the entire process once the candle is reignited.

If you follow these guidelines, the element of Fire will most likely appreciate the respect you have demonstrated, which he rightfully deserves. In time, not only will he speak to you through candle communication, but through other venues, such as providing insight into matters of everyday life. In many cases, he will even become a protector and, without imploring his help, will even assert justice upon those who have wronged his favored people.

Even when his flames have engulfed terrains and structures, Fire will often spare the impending fate upon objects that are sacred to his favored people. For instance, the Shroud of Turin, a linen said to have been imprinted with the image of Jesus Christ after his crucifixion, has survived three distinct fires spanning hundreds of years. On June 10, 1194, the entire town of Chartres burned down, including their cathedral. But their beloved relic, a tunic allegedly worn by Mary as she birthed Jesus Christ, survived.

While some people believe that sacred objects are highly protected, others may profess that this displays Fire's proficiency of consciousness. Nevertheless, these are just two of many incidences occurring throughout history.

As a matter of fact, an article was published on January 14, 2025, by Ann Rodgers for the Catholic News. It was about a tabernacle surviving the incineration of an entire Catholic Church in Los Angeles, California, during the wildfires. She quoted Fire Captain Bryan Nassour as saying, *"Talk to any firefighter. In any religious building what usually survives is the cross and certain specific items that are highly religious, unless they've been specifically set on fire."*

THE FORMIDABLE NATURE OF FIRE

Some people proclaim that the element of Fire has a capricious nature, because he has the power to destroy, and does so on a frequent basis. My counterargument is that he can become intensely angry, just like any living being, if disrespected, neglected, imposed upon, misused, or exploited.

As a teenager in Cuba, my mother burned down the entire house after lighting a candle to a deity of Santería. Up to the day she died, she blamed the deity. But both of my uncles had a different version of the story. She neglectfully placed her altar by an open window, then closed the curtains for privacy. Fire, air, and curtains are not a good combination, so always ensure that any ventilation outlets are far from your candle flame. Also, do not place your candles near combustible materials.

In my book, *Hoodoo Cleansing and Protection Magic*, there was a story about a girl who became virtually manic in her attempts to follow numerous metaphysical practices simultaneously. Always having a multitude of candles lit at any given time in different areas of her home, the candles were misused, and she imposed upon the element of Fire. She ultimately died in a house fire.

Asking the Big Guns

After having explored fire rituals, fire worshippers, firewalkers, fire eaters, etc., it was time to ask myself, *"Who else knows fire?"* Obviously, it's got to be firefighters! After searching for the perfect person to question, my prayers were answered. It was an unprecedented honor to have been given the opportunity to interview an expert in this field.

Robert Anglin, the Captain of a fire station in Oregon, is a fourth-generation firefighter. It was both amazing and humbling to listen to this man talk about what he knows of fire.

He first explained to me that there are two types of firefighters. A structural firefighter primarily focuses on buildings and other structures. Whereas a wildland firefighter deals with terrain challenges, such as wildfires. Both are different sciences, and both types of firefighter specialists receive different training.

However, firefighters in rural areas have to be masters of both, and Captain (Cpt.) Anglin's district is considered a *"Wildland-Urban Interface."* This means that he and his crew must be ready for any type of fire at any time.

Fire as a Life Form

Being a metaphysical practitioner, my belief is that Fire is a living entity. After sharing my thoughts with Cpt. Anglin, he was asked for his view on the topic. It was a delight to hear his response:

> *It needs oxygen (O_2) to live, it consumes food, it grows, and it communicates. Of course it's a living being!"*

Communicating with Fire

While metaphysical practitioners interpret the language of candle smoke, an art called either *capnomancy*, or *libanomancy* (if reading the smoke of incense), firefighters practice a science called *"reading smoke."* Cpt. Anglin says:

> *We know what a fire is doing by reading its smoke. We analyze its color, density, volume, and velocity. This tells us where it is, the size of the fire, and what it plans to do. There's a wonderful video on the topic; you can find it on YouTube. It's called: The Art of Reading Smoke."*

The Basis of Candle Fires

When asked about the prevalence of candles as the source of fires, Cpt. Anglin replied:

> *Major fires have indeed been caused by candle burning due to a variety of factors. Candle placement is a major cause. These types of fires can be started by objects either above or next to the candle flame. This is due to the fact that there's actually two different types of heat transfer at play: "radiant" and "convective" heat. Both are equally important and well worth considering when lighting candles.*
>
> *Radiant heat is transferred directly through electromagnetic waves. With radiant heat, think of the sun heating the earth or people being warmed by a campfire. So, the air between the heat source and the object being warmed may not necessarily feel hot.*
>
> *Convective heat, on the other hand, transfers heat through air movement. Convective heat is transferred by the movement of hot air or gases—the actual heating of the surrounding air. This is why convection ovens are more efficient at cooking.*
>
> *It is unsafe to allow pets around lit candles. Cats are especially dangerous because they are not only attracted to fire, but they like to swat at the flames. We had one call when a cat became too friendly with a lit candle that was sitting on a coffee table. Its tail caught on fire, it ran to the curtains, and they too caught on fire. You can imagine the rest of the story!*
>
> *Another factor to consider are candle wicks. Most candles are sold with long wicks and, the longer the wick, the bigger the*

flame, which increases your chances of triggering a major fire. A long wick is also more likely to exhibit incomplete combustion.

If you see black smoke coming from your candle, that smoke contains the products of incomplete combustion and can lead to soot build-up on nearby walls/objects, and it can even cause health issues over time. If your candle is creating black smoke while burning, or if after extinguishing the candle, and the wick is curled, or looks like little knots, then the wick is way too long.

A neat trick you can try yourself to demonstrate this is immediately upon extinguishing the candle, hold a match in the black smoke a couple of inches above the wick. The smoke particles will ignite and travel down to the wick reigniting the candle. Always keep the wick trimmed short for fire safety purposes, and continue to trim it as the candle burns down.

Candle expulsions can also present a problem. These are tiny explosions caused by air bubbles, debris, or moisture pockets trapped in the candle wax. That's why you'll sometimes hear popping sounds. Cheaper candles can contain more air bubbles, especially pillar candles, when burned for more than 3 hours at a time. If a candle has herbs on it, they can pop off and cause a fire.

Also, because some cheap candle holders are less heat resistant, they can easily shatter. This is the reason I always recommend buying higher-quality candles from reputable sources.

All these factors can trigger major fires due to the proximity of highly combustible materials. These nearby objects are more prevalent than you realize."

How Fire Escalates in the Home

❝ *Understand that fire grows faster today than back in the 1960s. This is because the stuff that we put in our homes is full of new and highly flammable artificial fabrics and fibers. Unlike what was produced prior to, and around the 1960s, many materials are now petroleum-based, such as nylon and polyester, which causes fire to propagate much faster.*

So, the housing structure is not the problem, but what you put inside your home, such as the sofa, curtains, bedding, etc., are the prospective fire hazards. A smaller fire can double its size in less than two minutes, but these newer items have the potential of burning at a much faster rate. These newer synthetic fabrics and materials also create more toxic fumes, causing people to lose consciousness and be unable to escape the fire. Most people who die in structure fires do so because of the smoke inhalation, not because they were physically burned"

A Metaphysical Query

I told Cpt. Anglin of my belief that Fire can become *"angry"* if disrespected, neglected, imposed upon, misused, or exploited. His response was:

 *Fire does seem to affect many people whose lives are ruled by chaos. Here's a prime example:*

When I started with this department, my first structure fire involved a couple living in an RV. A gas line was not properly maintained and a fire ensued. Both occupants were able to escape with serious burns, but their RV, the neighboring RV, and several cars were destroyed. 3 or 4 months later, the same couple was involved in another RV fire in the next county over. Again, both were able to escape, however another 3 or 4 months later, the same couple was involved in a third RV fire, which ultimately, and sadly, cost the female occupant her life."

Later in this chapter, Cpt. Anglin will discuss safety tips. He will also tell us what to do if, God forbid, a fire does ensue.

CANDLE FIRE STATISTICS

The candle fire statistics reported by the National Fire Protection Association (NFPA) between the years 2018-2022, was startling. Some of the figures included:

- U.S. fire departments responded to an annual estimated average of 5,910 house fires started by candles.

- These candle fires caused an annual average of 74 civilian deaths, 558 injuries, and $257 million in property damage.

- 🔥 Candles were the second leading cause of bedroom fires, the fifth leading cause of living room fires, and the eighth leading cause of all home structure fires.

- 🔥 Half of the fires started were caused by candles being too close to flammable items.

Always Be Conscientious of Fire Safety

Again, it is worth repeating that we must continuously keep in mind that Fire reacts negatively if disrespected, neglected, imposed upon, misused, or exploited. If we handle our tools with prudence and thoughtfulness, the chances of creating a disaster are virtually eradicated.

A fire extinguisher and fire blankets ought to be readily available in the event of a mishap. Fire blankets are inexpensive and work well for small fires. But for larger ones, a fire extinguisher is warranted.

When working with incense, charcoal discs, candles, or any type of flames or fire, keep them away from combustible materials. As a former administrator of a world-renowned metaphysical forum, it was sadly devastating to read how numerous people performed candle spellwork in their closets. They did so to avoid being seen by their family members or significant others. Ultimately, one gal had a mishap, and her entire apartment burned down.

Dried herbs and paper are extremely flammable. When rolling your candles onto herbs, ensure that the herbs are finely crushed. Large pieces of herbs can catch fire and pop off the candle onto something flammable. If you plan to stuff a candle with dried herbs, use them sparingly. When stuffing a candle with a petition paper, ensure that the paper is very small.

Place your candle in a candle holder, on a dish, pan, aluminum cookie sheet, or another flat surfaced, fire-resistant foundation. Then adhere the candle to the base. Do so by melting the bottom of the candle so that it drips a little of the wax onto the holder, or onto a petition paper and/ or picture that has been set on the base. While the base of the candle is still soft, place it directly into the holder and press it firmly until the wax hardens and the candle is stable and doesn't wobble. Also ensure that neither the candle holder nor the altar wobbles.

My preference is to place the holder over two stacked cork coasters. Others place sand over their altar cloth and set the holder on the sand. Keep your candle at least twelve inches away from the wall.

Avoid cluttering your altar. Not only does clutter contribute to ineffective spellwork, but if an item is in close proximity to a candle, it can be a fire hazard.

When closing doors, do so slowly because it enhances the air flow. Rapid air movement causes the flame to momentarily behave in an erratic manner

If you must keep a candle lit, but unattended, remove anything combustible in the bathroom, such as shower curtains. Then, place your candle in either the bathtub or the shower.

Smoke is ignitable. So, when a candle is extinguished, ensure that the smoke, along with the flame, is completely extinguished before leaving your altar.

In addition to my safety precautions, Cpt Anglin adds his safety tips to the above suggestions:

- *"If someone is experiencing poltergeist activity, do not light any candles as mischievous spirits may knock them over."*

- *"Be cautious of curtains or hanging objects that could blow around in a breeze near your candles."*

- *"Keep the candle wicks trimmed to about ¼ inch."*

- *"Be aware of what is above, below, and beside the candle."*

- *"Keep the door closed in the room that has a lit candle. The door acts as a temporary barrier between fire and the rest of the house, and can slow down the spread of fire to other rooms."*

- *"When sleeping or leaving the home, close the doors of all rooms (this is also an everyday safety measure). Again, this can slow the spread of fire and toxic gases while giving you extra time to escape."*

- *"Have plenty of smoke alarms in place. You should have at least one in each room, placed at the highest point. There are two types of smoke alarms, the traditional type that uses a radioactive isotope, and a newer optical detector. Each type is better at detecting different kinds of smoke. Now, there are hybrid detectors containing the components of both."*

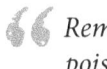 *"Keep pets away from lit candles."*

WHAT TO DO IF THERE'S A FIRE

Finally, Cpt Anglin gives us advice on how to handle a small fire or a large one:

> Remember that typically, people don't die from fires, but from poisonous smoke inhalation. If it's a small fire, your first goal should be to make sure everyone is out of the house and safe from smoke.
> Then try extinguishing it with a fire extinguisher and always aim for the base of the fire. The faster you can get it out, the better chance you have of saving your house. The best fire extinguisher to have on hand is an ABC dry-chem extinguisher, which is also effective on most household fires. If you're going to attack the fire yourself, stay as low to the ground as possible as this is where the cleaner and cooler air is.
> Depending on how big or small the fire was, you probably want to still call the fire dept as there may be hidden hotspots capable of rekindling a few hours later. But don't forget to close the door to that room, just to be safe.
> If it's a larger fire, get everyone out of the house. If possible, close the door of the room where the fire is, and call 911 or the fire department. Never attempt to fight a larger fire yourself."

HOMAGE TO FIREFIGHTERS

A firefighter is responsible for rapidly, efficiently, and safely performing various duties under emergency conditions. These conditions frequently involve considerable danger. Firefighters put their lives on the line every single day in order to save ours.

They have the courage to confront and tackle the rage and fury of formidable fires. But they also respond to accidents, collapsing buildings, earthquakes, hurricanes, and other disasters. They risk their own lives to rescue and treat the injured and dying.

When you think of a person entrapped in a car that is about to explode, who is there to come to the rescue? The firefighters! When heavy equipment or structures fall upon a person, who is there to come to the rescue? The firefighters! Whether it's a plane crash, wildfire, or any catastrophe, they are always here for us

Yet, they don't get the recognition that is duly deserved. These men and women are the unsung heroes of the world. If you see any firefighter, please thank them for their service. May God/Goddess bless every single one of them.

Now, on to candle communication…

CHAPTER FIVE
THE SECRET LANGUAGE OF FIRE
Interpreting the Messages of Flame, Smoke, and Wax

The candle feedback mechanism, or what the candle is communicating back to you, is conveyed through three processes. The first is pyromancy, which consists of observing and interpreting the movement of a flame. The second is capnomancy, or the observation and interpretation of the smoke produced by fire. The last is ceromancy, the art of interpreting candle wax movement and symbols.

Most of my clients completely ignore both pyromancy and capnomancy while solely concentrating on the remaining wax symbols from a completed candle burn. When asked why the behaviors of both the flame and smoke have been discounted, the usual response is: *"…it's too complicated."*

Sadly, they've missed a large portion of spiritual messages being conveyed due to misinformation regarding complexity. The truth? It's not that difficult if we are familiar with the very basic guidelines, which will be provided in this chapter. The foundation of effective interpretation is to familiarize yourself with the witches' compass.

THE CARDINAL DIRECTIONS

To understand fire and candle communication effectively, a proficient magical practitioner must first know the cardinal directions. From a clockwise direction, they are the primary points of east, south, west, and north on a compass.

My distinction is made by starting in the east (as opposed to the conventional examples of cardinal directions being north, south, east, and west) for two reasons. The first being that numerous practitioners will create a circle of protection starting in the east, work their way clockwise, and return to the east in order to complete the circle. The second reason is that some magical practitioners prefer to perform specific spellwork facing a particular direction. In most cases, they prefer only to face east; thus, it is the primary cardinal point for us.

The Elements

Each cardinal direction represents one of the four elements of Western culture. They are as follows:

- **East:** Represents *Air*.
- **South:** Represents *Fire*.
- **West:** Represents *Water*.
- **North:** Represents *Earth*.

The Conditions

In synchrony with their assigned elemental representations, the cardinal directions give rise to connections with actions, conditions, or emotions. They also have planetary and deity associations. However, due to the abundance of deities within the numerous metaphysical practices of the world, the examples below will not be exhaustive.

THE EAST

Spellwork may involve conditions related to communication to (or through) the spirit world, confidence, energy, physical healing, prayers, personal protection, travel by air, or uncrossing. This direction is associated with the Sun, which also represents leadership, power, fame, self-expression, individuality, and awareness.

THE SOUTH

Conditions associated with this direction may include ambition, command, control, cursing, crossing, dark thoughts, mastery, and forceful power. The planet associated with the south is Mars, and it's related to action, conflict, and assertiveness.

THE WEST
This direction is associated with situations involving attraction, emotions, emotional healing, justice, love, lust, passion, and romance. Saturn is most commonly associated with the west cardinal direction and represents such attributes as discipline, responsibility, structure, and long-term goals. The moon, widely linked with love magic, is associated with the direction of northwest.

THE NORTH
Conditions pertaining to agriculture, business, communication with people, materialistic desires or needs, luck, money, road opener, or steady work. In many astrological traditions, the North direction is considered to be governed by Mercury, a planet known for preserving and protecting nature and mankind.

Cardinal Directions as Translators
The cardinal directions play an important role when interpreting why a candle flame, smoke, and/or wax remains may favor, or disfavor, a certain direction. For example, if performing a love spell and the flame or clear smoke wafts to the west, we know that this direction can represent romance. Therefore, the behavior of the flame and/or smoke may be interpreted as spiritual assistance being provided regarding your request. However, if the behavior is unfavorable and the candle exhibits unwanted signs, such as the wafting of sooty smoke toward that direction, it may indicate obstacles.

If the flame, smoke, or wax favors a particular direction, also consider the conditions associated with that cardinal point. For instance, if you are seeking reconciliation but the communication favors directional south, it could mean conflict still exists. If this happens, a healing or forgiveness spell might be indicated.

Moreover, the communication could simply represent a literal geographical location. In my practice, figural candles, dolls, jars, and other paraphernalia are utilized in spellwork. However, my two German Shepherd Dogs (GSDs) prevent me from lighting long-term glass-encased (vigil) candles. Because these types of candles are also employed in my practice, Nathen, my candle server, lights them concurrently during my spellwork. He lives three states and hundreds of miles away from me.

In almost all cases, my figural candles and his vigil candles communicate the same messages. Once, a client had hired us for justified retribution spellwork. Both my assistant and I received continuous messages of obstacles stemming from the direction of northeast.

Unbeknown to us, in anger, the client had erroneously forewarned the target of her intentions to curse him. We later learned that, upon her warning, the target immediately hired a powerful Babalawo in New York to protect him from any spellwork. New York, by the way, is northeast of both me and my assistant.

A common query is job opportunities. All components of the candle may try to tell the spellcaster or the client where to geographically seek employment.

Nevertheless, consider all aspects associated with directional communication. Flames, smoke, and/or wax could be talking about conditions, locations, or the chances of successful or unsuccessful spell outcomes. If the candle is communicating an unfavorable outcome, complete the spell anyway. Then, consider a new strategy and try a different approach.

Utilizing Your Altar as a Compass

My sense of direction is, and always has been, disgraceful. But when facing my altar, it becomes so easy to determine the cardinal directions. Even more astounding, it's just as effortless for me to identify the intercardinal, or ordinal, directions of northeast (NE), southeast (SE), southwest (SW), and northwest (NW).

This is accomplished by placing only one item in each cardinal direction that represents the elemental association with that point. When the candle flame or smoke wafts towards any direction, all one needs to do is to look at the proverbial *"compass points,"* or items, on the altar. Then, look to the representations associated with that specific elemental direction in order to identify a possible incoming message from Fire, a deity, or a spirit.

To avoid a potential fire mishap, place each item toward the edge of the altar in order to avoid the candle that is centered in the middle. My preference is to rest a small feather on the altar to represent east, a lava rock to represent south, a seashell for west, and a little bit of soil to denote north. But there are alternatives to my selections and a multitude of options. Here are just a few examples:

CARDINAL EAST

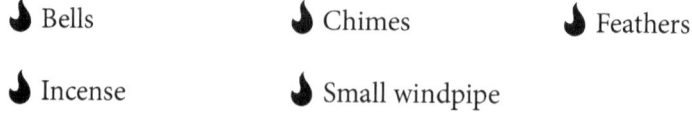

- 🔥 Bells
- 🔥 Chimes
- 🔥 Feathers
- 🔥 Incense
- 🔥 Small windpipe

CARDINAL SOUTH

- Igneous stones*
- Lava rocks**
- Volcanic ash
- Small red candle

Andesite, basalt, obsidian, pumice, or rhyolite.
**Also called "scoria," widely available and used for garden decorations.*

CARDINAL WEST

- Chalice
- Conch shell
- Seashell
- Seaweed
- Water

CARDINAL NORTH

- Roots of a plant.
- Pebbles and rocks
- Pentacle
- Seeds
- Soil

Now that you understand the cardinal directions, you're halfway there. Congrats!

CONSIDERATIONS PRIOR TO LIGHTING THE CANDLE

Before lighting your candle, first consider the physics of the candle placement, the ingredients on or inside your candle wax, and the quality of the wax because they will have a bearing on the candle burn. These disruptions are not related to candle communication.

Candles ought to be placed away from any drafts such as open windows, air vents, fans, or fast body motions. Rapid wafting airflow will artificially manipulate the candle flame and smoke, thus producing false communicative feedback. It can also cause the flame to either extinguish itself or to grow exceptionally tall and possibly burn something nearby.

If your candle has been dressed in herbs and/or glitter, you will frequently hear popping sounds after the candle is lit. If your candle has been stuffed with herbs or petition papers, popping sounds also occur once the flame comes in contact with them. When fire is consuming an ingredient and produces sounds, as well as a temporarily erratic flame, it is not candle talk. The behaviors are simply physics in action.

Also consider the consequences of purchasing low-cost candles. They are usually made of poor-quality wax, which also has tons of bubbles inside. You might hear lots of popping sounds, which are called expulsions or tiny explosions. They can produce a weak flame, resulting in an incomplete candle burn. But if the wick is sturdy, the wax of the figural candle will melt and pool too fast. Frequently, a vigil glass container will shatter. Remember, you get what you pay for!

ONCE THE CANDLE IS LIT

Remember that Fire is an entity who sees and hears everything. Additionally, the flame also pierces the veil between our mundane world and the spirit world. When this happens, communication with other spirits commences. So everything said after the candle is lit will be heard by many entities. Therefore, avoid any conversations with people or pets when near the flame, as there can be miscommunication between you and the entities.

Even if a spouse, child, or pet is on the other side of a closed door, it can be disruptive. If they're making annoying sounds, it is instinctive to shout out commands like *"No!,"* *"Shut up!,"* or *"Stop it!"* But if the entities hear these commands, don't just assume that they know who you're talking to. Instead, they'll probably believe that you are speaking to them. They could cease to assist you. This is another reason that seasoned metaphysical practitioners wait until they're alone to cast a spell.

Last, but certainly not least, do not engage in any telephone conversations or text messaging while casting a spell. Effective spellwork requires consistent, unform energy output. Additionally, entities ought to be given our respectful and undivided attention. For these reasons, it is my habit to keep the phone in a different room or turn the ringer off to prevent being interrupted

Pyromancy
Interpreting Fire Talk

Imagine it's ancient Greece, around the years 8,000-9,000 B.C. Multitudes of people of commoners and royalty alike, dressed in long tunics fastened at the shoulder, or wearing cloaks, flocking to the slopes of Mount Parnassus in order to reach Delphi. Envision these gathered people anxiously anticipating the chance to receive messages and divination from the Sun God, Apollo, through the entranced high priestess, called *"Pythia."* Today, we simply call her *"The Oracle of Delphi."*

But Delphi was also home to other oracles, who were the priests and/or priestesses acting as mediums. As visitors awaited a chance to speak to Pythia, they also sought divination from priests who performed pyromancy, the practice of interacting with fire or flames for divinatory purposes. In my imagination, these people sat around a huge bonfire while the priests conversed with, and conveyed messages from, the entity of Fire.

The craft of pyromancy has been practiced all around the world for millenniums. As a matter of fact, we already know that this art most likely began in the Middle Old Stone Age, or *"caveman"* era. It is one of the few ancient practices that still exists today because the element of Fire is a timeless, fostering, and foreboding entity.

So how can we perform pyromancy? It just takes a little bit of patience and observation. Although none of us can achieve expertise after just one attempt at interpreting fire-talk, remember that it takes practice in order to achieve proficiency. However, there are some people who immediately bond with the entity of Fire, while instantaneously grasping his language. My guess? It's because they displayed unadulterated respect in his presence.

Before defining the language of Fire, it is essential to first look deep into his nature. We do this in order to understand his personality, as well as to appreciate his splendor.

Begin the Communication Process

If you have followed the exercises in the previous chapter, you already know that the first few encounters require a little bit of time, concentration, and good observational skills. But with practice, it will become second nature in a short while.

STEP #1
Light the candle and wait five minutes in order to give the flame time to pierce the veil between our mundane world and the spiritual world.

STEP #2
Introduce yourself. Then, tell the element of Fire about your spell intentions.

STEP #3
Perform your spellwork.

STEP #4
Once your spellwork is in progress, the flame ought to have a consistent radiance. If it's strong, focus your vision on the center of the flame for about five minutes. Relax and try to imagine that nothing else matters except you and his light. Do not become one with the fire; instead just bond with it.

STEP #5
By this time, the flame will begin providing communicative feedback. Do keep in mind that disrupting the flame (such as breathing heavily upon it), or abruptly extinguishing it without prior notice, could change the message. It's akin to someone talking, but then another comes along and covers his or her mouth. That person might think twice about speaking freely ever again!

STEP #6
Attempt to define the behavior of the flame. If there's a mechanical problem, such as a faulty candle or wick, correct the problem. If the flame is behaving erratically, consider the physics. This type of behavior is usually caused by rapid wafting airflow arising from open windows, air vents, fans, etc. If this is the case, move the candle away from the draft.

STEP #7
Once the behavior of Fire is understood, don't forget to verbally express gratitude for his input.

Defining The Language Of Fire

There are several omens and portents associated with candle flame divination throughout the world. For example, the old Hoodoo practitioners professed that upon immediately lighting a candle, if the flame is short, a short visitor will arrive, whereas if the flame is tall, expect a tall visitor. They also believed that if a candle extinguishes itself before burning to the end, expect to hear news of a death.

Based on centuries of interactions and experience with candle divination, the numerous beliefs throughout the world are most definitely trustworthy. Do not negate the beliefs. Just keep in mind that others are practicing different divination systems that do not apply to the following interpretations:

- **A strong, tall, steady flame:** Your prayers and petitions are being heard by those in the spiritual realm. If the flame is consistent in its character, you will receive assistance with your request. Keep in mind that it does not necessarily mean that your wish will be granted. Instead, it indicates support from the entities whom you petitioned.

- **A strong, tall, bouncing or *"happy"* flame:** This usually indicates that the target is being affected by your spellwork.

- **A strong, tall flame that leans toward a particular direction:** Usually a positive sign, so look to the cardinal directions, and their interpretations, for a better understanding of the message.

- **A strong, short flame:** Either the candle wick is too short, or it is an indication of low energy output. In other words, the smaller the flame, the more vivacity that you must add to the spell. When you do so, the flame will usually increase in size.

- **A strong blue candle flame:** Powerful spiritual energy is present and assisting with the spellwork.

- **A strong red flame:** This indicates that there is minimal spiritual assistance being provided. You must again call on your petitioned entities or request additional spirits to assist you with your spellwork.

- **A strong flame that hisses, sizzles, crackles, or pops:** This can either indicate candle expulsions, due to cheap wax, or an incoming message from the spiritual realm. If the latter, it means that either the element of Fire, an ancestor, or another entity is trying to convey a message to you. Just relax and concentrate on the flame while asking spirits for clarity.

🔥 **A strong flame that burns only on one side:** Either you have a faulty candle, a faulty wick, or it could indicate an incomplete manifestation of your desired outcomes.

🔥 **A strong flame causing the candle to explode:** If this is not a faulty candle, then an explosion is a sign of failed spellwork. If something catches on fire, it also foretells imminent danger ahead for either the spellcaster or for their client (but not the target). The danger does not necessarily indicate physical harm. This once happened to me while performing a spell for a client. A week later, he was served with legal papers and sued for back-pay child support. The poor guy didn't even know that the child had ever existed.

🔥 **A strong, but unsteady flame that repeatedly flares, dips, bends, or gutters:** If this is not a faulty candle, or there are no incoming drafts, then you are receiving opposition from your target. More and/or different spellwork is highly suggested.

🔥 **Multiple flames arising from one wick:** Two or more flames can indicate that one or more people, depending on the number of flames, are either working to help or to oppose you.

🔥 **A strong flame causing a fast-burning candle:** In any kind of spellwork, fast movement usually indicates short-term results. For this reason, any type of *"fast luck"* products are not recommended in my practice. Thus, a fast-burning candle usually indicates that part of the spell will manifest, but only for a brief period of time. Repeating the candle work is highly recommended.

🔥 **A strong flame with a slow candle burn:** Usually indicates that the spell will take a longer-than-expected time to manifest.

🔥 **A weak flame with a slow candle burn:** Usually indicates that the practitioner has performed either a weak or incorrect spell. Attempt to strengthen the spell by increasing energy output. If the flame does not grow, do not extinguish the candle. Instead, allow a complete candle burn, then perform other types of spellwork.

- **The flame extinguishes itself:** Just as with a weak slow burn, it could also indicate that the practitioner has performed either a weak or incorrect spell. Attempt to strengthen the spell by increasing energy output. However, if you have had to relight the candle on the third try and it again extinguishes itself, this is a clear message from the spirit world that your spell will not manifest.

- **An extinguished candle that continues to glow:** Although this is a rare event, when it does happen, there will be misfortune for either the spellcaster or the client.

While Burning Two Candles or Two Wicks

Some figural candles are made as one unit representing two people. These candles have two wicks in order to distinguish one person from another. Examples include candles symbolizing lovers, marriage, divorce, etc. A practitioner will either use the single unit candle representing two people or employ separate candles to represent each individual person. Nevertheless, the language of Fire remains the same, with two additional indicators to explore. The signs to look for are attraction and repulsion.

When the flame of one candle leans toward the other, it is a sign of attraction. When they both lean toward one another, there is a mutual attraction. Conversely, if the flame is leaning away from the other, it is a sign of resistance, or repulsion, to that person. If they both lean away from each other, the feelings are mutual!

Seek Answers

Keep in mind that the element of Fire is your friend. If his flame is behaving in an undesirable manner, talk to the fire. Ask him questions, one at a time, and await his answer. You may receive further communication from him. Maybe you'll hear his voice or receive a profound psychic impression such as a vision or a thought. Just be patient.

CAPNOMANCY
Interpreting the Smoke of Fire

One of my goals is to teach everyone how to distinguish the difference between capnomancy and libanomancy. *Libanomancy* deals with divining and interpreting the language of smoke that is emitted from incense. On the other hand, *capnomancy*, which is the focus of this section, is divining, or interpreting the language of smoke emitted from fire. Upon careful consideration regarding how to emphasize the latter, the old Western movies and television programs came to mind.

A Story to Remember

Having watched a multitude of these Western shows throughout the decades, it became clear to me that the Native Americans of this land might be masters of capnomancy. Since they appeared to be exceptionally gifted at corresponding with others, in great detail, through *"smoke signals,"* they are probably experts in smoke divination too.

After all, millions of us viewed groups of Native Americans sitting around a bonfire wearing headbands or *"caps"* (*as in capnomancy!*) adorned with feathers. Then, large pieces of deerskin cloths were fanned over the fire and smoke in order to construct words and sentences. We know this because, on television and in the movies, there was always someone around to interpret the smoke signals to their gullible viewers, such as myself.

My misconstrued belief was that all Native American people could both create and interpret detailed smoke signals from fire. So, it inspired me to contact my dear friend, a native Ojibwe, in order to obtain more information from his tribe regarding the topic of capnomancy. His very short, but polite, response was that nobody ever talked about this topic.

Upon further research, I learned that the media had grossly misrepresented our Native American compatriots for decades. No such scenarios ever existed. Neither words nor complex languages have ever been fashioned from smoke. Although there were a handful of tribes, such as the Apache and Navajo, capable of creating brief warning signals of danger or approaching enemies, the rest of what was aired through the media industry was sorely exaggerated and ridiculed. Last, and most importantly, a sincere apology was conveyed to my Ojibwe friend!

The art of capnomancy probably originated in the Stone Age period, around the same time as did the art of pyromancy. My educated guess is that most Native American medicine men are more than capable of divining with fire and smoke, but do so in seclusion. Nevertheless, it is my hope that this little story has helped you to remember the term *"Capnomancy."*

The Physics

Smoke is a byproduct of incomplete fire combustion. Therefore, when performing capnomancy, remember that you are still communicating with the element of Fire. He's just using a different mode of expression. Think of it as a person attempting to communicate a message that you just don't understand. So, that person might say: *"In other words…"* and change his or her verbiage in order for you to understand what is being said.

Keeping this in mind, there are four behaviors to first consider when attempting to interpret the language of smoke.

1. **Color:** Although fire can produce black, blue, brown, or grey smoke, the most common colors produced by candle flames are black and light grey to white.

    A light color is usually a favorable sign. Black or sooty smoke, on the other hand, can indicate an unfavorable sign for most spells. However, if the spell is to curse, hex, or cross someone, it could either be a favorable sign, indicating assistance with the spell, or an unfavorable sign denoting resistance. Look to the accompanying patterns, shapes, and/or symbols for clarification.

2. **Volume:** Depending on the message being transmitted, a lot of smoke is a strong message whereas, a little bit of smoke may indicate a suggestion or simple continuity alongside your spellwork.

3. **Velocity:** The speed in which the smoke is travelling, accompanied by color, shapes, etc., can be an indicator of the speed of manifestation. However, if the accompanying volume and/or color is unfavorable, it could indicate strong resistance.

4. **Odor:** With the exception of negative spellwork, a pungent odor is a sign of resistance.

The Movement of Smoke

- 🔥 **Thin, straight, vertical, unbroken single line:** If it's in light color, it's a good omen.

- 🔥 **Heavy, straight, vertical line:** Also called a smoke plume, may indicate that your spell will not manifest.

- 🔥 **Broken vertical line:** Resistance to spellwork.

- 🔥 **Moves toward a particular horizontal or vertical direction:** Usually a positive sign, so look to the cardinal directions and their interpretations for a better understanding of the message.

- 🔥 **Shifts toward the spellcaster:** Something is coming to you.

- 🔥 **Shifts away from the spellcaster:** Could either mean a successful banishing spell, or the end of something that is related to the spellwork.

- 🔥 **Moves downward:** Either the wrong spell was implemented, or the spell will not manifest.

- 🔥 **Smoke touches the ground:** Immediate action must be taken to prevent problems.

- 🔥 **Smoke in all directions:** Confusion, disruptions. Try a different spell.

- 🔥 **Smoke struggles to move upward:** There are challenges to the spellwork. More, or different, spellwork is needed.

- 🔥 **Smoke breaks into separate wafts:** Other people are involved in the situation at hand.

Defining Smoke Patterns and Shapes

Below are just a few of the most common patterns and shapes produced by the smoke of candle flames:

- 🔥 **Swirls or spirals:** Spell intentions are not clear. Be more specific with your verbal and written petitions.

- 🔥 **Unbroken, complete circle:** This indicates success with spellwork.

- 🔥 **Broken circle:** The Spell will manifest if more energy output is provided.

- 🔥 **Ladder:** Spell will manifest, but it will take more work, either in the mundane world or with your spellcasting, to achieve success.

CEROMANCY
Interpreting the Shapes of Wax Left Behind

The history of candle wax divination might be traced back hundreds of years, to the Greeks. They interpreted the shapes and patterns of the wax to predict the outcome of battles and other important events.

Candle wax divination also played a significant role in medieval Europe. Because candles were often used for religious ceremonies, they were considered to possess powerful spiritual properties. Therefore, many people believed that the symbols formed by candle wax were messages being conveyed from the spiritual world.

Later in the 17th century, candle wax divination became popular in England, where it was often used by fortune tellers and mystics. It was during this time that the practice became known as *"ceromancy,"* a term derived from the Greek word *keros*, meaning wax.

During the 19th and 20th centuries, candle wax divination gained popularity in the United States and was widely practiced by spiritualists and psychics. Today, it remains a popular form of divination.

Although the technique of divination using wax is popularly known as ceromancy, the art is also interchangeably termed *ceroscopy* or *carromancy*. However, it is my preference to distinguish the varying terms from one another.

CEROSCOPY
This is a system of wax divination employed by placing hardened wax into a heated vessel and then melting it until it becomes a liquid. That wax is then carefully poured, a little at a time, into a container of cold water. The wax immediately hardens and forms shapes and symbols that are

interpreted by the reader. In ancient times, people melted their wax in brass vessels. Today, wax can be melted through various heating vessels such as a double boiler.

CARROMANCY

This method of divination simply involves dripping the melted wax from a burning candle into a bowl of cold water, then interpreting the hardened wax symbols. It is believed that around the year 500 A.D., this system was also practiced by the ancient Druids.

Today, the technique remains a widely employed divination tool. Because the terms are interchangeable, it is considered to be a second style of ceromancy.

CEROMANCY

This is the art of reading melted and hardened candle wax symbols, shapes, and forms. Unlike carromancy, the liquid wax is not poured into water. Instead, the hardened remnants, after the candle spell is completed, are interpreted. The shapes taken on by the hardened wax are called *"persistent images."* Ceromancy will be the focus of this section, but before we get started, there are a few things to consider prior to your divinatory pursuit.

Physics, AGAIN???

This will be a short paragraph. Promise! But, because an ideal candle burn is desired in order to receive accurate wax communication, we must consider the climate.

Ambient air temperatures affect a candle's burn patterns. In a cold room, they will burn at an unusually slower rate. Whereas, in a hot room, they will burn excessively fast. Sometimes, high ambient temperatures may even cause the candle to bend.

Consequently, an artificially induced burn rate will also produce false symbols, forms, and shapes. So, please ensure an ideal room temperature while burning candles.

Resist Pareidolia

Pareidolia (pronounced *"par-i-DOH-lee-a"*) is a psychological phenomenon in which the human brain sees recognizable images—most often faces—in random arrangements of shapes. Many see human faces in inanimate objects, such as the face of Jesus on their sandwich or the face of the man on the moon. This most often occurs in people who are religious or strongly believe in the supernatural.

Images in candle wax remnants can be extremely confusing to neophyte practitioners. But anybody, including myself, can be easily misdirected into pareidolia when working with figural candles. This is because they generate large amounts of residual wax, which is initially difficult to interpret. When we can't recognize a shape, form, or symbol in the wax, there is a sudden sense of distress. Although there are many theories regarding this phenomenon, it is my suspicion that our brains compensate for these feelings of uneasiness. The brain does so by providing a false recognizable image to eliminate any stress. Again, if we are religious or believe in the metaphysical, a face is that comforting image.

One of the best ways to overcome the tendency to see faces in the wax is to initially glance at the wax remains, recognize the face(s), remember what you've seen, and then walk away. Wait for at least at least twenty-four hours, and remember the face (s) observed. Before returning to the residual wax s, make a concerted effort to ignore or dismiss those images.

Knowing that my brain is preprogrammed to pick out faces and not a true communication from spirit, I will look at everything else in and around the misperceived faces. Once my brain has accepted the fact that it was merely an illusion, the pareidolia begins to dissipate and relevant symbols begin to appear.

Three Common Figural Candle Burn Outcomes

1. **The candle wax is completely consumed:** This is known as a *"clean burn"* and is viewed as a highly favorable sign.

2. **The wick disappears and the figural candle still has most of its original form:** This is also called an incomplete burn. Either the wrong spell was implemented, or the spiritual world is denying your request.

3. **The candle leaves puddles of wax:** Don't worry! This is the most frequent outcome of figural candle burns for which we will now explore.

The Figural Flow

The benefit of figural candles is that they assist the practitioner to intensely focus on their desires. The disadvantage, however, is that the wax is usually not fully consumed during the candle burn. Instead, there are puddles of wax left behind, having flowed in different directions, and creating a variety of both relevant and irrelevant shapes and forms. The practitioner is forced to closely scrutinize each and every possible symbol to determine applicability. A taper candle without a holder will often behave in the same manner.

After a figural candle has self-extinguished, what is frequently observed are symbols resembling mounds, the waves of an ocean, or numerous flower petals. This is just residual candle wax overflow, or physics in action. However, do examine every area to identify any possible hidden symbols. Once, when attempting to prompt my workaholic boyfriend into taking a rest, there appeared to be a tiny rowboat within the waves of the residual candle wax. Two weeks later, he surprised me with tickets for a Caribbean cruise!

A candle set on the lid of a jar will frequently leave streams of wax starting from the candle all the way down to the base of the jar. In order to elude this nuisance, focus your attention on the area where the candle was initially placed. Look for symbols in and around that area. Then gradually expand your attention outward and continue to look for pertinent symbols.

If the wax has flowed to one side, observe the direction, then look to the cardinal points and their interpretations for a better understanding of the message. Try to connect the interpretations with other wax symbols in an attempt to unfold a story.

If performing a spell to bring something or someone to you, and most of the wax settles toward your position, it is usually a favorable sign. But if it settles furthest from you, it is viewed as an unfavorable outcome. Conversely, if attempting to banish something, such as an illness, the opposite symbolisms apply.

When a figural candle represents two people, such as lovers or a bride and groom, the seepage could represent tears of sorrow, or either the willingness or unwillingness of one person to let go of a relationship or situation. This behavior is also displayed when separate candles are used to represent two or more people.

Interpreting The Persistent Images

It is important to note that the reading of shapes and symbols can be highly subjective and will vary among different people. This is especially true if the practitioner has developed his or her own method of interpretations based on their intuition or experiences. My system of analysis is based upon personal symbols and traditional meanings.

Personal messages from spirit can be presented as meaningful numbers, letters, shapes, and symbols. Oftentimes, when performing justified cursing spells on behalf of clients, the residual wax of a figural candle will produce surprising shapes. They sometimes look like monsters, or they demonstrate unpleasant gestures. These forms represent the target's true character, thus providing me personal confirmation that he or she is indeed an awful person.

A traditional system consists of having specific meanings for the different shapes and patterns. Here are a few examples frequently seen with my candle burns, along with the traditional meanings that I use:

- **Acorn:** Good fortune
- **Bird:** Good news, good luck
- **Clouds:** Trouble, obstacles
- **Dove:** Unadulterated success
- **Flower:** Spell will manifest
- **Lion:** Strength
- **Mouth:** Expect news
- **Snake:** Enemies, evil

- **Apple:** Happiness, success
- **Circle:** Completion
- **Dog:** Loyalty
- **Fish:** Excellent sign
- **Heart:** Romance
- **Moth:** Caution
- **Octopus:** Entanglement

For traditional definitions, look to tea leaf interpretations in order to translate the messages. Unfortunately, Google searches appear to provide a multitude of different and confusing explanations. Therefore, my go-to book for the interpretations of shapes and symbols, presented by both smoke and wax, is: *Tea-Cup Reading A Quick and Easy Guide to Tasseography*, by Sasha Fenton.

Perfecting the art of ceromancy requires patience, good observational skills, and practice. But with a little bit of time, this formula will yield great results.

CHAPTER SIX
A FIGURAL CANDLE MAGICAL GRIMOIRE
A Compendium of Spells for Every Intention

This chapter is a complete grimoire of magical spells designed for nearly every magical intention and figural candle type you can think of. Whether you're looking for love, in need of money, trying to remove a curse, spice up your marriage, or bring healing to the sick, these powerful spells will aid you in every area of your life!

DECIPHERING THE FORMAT

Symbolism
First, the symbolism represented by each candle will be explained. In some sections, color associations with the desired conditions will also be reiterated.

Suggested Spellwork
Then, you will be provided with suggested spellwork associated with each candle type. Some candles offer multiple spells. Please consider that, with every candle, there are numerous ways to perform spellwork. Therefore, feel free to use your God/Goddess-given talent of ingenuity to either create your own spells or to modify the ones presented here.

YOU WILL NEED:

- A list of items you will need for the spell, marked by a checkmark.

SUGGESTED CANDLE DRESSINGS

- Next, a list of suggested dressings for candles is recommended, each marked by a leaf icon. You may use as many as you wish, but just remember that finely crushed herbs, as opposed to large bits, will avert fire hazards.

SUGGESTED PRAYER

- Finally, prayers to enhance your spellwork are also frequently offered, and are drawn from Christian, Jewish, and other faiths, and are marked by a bible icon. They are presented, in their entirety, in the last chapter. However, with the exception of a few workings, they are purely discretionary. Feel free to utilize them, recite prayers within your own spiritual belief system, or simply plead your petition.

Today, there is a vast array of candle molds available. However, only the most readily obtainable figural candles will be explored in this chapter. Only use unscented candles, as, in most cases, they are either artificially or improperly scented, which could ruin your spellwork.

Now that we have examined almost every aspect of how to perform a figural candle spell, it's finally time do actually do the work!

ANGEL CANDLE
(Large)
For Veneration, Guidance, or Protection

Symbolism

An angel is defined as a spiritual, heavenly, or spiritual being created by God. Some act as messengers, or intermediaries, between God and man.

Although we don't know how many exist, in Hebrews 12:22 of the Holy Bible, it states "...*an innumerable company of angels.*"

The hierarchy of angels is described, in some religious belief systems, as having three orders: highest, middle, and lower. Each order contains choirs that are classified from the highest to lowest positions on the ladder. Beginning with the highest ranking and descending down to the lowest, they are: Seraphim, Cherubim, Thrones, Dominions, Virtues, Powers, Principalities, Archangels, and finally (guardian) Angels. Most of us interact solely with our guardian angels or the archangels.

From infancy to death, our guardian angels are assigned to guide and protect us. This belief holds true today as it did throughout all antiquity, beginning with various pagan religions. Although we are not to worship them, we often pray to our angels for gratuitous purposes or to seek their intercession.

Archangels are the second-lowest ranking in the Christian hierarchy of angels. However, they are of the highest rank to interact directly with humans, while remaining close to God.

There are diverse opinions as to how many exist. Depending on the varying religious doctrines, it is believed that there might be anywhere from three to twelve archangels, with seven being the widely accepted number. The most popular ones are Gabriel, Michael, Rafael, and Uriel

In several metaphysical practices, Gabriel, associated with the cardinal direction of east, is often asked to help in matters of communication. Michael, whose domain is the cardinal direction of south, is frequently called upon for protection, especially against malicious spiritual forces. Rafael, ruler of the cardinal direction of west, not only guides humans on the path to healing, but he is also considered to be the patron saint of romantic love, educators, and pharmacists. Uriel rules the cardinal direction of north and is called upon to assist in matters concerning nature, the environment, and materialistic desires.

#1: A Spell for Guardian Angel Veneration

YOU WILL NEED:

- An angel candle
- Holy Water
- Olive oil

This candle is not to be burned, but instead used in lieu of a statue. First, completely remove the wick with a pair of scissors. Spray the candle with Holy Water, followed by ritually asking the entity to live within the candle.

To do so, anoint the back of the head of the candle with either olive oil or Holy Oil. Next, recite a prayer specific to that entity. Before ending the prayer with the word *"Amen,"* introduce yourself with both your birth name and birth date. Then tell the entity that the candle belongs to him/her and to view the candle as a second home. Promise to offer him or her fresh water on a frequent basis. Thank the entity and close the communication with the word *"Amen."*

If the entity agrees to your request, an essence of its divine being will be within the candle. Therefore, you must never, under any circumstances, burn the candle. Remember to offer fresh water on a frequent basis. Never allow the water to become stale.

SUGGESTED CANDLE DRESSINGS

- The Holy Bible speaks only of olive oil for anointing candles

SUGGESTED PRAYER

- Guardian Angel Prayer *(page 188)*

#2: A Spell for Guidance from Guardian Angels

Both religious and spiritual practitioners frequently request guidance from their guardian angels. An angel candle is absolutely perfect for this type of petition.

YOU WILL NEED:

- An angel candle
- Olive oil
- A picture of yourself with eyes showing

After cleansing the candle, inscribe the candle with the words: *"Guardian Angel of ___ [your name]."* Anoint the entire candle with olive oil.

On a picture with your eyes showing, write your petition over the forehead image. Place it on your candle holder, image facing upward, then set the candle over your picture. Light the candle and recite your prayer.

SUGGESTED CANDLE DRESSINGS

🍃 The Holy Bible speaks only of olive oil for anointing candles

SUGGESTED PRAYER

📖 Guardian Angel Prayer *(page 188)*

ANGEL CANDLE
(Small)
For Health or Reconciliation

Symbolism

As previously discussed, the archangels are of the highest rank to interact directly with humans, while remaining close to God. Because He grants the archangels domains to rule, and thus, they have the ability to grant specific wishes, in accordance with the realm for which they rule. This spell specifically asks for success in protection, communication, and healing. It is an ideal spell for healing or reconciliation.

A 3-Day Wishing Spell to the Archangels

YOU WILL NEED:

- A large, flat, heat-resistant white plate
- ½ cup White cane sugar
- Three small white angel candles

After cleansing the candles, inscribe one candle with the words: "*Saint Michael,*" another with the words "*Saint Gabriel,*" and the last with "*Saint Rafael.*" Anoint all three of them with olive oil.

Set an open-faced petition paper stating your petitions in the middle of the dish. Completely cover the petition with the sugar. Place the candles toward the rim of the dish to face and encircle, but not to touch, the mound of sugar **(see illustration #1)**.

On the first two days, light the candles for about fifteen to twenty minutes and recite the mandatory prayer. Each day, promise to publicly acknowledge the archangels' intercession. On the third day, allow the candles to completely consume. When your petition is granted, publicly acknowledge the archangels on your social media venues.

Illustration #1: 3-Day Wishing Spell to the Archangels

SUGGESTED CANDLE DRESSINGS

🍃 The Holy Bible speaks only of olive oil for anointing candles

SUGGESTED PRAYER (MANDATORY)

📖 Archangels Michael, Gabriel, and Rafael Prayer *(page 184)*

Animal Candle
For Healing

Symbolism

An effigy is an image or representation of a person or an animal. It is believed that this word is derived from the French word *effigie*, meaning "*copy, image, likeness, portrait, and statue.*"

Although dictionaries state that effigies are designed to represent hated people, this is not the case in the metaphysical practices. Instead, they are employed to efficiently manipulate a person or animal toward a desired outcome, including healing.

When healing spells are employed using figural candles, not only can we pray for a favorable outcome, but we can also apply medicinal healing properties to the effigy. However, just remember that your magic and your behaviors must complement each other. Therefore, ensure that your beloved pet is also being seen by a qualified veterinarian.

A Spell for Healing

YOU WILL NEED:

- A white or light blue figural candle resembling your pet
- Olive oil or a condition oil
- A little bit of your pet's personal concerns *(page 39)*, such as fur, feathers, or shedding (depending on the type of animal).
- Small petition paper
- Soldering iron
- Your pet's picture with eyes showing
- Candle dressing

Cut the personal concerns into tiny pieces, keeping in mind that fur and feathers are highly combustible, bore a small hole into the abdominal portions of the candle and insert the personal concerns and the paper. Refill the hole with wax.

Cleanse, inscribe, baptize, and name the candle. Anoint the candle with either a healing condition oil or olive oil. Sprinkle the entire candle with finely crushed healing herbs.

Place your pet's picture on the candle holder, image facing upward. Set the candle over the picture. Light the candle and recite the appropriate prayer at least twice a day.

SUGGESTED CANDLE DRESSINGS

- **All Heal/Self Heal** *(Prunella vulgaris)*: Used to improve health
- **Althea** *(Althaea officinalis, Althea spp.)*: Employed for medicinal and spiritual healing
- **Angelica** *(Angelica archangelica, Angelica spp.)*: A powerful healer

SUGGESTED PRAYERS

- **St. Francis of Assisi Prayer:** Patron Saint of all animals *(page 193)*
- **St. Gertrude Prayer:** Patron Saint of cats *(page 193)*
- **St. Roch Prayer:** Patron Saint of dogs *(page 195)*

ANKH CANDLE
For Long Life

Symbolism

The ankh is an ancient Egyptian symbol that represents life, immortality, and rebirth. Oftentimes, people employ this symbol in order to prolong their lives.

If suffering from a debilitating illness, the ankh spell is by no means an alternative to receiving ongoing professional health care. Instead, it is designed to live a longer life.

A Spell for Long Life

YOU WILL NEED:

- A white or purple Ankh candle
- A picture of yourself with your eyes showing
- Petition paper
- Olive oil
- Candle dressings.

Cleanse, inscribe, and anoint the candle, then sprinkle crushed herbs over it. On a picture with your eyes showing, write your petition over the forehead image. Place it on your candle holder, image facing upward, then set the candle over your picture. Light the candle and recite your prayer.

SUGGESTED CANDLE DRESSINGS

- **Life Everlasting** *(Gnaphalium dioicum, Gnaphalium spp.)*: Said to prolong one's life

SUGGESTED PRAYER

- **Psalm 61:** For a longer life *(page 206)*

BRIDE & GROOM CANDLE
(Heterosexual)
For Marital Matters

Symbolism

These candles, shaped like a bride and groom standing together, represent the unity of a man and woman in marriage. Oftentimes, they are used in spellwork to magically entice a marital commitment from a reluctant mate. But they are also employed to repair specific marital problems or to break up a marital union.

In this segment, five different spells are offered. One is to encourage a marriage, three are to repair the most common marital discords, and finally, one to justifiably divide a marital bond.

#1: A Spell to Inspire Marital Commitment

YOU WILL NEED:

- A white bride and groom candle
- A picture of the female, with her (or your) eyes showing
- A picture of the man with his (or your) eyes showing
- Petition paper
- A condition oil or olive oil

- ¼ teaspoon honey
- Candle dressings
- 5 real or imitation gold wedding bands
- ¼ cup uncooked rice
- White altar cloth (must be white)

Cleanse the candle. Inscribe the male portion of the candle with the man's name then, name and baptize it. Inscribe the female portion of the candle with her name, name and baptize it. Next, inscribe the word *"marriage"* seven times, in a circular fashion, starting from the base of the candle to the highest possible point. Anoint the candle with the oil and sprinkle crushed herbs on it.

The honey will act as a glue. Spread the honey over the images of both people, then set the pictures together, face-to-face. Place the cloth on the altar, followed by the candle holder. Put your petition paper and the pictures (images facing upward) in the candle holder, then set the candle on the pictures. Surround the candle with the five rings and scatter the rice around the candle. Light the candle and recite the prayer.

SUGGESTED CANDLE DRESSINGS

- **Myrtle** *(Myrtus communis)*: Used in marital work
- **Red Clover** *(Trifolium pratense)*: Employed to encourage marriage

SUGGESTED PRAYER

- Interfaith Wedding Vows *(page 189)*

#2: A Spell to Enhance Love in a Marriage

YOU WILL NEED:

- A pink bride and groom candle
- A picture of the female, with her (or your) eyes showing
- A picture of the man with his (or your) eyes showing
- Petition paper
- A condition oil or olive oil
- ¼ teaspoon honey

✅ Candle dressings

Cleanse the candle. Inscribe the male portion of the candle with the man's name then, name and baptize it. Inscribe the female portion of the candle with her name, name and baptize it. Next, inscribe the words: *"love me"* seven times, in a circular fashion, starting from the base of the candle to the highest possible point. Anoint the candle with the oil, and scatter candle dressings on it.

The honey will act as a glue. Spread the honey over the images of both people then, set the pictures together, face-to-face. Place the cloth on the altar, followed by the candle holder. Put your petition paper and the pictures (images facing upward) in the candle holder, then the set candle on the pictures. Light the candle and recite the prayer.

SUGGESTED CANDLE DRESSINGS

- **Caraway Seeds, crushed** *(Carum Carvi)*: for marital faithfulness
- **Marjoram** *(Organum majorana)*: Enhances love in marriage
- **Myrtle** *(Myrtus communis)*: A love herb
- **Passionflower** *(Passiflora incarnata)*: Incites a *"clingy"* type of love

SUGGESTED PRAYER

📖 **Psalm 45:** To obtain love *(page 204)*

#3: A Spell to Enhance Lust in a Marriage

Follow all of the instructions for **Spell #2: A Spell to Enhance Love In a Marriage** *(page 87)*, but with two exceptions:

1. Use a red bride and groom candle instead of a pink one.

2. Replace the words *"love me"* with *"make love to me"* (or other words that can't be published!).

SUGGESTED CANDLE DRESSINGS

- **Damiana** *(Turnera aphrodisiaca)*: For a better sex life

- **Cinnamon** *(Cinnamomum aromaticum)*: Heats up a love affair
- **Dittany of Crete** *(Origanum Dictamnus)*: Promotes passionate desires

SUGGESTED PRAYER

- Intimacy With Spouse Prayer *(page 189)*

#4: A Spell to Mend A Broken Marriage

This spell is employed to mend a failing marriage when the spouse is still residing with you. Follow all of the instructions for **Spell #2: A Spell to Enhance Love In a Marriage** *(page 87)*, but with two exceptions:

1. Use a light blue bride and groom candle instead of a pink one.

2. Replace the words *"love me"* with *"forgive me."*

SUGGESTED CANDLE DRESSINGS

- **Basil** *(Ocimum basilicum)*: Promotes peace in the family
- **Borage** *(Borago officinalis)*: For peace in the home
- **Chickweed** *(Stellaria media)*: To keep a marriage happy
- **Forget-Me-Not** *(Myosotis spp.)*: Promotes reconciliation

SUGGESTED PRAYER

- **Psalm 41:** For emotional and physical healing *(page 203)*

#5: A Spell to Break Up a Marriage

Breakup spells should only be performed in situations when someone has stolen your significant other or if the breakup will save one party from present or future harm.

YOU WILL NEED:

- ✅ A black bride and groom candle
- ✅ A picture of the female, with her eyes showing
- ✅ A picture of the man with his eyes showing
- ✅ Petition paper
- ✅ A condition oil or olive oil
- ✅ Candle dressings
- ✅ A knife, torch lighter, or soldering iron

Illustration #2: A Spell to Break up a Marriage

Cleanse the candle. Inscribe the male portion of the candle with the man's name, then name and baptize it. Inscribe the female portion of the candle with her name, name and baptize it. Next, inscribe the words: *"breakup"* thirteen times, in a circular fashion, starting from the top of the candle down to the base or to the lowest possible point. Anoint the candle with the oil, and scatter candle dressings over the candle.

Set your petition paper in the candle holder. Over the petition paper, place her picture, image facing upward, where the female effigy will sit in the candle holder, and his picture where his candle image will rest. Light the wicks and frequently demand that either he leaves her or she leaves him. About twenty to twenty-five minutes after the candle has been lit, heat the blade of the knife then, separate the two images, about ¾ down, while screaming *"Break up!"* **(see illustration #2)**. Alternatively, the images can be separated with a torch lighter or a soldering iron.

If using a knife, leave it in between the two images until the effigies have been completely consumed. If there are any candle wax remains, separate them and deploy the remnants of the male and female in different areas, far apart from one another.

SUGGESTED CANDLE DRESSINGS

- **Black Snake Root, crushed** *(Cimicifuga spp.)*: To make someone in the home move away
- **Couch Grass** *(Agropyron repens, Elytrigia repens)*: To break up lovers
- **Lemon Verbena** *(Aloysia spp.)*: To cause strife between lovers
- **Poppy Seeds** *(Papaver spp.)*: Causes confusion

SUGGESTED PRAYER

- Break Up Relationship Prayer *(page 185)*

> **Note:** please do not, under any circumstances, perform breakup spells on abusive relationships. These spells cause anger and arguments, and if an abuser is provoked, that person may become physically violent toward his or her partner. Instead, cast send-away spells on the abuser. The second step is to encourage the partner to seek help from professional counselors of domestic violence. A great starting point is to have the victim contact the National Domestic Violence Hotline at *www.TheHotline.org*.

Bear Candle
For Courage And Emotional Strength

Symbolism

Bears are capable of incredibly amazing feats of courage, strength, and power. In addition to these attributes, many Native American tribes also hold them in high regard for their abilities to keep fighting, even when wounded.

Likewise, passages in the the Holy Bible, including 2 Samuel 17:8, Proverbs 17:12, 28:15, Isaiah 11:7, 59:11, Lamentations 3:10, Daniel 7:5, Hosea 13:8, Amos 5:19, and Revelation 13:2 speak of these aforementioned attributes while also embracing the bears' ferocity, protective, and divine powers.

Spells implementing images of bears are often utilized to strengthen victims of oppressors who often harass them. These tyrants include bullies at school or in the workplace, gossipers, interlopers, etc.

A Spell for Courage and Emotional Strength

YOU WILL NEED:

- A bear candle, either white or purple
- A picture of yourself with eyes showing
- Petition paper
- Your personal concerns *(page 39)*
- A condition oil or olive oil
- A soldering iron
- Candle dressings

Bore a hole into the widest portion of the bear candle, and insert your personal concerns into it. Then restore the candle to its original form by filling the hole with melted wax of the same color.

Cleanse the candle, then inscribe your name onto it in five random separate areas, and then cross over your name with the inscription *"Courage Strength."* Anoint the candle with oil and scatter candle dressings over it.

Place the petition paper in the candle holder, followed by the picture, image facing upward. Set the candle over the picture. Light the candle and pray.

SUGGESTED CANDLE DRESSINGS

- **Mullein** *(Verbascum Thapsus)*: Provides courage and protection
- **Sampson Snake Root, crushed** *(Echinacea spp.)*: Brings respect from others
- **Yarrow** *(Achillea millefolium)*: Aids with bravery

SUGGESTED PRAYER

- Courage & Strength Prayer *(page 187)*

BUTTERFLY CANDLE
For Freedom

Symbolism

The butterfly represents happiness, transformation, rebirth, and most importantly, freedom. This is an ideal candle for use in spellwork to escape feelings of entrapment, or abuse. It also assists one to flee from spiritual slavery, which is the act of being forced into behaving in a manner that others demand of a person.

A Spell for Freedom

YOU WILL NEED:

- Either a white or purple butterfly candle
- A picture of yourself with your eyes showing
- Petition paper
- A condition oil or olive oil
- Candle dressings

Cleanse the candle and inscribe the person's name and birth date onto it. Then, in five random areas on the candle, inscribe the word *"freedom."* Anoint the candle with oil and scatter candle dressings over it.

Place the petition paper in the candle holder, followed by the picture, image facing upward. Set the candle over the picture. Light the candle, pray, and imagine yourself being that butterfly, ecstatically soaring in the air.

SUGGESTED CANDLE DRESSINGS

- 🌿 **Master Root, crushed** *(Imperatoria ostruthium)*: Aids in strength and mastery
- 🌿 **Master of the Woods** *(Asperula odorata)*: Assists with personal strength

SUGGESTED PRAYER

- 📖 **Saint Josephine Prayer:** Once a slave herself, she is the patron Saint of victims of slavery *(page 194)*

CAT CANDLE
(Black)
For Protection From Negative Spiritual Forces

Symbolism

Revered for their association with magic, independence, and secrecy, cats also possess protective powers. Although available in different colors, to represent various symbology, the black cat will be featured here for its protective powers against malicious spiritual influences.

A Spell to Protect from Negative Forces

YOU WILL NEED:

- ✅ A black cat candle
- ✅ Your picture, with eyes showing
- ✅ A condition oil or olive oil
- ✅ The herb rue, finely crushed (if pregnant, avoid this herb)

Cleanse the candle. In thirteen different areas on the candle, inscribe your name, then cross your name with the word *"protection."* Anoint the candle with the oil and scatter crushed rue onto it. No petition paper is needed.

Place your picture, image facing upward, in the candle holder. Scatter a little more rue over it. Set the candle atop your picture. Light the candle and recite your prayer.

SUGGESTED CANDLE DRESSINGS

- 🌿 **Rue** *(Ruta graveolens)*: One of the oldest and most powerful protection herbs
- 🌿 **Eucalyptus** *(Eucalyptus spp.)*: Use as an alternative to rue. Repels evil forces

SUGGESTED PRAYER

- 📖 **Psalm 121:** To repel evil entities *(page 212)*

COFFIN CANDLE
For Justifiable Revenge

Symbolism

A coffin is a powerful symbol representing a final conclusion. Although most of us think of it as the last physical space that a living being will occupy, it can also denote the end of a relationship, a chapter in one's life, a career, or a disease.

That being said, due to its diverse symbology, including physical death, it is not advisable to perform spellwork on oneself employing a coffin-shaped candle. In my practice, it is only used for justifiable payback. For instance, when one of my dogs was purposely killed, my boy's death was avenged with numerous retaliative spellwork, including a coffin candle spell. Although the perpetrator did not die, he was instead suddenly afflicted with numerous health problems and became suicidal.

However, when utilizing any type of negative spellwork, always remember that justice is the administering of a deserved punishment that is proportionate to the crime. Otherwise, you will be as culpable as your rivals. So, please think twice before performing any type of revenge spell.

A Spell for Justifiable Revenge

YOU WILL NEED:

- ✅ Holy Water, or Florida Water
- ✅ Protection amulets

- A black coffin candle
- A picture of your target, with eyes showing and/or his or her personal concerns *(page 39)*
- Petition paper
- A condition oil or olive oil
- Candle dressings
- A soldering iron

To ensure self-protection, first spray yourself with the water and don protection amulets before proceeding with this spell. With your soldering iron, bore a hole into it, through the widest portion of the candle. It must be large enough to hold the picture, petition paper, personal concerns, and cursing ingredients. Then, fill the candle with the aforementioned items. Restore the candle to its original form by filling the hole with melted wax of the same color.

Cleanse the candle, then, in thirteen random areas on the candle, inscribe the target's name, then cross over the name with the inscription *"Rest in peace"* (do not use the abbreviation: R.I.P.). Anoint the candle with the oil, then scatter the dressing/cursing ingredients all over it.

There are two options for employing this spell. Because this candle implies death, avoid

any negative lingering energies within your dwelling. Instead, either burn the candle outside, away from anything combustible, or simply bury it in a cemetery.

SUGGESTED CANDLE DRESSINGS

- **Black or Brown Mustard Seeds** *(Brassica spp.)*: Confuses rivals
- **Blueberries, Dried** *(Vaccinium frondosum)*: Brings sorrow to enemies
- **Cactus Spines** *(Cactaceae spp.)*: Used to jinx people
- **Chicory Root, Crushed** *(Cichorium intybus)*: Curses enemies
- **Red Pepper** *(Capsicum annum)*: To hurt a foe

SUGGESTED PRAYER

- **Psalm 109:** This is the most powerful text for retribution *(page 211)*

CROSS CANDLE
(Red)
For Saint Michael's Protection

Symbolism

The cross is the central symbol of Christianity, symbolizing Jesus Christ, as well as faith, mercy, redemption, sacrifice, salvation, and triumph. These candles are used in spells and rituals centered on protection, divine blessings, and spiritual strength. The colors most often used are white for peace and purity, green for abundance, and red for protection.

As we already know, St. Michael is frequently called upon for protection, especially against evil people and malicious spiritual forces. In my practice, the most powerful and successful protection spell implements both the intercession of St. Michael along with a red cross candle. It has yet to fail me.

A Cross Candle Protection Spell

YOU WILL NEED:

- Either a statue or framed image of St Michael
- A sturdy St. Michael prayer card
- On photo quality paper, a wallet-sized picture of yourself, with your eyes showing
- Clear tape
- A small, clear, or plain white bowl
- About ½ cup of Holy Water
- Olive oil

Cleanse the candle, and on its vertical portion, from the base of the candle to the top, inscribe the word *"protection"* three time. Sprinkle about a teaspoon of Holy water over the candle, then anoint it with olive oil.

Pour the remaining Holy Water into the bowl, add a small handful of suggested dressings to it, and gently stir with your finger.. Generously tape your picture to St. Michael's picture, face-to-face and set it into the bowl containing the water and herbs. Set the candle over it (**see illustration #3 on following page**).

Place either the statue or the framed picture on your altar, facing the bowl. Light the candle and recite the mandatory prayer.

Once the candle has been completely consumed, if the arms fall off, it's a positive sign. Place the bowl of water and herbs near a window. Allow the water to completely evaporate (this ought to take about 1 to 3 days). Remove the taped images from the bowl and keep them under the statue or framed image of St. Michael.

Every Sunday thereafter, light a small red or white candle in front of the image of St. Michael and continue to pray for his protection.

Illustration #3: Cross Candle Protection Spell

SUGGESTED DRESSINGS

- **Agrimony** *(Agrimonia eupatoria)*: Wards off curses, provides protection
- **Eucalyptus** *(Eucalyptus spp.)*: Wards off evil and repels enemies
- **Rosemary** *(Rosmarinus officinalis)*: Cleanses and purifies
- **Rue** *(Ruta graveolens)*: One of the oldest and most powerful, protection herbs

SUGGESTED PRAYER (MANDATORY)

📖 **St Michael Prayer:** for Protection *(page 194)*

Dog Candle
For Loyalty

Symbolism

As most dog owners know, these beloved creatures have always strived to be man's best friend. In both ancient and modern art, they have perpetually symbolized loyalty, companionship, and unconditional love. Due to these attributes, dog candles are used in gentle spells to create loyalty, faithfulness, fidelity, or unconditional love from another.

This is not a domination spell. To command another, see the mouse candle spell.

A Spell for Loyalty

YOU WILL NEED:

- A puppy dog candle
- Depending on your own gender, a white or pink male or female human candle
- A picture with your eyes showing
- A picture with your target's eyes showing
- The target's personal concerns, if available *(page 39)*
- A petition paper
- A condition oil or olive oil
- A soldering iron
- Suggested dressings

Bore a hole into the widest portion of the dog candle, and insert your target's personal concerns into it. Then restore the candle to its original form by filling the hole with melted wax of the same color.

Cleanse the candle, then inscribe your target's name onto it in seven random separate areas. Cross over your name with the inscription *"Follow _____ [your name]."* Anoint the candle with oil and scatter candle dressings over it.

For the human candle, cleanse it and inscribe your name and birthdate onto it in five random areas. No other inscription is necessary. Anoint the candle with oil and scatter candle dressings over it.

Place the dog petition paper in the candle holder, followed by the target's picture, image facing upward. Set the dog candle over the picture. Place your petition paper in a separate candle holder, followed by your picture, image facing upward, then set the human candle over it.

The candles must face each other. Try to arrange them as close together as possible. Light the candles and pray.

SUGGESTED CANDLE DRESSINGS FOR THE DOG CANDLE

- **Coriander Seeds, crushed** *(Coriandrum sativum)*: Stops a mate from running around

SUGGESTED CANDLE DRESSINGS FOR THE HUMAN CANDLE

- **Dittany of Crete** *(Origanum Dictamnus)*: Creates passionate desire in another
- **Dried Pink or Red Rose Petals** *(Rosa spp.)*: A love drawing ingredient

SUGGESTED PRAYER

- Loyalty and Faithfulness Prayer *(page 190)*

DOUBLE-ACTION CANDLE
To Reverse Bad Luck In Various Matters

Symbolism

Although not technically figural candles, they are being explored here for their unusual colors, which are half black and half of an alternate color. Traditionally sold as nine-inch candles, but also offered in six-inch varieties, they are called *"double-action"* because their purposes are twofold. The black segment of the candle is employed to banish bad luck with a particular problem, while the other color is used to attract positive energies regarding the same situation.

Because double-action candles are offered in a variety of colors, it would be careless to disregard the symbology of each one. Therefore, nine different spells are offered to correlate with the most common problems faced by thousands of people.

SPECIAL INSTRUCTIONS: "BUTTING" THE CANDLE

The black half of the candle must burn first, thus, the candle must be *"butted"* prior to preparing it. This means that the original wick on the alternate color is completely snipped off and a new wick is created by burrowing into the middle of the black portion in order to extend the wick. Once this task is accomplished, the candle is ready for preparation.

#1: A Spell for Uncrossing

YOU WILL NEED:

- A white and black double action candle
- A condition oil or olive oil
- A petition paper
- A picture of yourself with your eyes showing
- Candle Dressing

First butt the candle then cleanse it. Beginning at the top of the black portion, inscribe the words *"Banish Negativity,"* three times, in a spiral fashion, moving downward. At the base of the white portion of the candle, inscribe the words *"Purification"* three times, in a spiral fashion, moving upward and ending where the black color begins **(see illustration #4 on following page)**.

Anoint the candle with oil. Sprinkle asafoetida (Ferula assa-foetida), a banishing ingredient, to the black portion of the candle and the suggested dressings to the white portion. Place your petition paper in the candle holder, followed by your picture (face-up), then set the candle on it. Light the candle and pray.

SUGGESTED CANDLE DRESSING
FOR THE BLACK PORTION
(used in all double-action candle spells)

- **Asafoetida** *(Ferula assa-foetida)*: A banishing ingredient

SUGGESTED CANDLE DRESSINGS FOR THE WHITE PORTION

- **Agrimony** *(Agrimonia eupatoria)*: Wards off curses, provides protection
- **Eucalyptus** *(Eucalyptus spp.)*: Wards off evil and repels enemies
- **Rosemary** *(Rosemarinus officialis)*: Cleanses and purifies
- **Rue** *(Ruta graveolens)*: One of the oldest, and most powerful, protection herbs. Do not handle if you are pregnant

SUGGESTED PRAYER

📖 **Psalm 37:** For uncrossing *(page 201)*

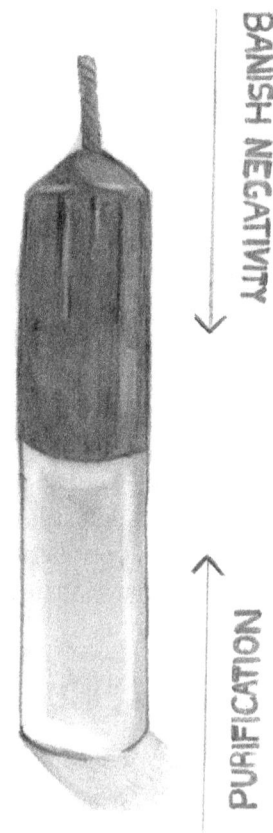

Illustration #4: Double Action Candle Spell For Uncrossing

#2: A Spell for Attraction

YOU WILL NEED:

- A pink and black double action candle
- A condition oil or olive oil
- A petition paper
- A picture of yourself with your eyes showing
- Candle Dressing

Follow all of the instructions for **Spell #1: A Spell for Uncrossing** *(page 101)*, with the exceptions of the inscriptions, candle dressing for the pink portion, and the prayer.

Beginning at the top of the black portion, inscribe the words *"Banish attraction blockages,"* three times, in a spiral fashion, moving downward. At the base of the pink portion of the candle, inscribe the word *"Attraction,"* three times, in a spiral fashion, moving upward and ending where the black color begins

SUGGESTED CANDLE DRESSINGS FOR THE PINK PORTION

- **Dill** *(Anethum graveolens)*: For luck in finding love
- **Dried Pink or Red Rose Petals** *(Rosa spp.)*: For luck in all love matters
- **Verbena/Vervain** *(Verbena officinalis)*: A love drawing herb

SUGGESTED PRAYER

- **Psalm 45:** For love *(page 204)*

#3: A Spell to Improve Your Communication

YOU WILL NEED:

- A yellow and black double action candle
- A condition oil or olive oil
- A petition paper

- ✓ A picture of yourself with your eyes showing
- ✓ Candle Dressing

Follow all of the instructions for **Spell #1: A Spell for Uncrossing** (page 101), with the exceptions of the inscriptions, candle dressing for the yellow portion, and the prayer.

Beginning at the top of the black portion, inscribe the words *"Banish speech inhibitions"* three times, in a spiral fashion, moving downward. At the base of the yellow portion of the candle, inscribe the word *"Dynamic Speaker"* three times, in a spiral fashion, moving upward and ending where the black color begins.

SUGGESTED CANDLE DRESSINGS FOR THE YELLOW PORTION

- 🍃 **Bay Laurel** (*Laurus nobilis*): For victory
- 🍃 **Deer's Tongue Herb/Vanilla Leaf** (*Achlys triphylla, Trilisa spp.*): Grants eloquent and pleasant speech
- 🍃 **Master Root, crushed** (*Imperatoria ostruthium*): Aids in strength and mastery

SUGGESTED PRAYER

- 📖 **Archangel Gabriel Prayer:** For Clear Communication (page 184)

#4: A Spell For Courage

YOU WILL NEED:

- ✓ A purple and black double action candle
- ✓ A condition oil or olive oil
- ✓ A petition paper
- ✓ A picture of yourself with your eyes showing
- ✓ Candle Dressing

Follow all of the instructions for **Spell #1: A Spell for Uncrossing** (page 101), with the exceptions of the inscriptions, candle dressing for the purple portion, and the prayer.

Beginning at the top of the black portion, inscribe the words *"Banish fear"* three times, in a spiral fashion, moving downward. At the base of the purple portion of the candle, inscribe the word *"Courage Bravery"* three times, in a spiral fashion, moving upward and ending where the black color begins

SUGGESTED CANDLE DRESSINGS FOR THE PURPLE PORTION

- **Mullein** *(Verbascum Thapsus)*: Provides courage and protection
- **Sampson Snake Root, crushed** *(Echinacea spp.)*: Draws respect
- **Yarrow** *(Achillea millefolium)*: Aids with bravery

SUGGESTED PRAYER

- Courage & Strength Prayer *(page 187)*

#5: A Spell For Court Case Obstacles

YOU WILL NEED:

- A brown and black double action candle
- A condition oil or olive oil
- A petition paper
- A picture of yourself with your eyes showing
- Candle Dressing

Follow all of the instructions for **Spell #1: A Spell for Uncrossing** *(page 101)*, with the exceptions of the inscriptions, candle dressing for the brown portion, and the prayer.

Beginning at the top of the black portion, inscribe the words *"Banish Legal Obstacles"* three times, in a spiral fashion, moving downward. At the base of the brown portion of the candle, inscribe the word *"Win Court Case"* three times, in a spiral fashion, moving upward and ending where the black color begins.

SUGGESTED CANDLE DRESSINGS FOR THE PURPLE PORTION

- **Cascara Sagrada, crushed** *(Rhamnus purshiana, Frangula purshiana)*: Gives luck in legal matters
- **Celandine** *(Chelidonium majus)*: Keeps law away
- **Shame Brier** *(Mimosa nuttallii)*: May get a lawsuit against you dropped

SUGGESTED PRAYER

Just Judge Prayer *(page 190)*

#6: A Spell For Health Matters

YOU WILL NEED:

- A light blue and black double action candle
- A condition oil or olive oil
- A petition paper
- A picture of yourself with your eyes showing
- Candle Dressing

Follow all of the instructions for **Spell #1: A Spell for Uncrossing** *(page 101)*, with the exceptions of the inscriptions, candle dressing for the blue portion, and the prayer.

Beginning at the top of the black portion, inscribe the words *"Banish Illness"* three times, in a spiral fashion, moving downward. At the base of the blue portion of the candle, inscribe the word *"Healing"* three times, in a spiral fashion, moving upward and ending where the black color begins.

SUGGESTED CANDLE DRESSINGS FOR THE BLUE PORTION

- **Althaea leaves** *(Althaea officinalis)*: A healing herb
- **Angelic Root Powder** *(Angelica archangelica)*: Provides emotional and physical healing
- **Boneset Leaves** *(Eupatorium ageratoides)*: A powerful healer

- **Self-Heal/All Heal** *(Prunella vulgaris)*: A popular healing herb

SUGGESTED PRAYER

Psalm 41: For Emotional and Physical Healing *(page 203)*

#7: A Spell To Restore Lust

YOU WILL NEED:

- A red and black double action candle
- A condition oil or olive oil
- A petition paper
- A picture of yourself with eyes showing.
- Candle Dressing

Follow all of the instructions for **Spell #1: A Spell for Uncrossing** *(page 101)*, with the exceptions of the inscriptions, candle dressing for the red portion, and the prayer.

Beginning at the top of the black portion, inscribe the words *"Banish Love Jinx"* three times, in a spiral fashion, moving downward. At the base of the red portion of the candle, inscribe the word *"Bring Passionate Love"* three times, in a spiral fashion, moving upward and ending where the black color begins.

SUGGESTED CANDLE DRESSINGS FOR THE RED PORTION

- **Damiana** *(Turnera aphrodisiaca)*: For a better sex life
- **Cinnamon** *(Cinnamomum aromaticum)*: Heats up a love affair
- **Dittany of Crete** *(Origanum Dictamnus)*: Promotes passionate desires

SUGGESTED PRAYER

Restore Sexuality Prayer *(page 192)*

#8: A Spell For Money

YOU WILL NEED:

- A green and black double action candle
- A condition oil or olive oil
- A petition paper
- A picture of yourself with your eyes showing
- Candle Dressing

Follow all of the instructions for **Spell #1: A Spell for Uncrossing** *(page 101)*, with the exceptions of the inscriptions, candle dressing for the green portion, and the prayer.

Beginning at the top of the black portion, inscribe the words *"Banish Money Problems"* three times, in a spiral fashion, moving downward. At the base of the green portion of the candle, inscribe the word *"Money Come To Me"* three times, in a spiral fashion, moving upward and ending where the black color begins.

SUGGESTED CANDLE DRESSINGS FOR THE GREEN PORTION

- **Alfalfa** *(Medicago sativa)*: Attracts money
- **Bayberry Root, crushed** *(Pimenta acris)*: Known for centuries to attract money
- **Blue Flag** *(Iris versicolor)*: Attracts prosperity
- **Earth Smoke/Fumitory** *(Funaria spp.)*: Brings fast money

SUGGESTED PRAYER

- **Psalm 37:** Not only an uncrossing prayer—it also attracts money *(page 201)*

#9: A Spell To Open The Roads

YOU WILL NEED:

- An orange and black double action candle

- A condition oil or olive oil
- A petition paper
- A picture of yourself with your eyes showing
- Candle Dressing

Follow all of the instructions for **Spell #1: A Spell for Uncrossing** *(page 101)*, with the exceptions of the inscriptions, candle dressing for the orange portion, and the prayer.

Beginning at the top of the black portion, inscribe the words *"Tear Down Obstacles,"* three times, in a spiral fashion, moving downward. At the base of the orange portion of the candle, inscribe the word *"Open The Roads,"* three times, in a spiral fashion, moving upward and ending where the black color begins.

SUGGESTED CANDLE DRESSINGS FOR THE ORANGE PORTION

- **Abre Camino** *(Koanophyllon villosum)*: A well-known road opening herb
- **Lemon Grass** *(Cymbopogon citratus)*: Dissipates bad energies and attracts beneficial ones

SUGGESTED PRAYER

- **St Peter Prayer:** To Open the Roads *(page 195)*

DOVE CANDLE
Invoking The Holy Spirit For Favors

Symbolism

Doves have numerous symbolisms throughout the world and in history. In ancient Pagan practices, this bird represented Goddesses such as Aphrodite, Asherah, and Inanna-Ishtar. The dove also appears in the Hebrew Holy Bible as well as the Christian texts.

In Matthew 3:16 of the New Testament of the Holy Bible, it says: *"And Jesus, when he was baptized, went up straightway out of the water: and, lo, the heavens were opened unto him, and he saw the Spirit of God descending like a dove, and lighting upon him."* This is one of many reasons that most Christians believe that doves symbolize the Holy Spirit, or an aspect of God's divine quality.

Millions of people, including Catholics and Hoodoo practitioners of past and present, have been possessed by the Holy Spirit. Some people have seizures or become incredibly psychic. During religious worship, others speak in an unknown language, called *"speaking in tongues,"* which is regarded as one of the gifts of the Holy Spirit

In Galatians 5:22 of the Holy Bible, it is suggested that if we pray to the Holy Spirit, we can experience peace, love, joy, patience, kindness, goodness, faithfulness, gentleness, and self-control. Yet I have personally petitioned the Holy Spirit for trivial matters such as winning a dog competition, or delivering an effective lecture, etc. Every prayer was granted with phenomenal results far beyond my expectations. In one situation, a white dove actually appeared to me, and my group members, after granting my request. Therefore, it is my personal belief that one can pray to the Holy Spirit for almost anything. All that you need to provide is love and respect.

A Spell to Invoke the Holy Spirit for Favors

YOU WILL NEED:

- A white dove candle
- A petition paper
- Olive oil
- A picture of yourself, with your eyes showing

Cleanse the candle and anoint it with olive oil. No inscription is necessary. Place your petition paper on the candle holder, followed by your picture, facing upward. Set the candle over the picture. Light the candle and pray.

SUGGESTED CANDLE DRESSING

- No dressings are suggested for dove candles. The Holy Bible specifically speaks of olive oil.

SUGGESTED PRAYER

📖 **Holy Spirit Prayer:** For a favor *(page 189)*

Egg Candle
For Fertility

Symbolism

Eggs symbolize fertility, new life, and rebirth. Amongst Pagans, these beliefs hold strong today, as they did in the ancient past. Because spring represents rebirth, eggs are often incorporated into Pagan festivals that celebrate the arrival of spring. During these festivals, eggs are offered as gifts or sacrifices to their Gods. Early Christians borrowed the symbolism of eggs and applied it to the resurrection of Jesus Christ. Today, Easter eggs hold both Pagan and Christian associations. In metaphysical practices, eggs are often employed in fertility spells.

A Spell for Fertility

YOU WILL NEED:

- A white or light blue egg candle (widely available during the Easter season)
- Seven perfect pinecones (Pinus sylvestris, Pinus spp.)
- Petition paper
- A very small petition paper, about ½ inch by ½ inch
- Vaginal secretions
- Olive oil
- A picture of yourself with your eyes showing
- A soldering iron
- Candle Dressing

On the small piece of paper, write your birth name and birth date on it. Cross the name over with the word *"pregnancy."* Smear your vaginal secretions on both of your petition papers and the candle dressings.

Bore a hole in the middle and widest part of the candle. Insert the smaller petition paper, along with about ½ teaspoon of candle dressing, into the hole. Restore the candle to its original form by filling the hole with melted wax of the same color.

Cleanse the candle and inscribe your name to seven random areas of the candle. Cross your name over with the word *"pregnancy."* Anoint the candle with olive oil and sprinkle it with candle dressings. Place your larger petition paper on the candle holder, followed by your picture, image facing upward. Set the candle over the picture. Surround the candle holder with the seven pinecones, which promote fertility. Light the candle and pray.

Once the candle is completely consumed, place five of the pinecones under your bed, or the location where conjugation occurs. Keep one pinecone in the bathroom (where most miscarriages occur), and one on your person or in your purse.

SUGGESTED CANDLE DRESSINGS

- **Queen's Root** *(Stillingia sylvatica)*: Increases chances of pregnancy
- **Squaw Vine** *(Mitchella repens)*: Aids with the health of a woman's reproduction system

SUGGESTED PRAYER

- **Fertility Prayer:** for conception *(page 186)*

FOUR-LEAF CLOVER CANDLE
For Good Luck

Symbolism

Not to be mistaken with the common shamrock, which only has three leaves, the four-leaf clover, or *"clover,"* is a rare occurrence. In fact, you would have to examine over 5,000 shamrocks just to find one clover!

Nevertheless, it is a symbol with a long history. The druids are said to have believed clovers had magical powers and used them in ceremonies for their protective powers. The clover became associated with the Irish people after the druids were driven out of Ireland. It was seen as a lucky charm and often worn as a talisman for protection. Today, it is believed by most people that the first three leaves symbolize hope, faith, and love, while the fourth leaf brings good luck.

A Spell for Good Luck

YOU WILL NEED:

- A green or white four-leaf clover candle (widely available around St. Patrick's Day)
- A petition paper
- A condition oil or olive oil
- A picture of yourself, with your eyes showing
- Candle dressings

Cleanse the candle and inscribe your name and birth date onto it. Then, cross your name over with the words *"Good Luck."* Anoint the candle with oil and scatter candle dressings over it.

Place the petition paper in the candle holder, followed by the picture, image facing upward. Set the candle over the picture. Light the candle and pray.

SUGGESTED CANDLE DRESSINGS

- **Benzoin** *(Styrax benzoin)*: Brings good luck and peace of mind
- **Black Cohosh** *(Actaea racemosa)*: For good luck in the home
- **Cinquefoil** *(Potentilla simplex)*: Good luck in money matters
- **Snake Weed** *(Stachytarpheta spp.)*: Brings both money and good luck

SUGGESTED PRAYER

- Traditional Irish Blessing *(page 197)*

GARGOYLE CANDLE
For Home Protection

Symbolism

Have you ever seen those strange-looking creatures on the outside of religious structures? They are called *"gargoyles"* and are believed to be supernatural creatures who protect what they guard, such as a church, from any evil people or harmful spirits. They will protect any dwelling and fiercely guard and protect the people within it.

A Spell for Home Protection

YOU WILL NEED:

- A white, black, red, or purple gargoyle candle
- A condition oil or olive oil
- Candle Dressings

Cleanse the candle, anoint it and sprinkle candle dressings over it. Treat it with the utmost respect while acknowledging its role as a fierce protector. After specifying your request, adamantly thank it. Place it by your entryway, light the candle and pray.

SUGGESTED CANDLE DRESSINGS

- **Rue** *(Ruta graveolens)*: One of the oldest and most powerful protection herbs
- **Eucalyptus** *(Eucalyptus spp.)*: Use as an alternative to rue. Repels evil forces

SUGGESTED PRAYER

- **Gargoyle Prayer:** For Protection *(page 188)*

GHOST CANDLE
To Banish Haunting Memories

Symbolism

Ghosts are simply the souls of earth-bound humans or animals. Although the depiction of ghosts is oftentimes associated with a mischievous or malevolent entity, the symbolism actually has a broad array of interpretations.

Depending on one's cultural beliefs, ghosts may represent an omen of an impending death or a poltergeist intrusion. But they can also represent a person's *"past ghosts,"* which refers to the haunting or unrest memories of a previous unjust event. As an attempt to eradicate unresolved conflicts, ghost candles are ideal for this purpose. Please remember that this spell ought to be performed alongside professional counseling.

A Spell to Banish Haunting Memories

Because ghosts have numerous symbolisms, you must be concise in this spellwork. Do not inscribe your name onto the candle, and refrain from using any pictures of yourself, or of your client.

YOU WILL NEED:

- A white or black ghost candle (widely available during the Halloween/Samhain season)
- A petition paper
- A condition oil or olive oil
- Candle dressing

Cleanse the candle and inscribe it three times with the memory you wish to banish. For example, if one were to have endured or witnessed a car accident, the inscription might say *"Banish memories of car accident."* Anoint the candle with the oil and roll it in the candle dressing.

Place the petition paper in the candle holder, then set the candle over the petition paper.

Light the candle and pray.

SUGGESTED CANDLE DRESSING

- **Asafoetida** *(Ferula assa-foetida)*: A banishing ingredient

SUGGESTED PRAYER

- **Psalm 41:** For emotional and physical healing *(page 203)*

HEART CANDLE
(large and small)
For love

Symbolism

Before the 14th century, the heart shape was not a metaphor for love. In fact, beginning around 1,400 years ago, the ancient Japanese believed that the heart was symbolic of a boar's eye. Because the boar is associated with bravery and determination, the heart symbol was inscribed on numerous spearheads and hand guards of warriors.

Then, around the 15th century in Europe, the traditional heart shape began to symbolize love. Today, it also represents allure, attraction, passion, romance, and mending emotions. In addition to matters concerning intense feelings, these candles can be used to assist with physiological heart conditions. But the spell suggestions here will focus solely on love.

Illustration #5: Small And Large Heart Candles

There are numerous heart-shaped candles, both large and small. Some candles are shaped exactly as a human anatomical heart. My preference is to employ the traditional heart shaped candles because of their symbology. The larger candles can be used alone for a specific spell purpose. The smaller ones, called *"floating candles,"* are usually employed in jar spells or used as *"helper lights"* (**see illustration #5**). Heart-shaped candles as helper lights will be illustrated in the *"Lovers Candle"* section of this book.

#1 - A Love Spell with a Large Heart Candle

YOU WILL NEED:

- A large white, pink, or red heart candle
- A picture of yourself with eyes showing
- A picture of your target with eyes showing
- ¼ teaspoon honey
- A condition oil or olive oil
- Candle dressings

Cleanse the candle and starting from the top going to the bottom, inscribe both the front and back surfaces with your desire. For example, you might write "_____ [**target's birth name and birthdate**] *will love* _____ [**your name and birthdate**]." Anoint the candle and sprinkle candle dressing on it.

The honey will act as a glue. Spread the honey over the images of both people then set the pictures together, face-to-face. Place your petition paper in the candle holder, followed by the pictures. Set the candle on the pictures, light the candle, and recite the prayer.

SUGGESTED CANDLE DRESSINGS

- **Cubeb Berries** *(Piper cubeba)*: To seduce a lover
- **Lovage Root, crushed** *(Levisticum officianalis)*: Encourages someone to love you
- **Myrtle** *(Myrtus communis)*: A love herb
- **Passionflower** *(Passiflora incarnata)*: Incites a *"clingy"* type of love
- **Rose Petals** *(Rosa spp.)*: For luck in all love matters

SUGGESTED PRAYER

- **Psalm 45:** To obtain love *(page 204)*

#2 - A Love Spell with a Floating Heart Candle

YOU WILL NEED:

- A small white, pink, or red heart candle
- A condition oil or olive oil
- Honey Jar Spell (see below)

Cleanse the candle and inscribe the words *"Love Me"* on the top portion and anoint it with oil. A candle holder is not needed. Instead, heat the bottom of the candle until the wax is soft (about twenty seconds) and place it on the lid of your honey jar.

HONEY JAR SPELL

YOU WILL NEED:

- The anointed and inscribed heart candle
- 1 new glass jar with an unlettered metal lid
- 1 jar of honey
- 1 wallet-sized photo of your face with eyes showing
- 1 wallet-sized photo of the target's face with eyes showing
- 2 strong magnets
- White, pink, or red yarn
- Petition paper
- Any, or all, of the candle dressings listed in the spell for a larger heart candle

Remove about ½ cup of the honey from the jar in order to prevent overfill. Insert your dressings into the jar and stir. Then, add your petition paper.

Dab a bit of honey on both pictures, then stick the images together face-to-face. Place a magnet on either side to further bind the target to you. Next, wrap this up with the yarn to create a ball. Start with a long tail hanging to be used for tying knots when the ball is completed. When creating this ball, state both the target's name and the intention for this person to have sweet and kind thoughts of you. When the ball is completed, leave extra yarn to create knots. Tie the tails together, making seven knots while repeating the intention each time a knot is tied. Once this is completed, insert the ball deep into the honey jar.

Add more honey to fill the jar and replace the lid. On Mondays, Wednesdays, and/or Fridays of the waxing moon, set a small heart candle that has been anointed with either olive oil or a condition oil directly on the lid while praying or stating your petitions aloud.

SUGGESTED PRAYER

📖 **Psalm 45:** For love *(page 204)*

HUMAN CANDLE
For Attraction, Cursing, Healing, Mastery, & Money

Symbolism

Male and female image candles, another form of effigies, are designed to represent specific individuals in spellwork. These candles are frequently used in lieu of cloth, clay, or other types of dolls. Just remember to baptize and name the candle in order to bring life to it.

#1 - A Spell For General Attraction

This spell won't attract a specific person. Instead, it is designed to make yourself pleasant to others.

YOU WILL NEED:

- A white or pink gender specific candle
- A petition paper
- A condition oil or olive oil
- A picture of yourself, with your eyes showing
- ⅛ teaspoon powdered sugar
- Candle dressings

Cleanse the candle then, on both sides of the candle, from bottom to top inscribe your birthday and birth date on the candle. In a horizontal fashion, cross over your name with a word such as *"attraction."* Anoint the candle and roll it in the candle dressings.

Place the petition paper in the candle holder Then set the picture, image facing upward on the paper, and sprinkle the sugar on it.. Place the candle over the picture. Light the candle and pray.

SUGGESTED CANDLE DRESSINGS

- **Cloves, crushed** *(Syzygium aromaticum, Eugenia spp.)*: Draws good friendships
- **Forget-Me-Not** *(Myosotis spp.)*: Encourages friendships
- **Pink Rose Pedals** *(Rosa spp.)*: Enhances the aura to attract people to you

SUGGESTED PRAYER

- **Psalm 133:** For friendship *(page 213)*

#2 - A Spell For Cursing and Crossing

This is a pretty harsh spell. So, as always, please ensure that the spell is justified, and that the punishment is equal to the crime committed against you. The candle will not be lit. Instead it will be wrapped like a mummy, and beaten.

YOU WILL NEED:

- A white or black gender specific doll
- A condition oil or olive oil
- Candle dressing
- About ½ yard of black cloth
- A generous amount of duct tape
- A hammer

Cleanse the candle then, on both sides of the candle, from top to bottom inscribe your target's birth name and birth date on the candle. In a horizontal fashion, cross over the name with a word such as *"destruction."* Anoint the candle and roll it in candle dressings.

Wrap the candle in the cloth then use enough duct tape, about ⅓ of a roll, to completely cover the cloth. Take it outside and lay it over cement or any hard surface. Beat it with the hammer while screaming the target's name and demanding destruction. Do this for thirteen days. Then, deploy the remains.

SUGGESTED CANDLE DRESSINGS

- **Black or Brown Mustard Seeds** *(Brassica spp.)*: Confuses rivals
- **Blueberries, Dried** *(Vaccinium frondosum)*: Brings sorrow to enemies
- **Cactus Spines** *(Cactaceae spp.)*: Used to jinx people
- **Chicory Root, Crushed** *(Cichorium intybus)*: Curses enemies
- **Graveyard Dirt**: For any type of negative spellwork
- **Red Pepper** *(Capsicum annum)*: To hurt a foe

SUGGESTED PRAYER

- **Psalm 109:** The most powerful text for retribution *(page 211)*

#3 - A Spell For Healing

Spellwork alone will not cure an illness, whether emotional or physical. Healing spells are designed to complement the professional help that is being rendered.

YOU WILL NEED:

- A white or light blue gender specific candle
- A petition paper
- A picture of yourself, with your eyes showing
- A condition oil or olive oil
- Candle dressings

Cleanse the candle then, on both sides of the candle, from bottom to top, inscribe your birthday and birth date on the candle. In a horizontal fashion, cross over your name with a word such as *"healing."* Anoint the candle and roll it in the candle dressings.

Place the petition paper in the candle holder Then set the picture, image facing upward on the paper, and sprinkle the sugar on it. Place the candle over the picture. Light the candle and pray.

SUGGESTED CANDLE DRESSINGS

- **All Heal/Self Heal** *(Prunella vulgaris)*: Used to improve health
- **Althea** *(Althaea officinalis, Althea spp.)*: Employed for medicinal and spiritual healing.
- **Angelica** *(Angelica archangelica, Angelica spp.)*: A powerful healer

SUGGESTED PRAYER

- **Psalm 41:** For emotional or physical healing *(page 203)*

#4 - A Spell For Mastery and Power

If you are perceived by others as being weak, this spell is designed to strengthen your aura, as well as your self-esteem. Remember that magic and behaviors must complement each other so, please work on your posture and always maintain direct eye contact when speaking to others.

YOU WILL NEED:

- A white or purple gender specific candle
- A petition paper
- A condition oil or olive oil
- A picture of yourself, with your eyes showing
- Candle dressings

Cleanse the candle then, on both sides of the candle, from bottom to top, inscribe your birthday and birth date on the candle. In a horizontal fashion, cross over your name with a word such as *"power."* Anoint the candle and roll it in the candle dressings.

Place the petition paper in the candle holder. Then set the picture, image facing upward on the paper, and sprinkle the sugar on it. Set the candle over the picture. Light the candle and pray.

SUGGESTED CANDLE DRESSINGS

- **Bay Laurel** *(Laurus nobilis)*: For victory
- **Master Root, crushed** *(Imperatoria ostruthium)*: Aids in strength and mastery

- **Master of the Woods** *(Asperula odorata)*: Assists with personal strength
- **Rattlesnake Grass** *(Briza spp.)*: For power and luck

SUGGESTED PRAYER-

📖 **St. Joan of Arc Prayer:** For Victory *(page 193)*

#5 - A Spell For Money

YOU WILL NEED:

- A white or green gender specific candle
- A petition paper
- A picture of yourself, with your eyes showing
- A condition oil or olive oil
- Candle dressings

Cleanse the candle then, on both sides of the candle, from bottom to top, inscribe your birthday and birth date on the candle. In a horizontal fashion, cross over your name with words such as *"money"* or "abundance. "Anoint the candle and roll it in the candle dressings.

Place the petition paper in the candle holder Then set the picture, image facing upward on the paper, and set the candle over the picture. Light the candle and pray.

SUGGESTED CANDLE DRESSINGS

- **Alfalfa** *(Medicago sativa)*: Attracts money
- **Bayberry Root, crushed** *(Pimenta acris)*: Known for centuries to attract money
- **Blue Flag** *(Iris versicolor)*: Attracts prosperity
- **Earth Smoke/Fumitory** *(Funaria spp.)*: Brings fast money

SUGGESTED PRAYER

📖 Money Prayer *(page 191)*

Jack-O'-Lantern Candle
To Scare Away Malicious Spirits

Symbolism

Around 2,000 years ago, the celebration of Samhain began, which is a contemporary Gaelic word meaning the *"summer's end"* or *"death of the old year."* It is described as an ancient Pagan Holiday that celebrates the death of the old year and the rebirth of a new one. In other words, a New Year's Eve event that begins on the night of the full moon closest to October 31 or November 1. To this day, Samhain remains an important Pagan holiday.

However, it is also believed that during this time, the veil or barrier between this mundane world and the spirit world is broken. When this happens, most entities, both benevolent and malevolent, will freely roam the earth.

One of the numerous tactics employed to drive away the malicious ones is to frighten them off with bonfires. Pumpkins and other gourds were also used in ancient times for protection. It is believed that if an ugly face is carved on a gourd, it will scare away evil spirits. An ugly face on the pumpkin is called a *"Jack-O'-Lantern."* A candle is inserted into the gourd in order to illuminate the ugly face.

Today, we can purchase Jack-O'-Lantern candles that serve the same purpose. It is an ideal candle, all year round, for people who are bothered by entities. Just avoid lighting any candles if you're experiencing poltergeist activity, as they can get knocked over and cause a fire.

A Spell to Scare Away Malicious Spirits

YOU WILL NEED:

- An ugly Jack-o'-Lantern Candle
- A condition oil or olive oil
- Candle Dressing
- Cleanse the candle, anoint it with the oil, and sprinkle candle dressings on it. Place it in a candle holder. Light the candle and pray.

SUGGESTED CANDLE DRESSINGS

- **Rue** *(Ruta graveolens)*: One of the oldest and most powerful protection herbs. Avoid this herb if pregnant
- **Eucalyptus** *(Eucalyptus spp.)*: Use as an alternative to rue. Repels evil forces.

SUGGESTED PRAYER

- **Psalm 121:** To repel evil entities *(page 212)*

LIP CANDLE
For Communication, Eloquent Speech, or to Stop Gossip

Symbolism

Lips are often depicted in art and culture to represent sensuality, emotion, beauty, and alluring sexuality. They also represent oral intake, such as eating, and oral output, such as speaking. Therefore, lip candles are perfect tools to employ in communication spells.

#1: A Spell To Receive Communication

Because parrots are notorious talkers, their feathers are often used in communication spells. Just use a little amount because feathers are highly combustible.

YOU WILL NEED:

- A white or yellow lip candle
- A petition paper
- A condition oil or olive oil
- A picture of yourself, with your eyes showing
- A picture of your target with eyes showing
- A small parrot feather, cut into tiny portions
- ¼ teaspoon of honey
- Candle dressings
- A soldering iron

Bore a hole between the upper and lower lip image. Insert the parrot feather pieces and about ½ teaspoon of the dressing into the hole. Restore the candle to its original form by filling the hole with melted wax of the same color.

Cleanse the candle and inscribe your desire in seven random areas of the candle. Examples include "_____ [target's name] *contact* _____ [your name]" or "____ [target's name] *talk to* _____ [your name]." Then, anoint the candle with olive oil and sprinkle it with candle dressings.

The honey will act as a glue. Spread the honey over the images of both people, then set the pictures together, face-to-face. Place your petition paper on the candle holder, followed by the pictures. Set the candle on the pictures. Light the candle and recite the prayer.

SUGGESTED CANDLE DRESSINGS

- **Deer's Tongue Herb/Vanilla Leaf** *(Achlys triphylla, Trilisa spp.)*: Fosters communication, grants eloquent and pleasant speech

SUGGESTED PRAYER

- Communication Prayer *(page 186)*

#2 - A Spell To Obtain Eloquent Speech

This is a great spell to perform for anyone who is about to deliver an oral public presentation.

YOU WILL NEED:

- A white or yellow lip candle
- A petition paper
- A condition oil or olive oil
- A picture of yourself, with your eyes showing
- Candle dressings
- A soldering iron

Bore a hole between the upper and lower lip image. Insert about ½ teaspoon of the candle dressings into the hole. Restore the candle to its original form by filling the hole with melted wax of the same color.

Cleanse the candle and inscribe your name in five random areas of the candle. In a vertical fashion, from bottom to top, cross your name with the words *"Dynamic Speaker."* Then, anoint the candle with the oil and sprinkle candle dressings over it.

Place your petition paper on the candle holder, followed by your picture, image facing upward. Set the candle on the picture. Light it and recite the prayer.

SUGGESTED CANDLE DRESSINGS

- **Bay Laurel** *(Lauris nobilis)*: For victory
- **Deer's Tongue Herb/Vanilla Leaf** *(Achlys triphylla, Trilisa spp.)*: Fosters communication, grants eloquent and pleasant speech
- **Master Root, crushed** *(Imperatoria ostruthium)*: Aids in strength and mastery

SUGGESTED PRAYER

- **Archangel Gabriel Prayer:** For Clear Communication *(page 184)*

#3 - A Spell To Stop Gossip

YOU WILL NEED:

- A white or black lip candle
- A petition paper
- A condition oil or olive oil
- A picture of your target, with eyes showing
- Candle dressings
- A soldering iron

Bore a hole between the upper and lower lip image. Insert about ½ teaspoon of the candle dressings into the hole. Restore the candle to its original form by filling the hole with melted wax of the same color.

Cleanse the candle and inscribe your target's birth name and birth date in thirteen random areas of the candle. In a vertical fashion, from top to bottom, cross your name with the words *"SHUT UP."* Then, anoint the candle with the oil and sprinkle candle dressings over it.

Place your petition paper on the candle holder, followed by the picture, image facing upward. Set the candle on the picture. Light it and recite the prayer.

SUGGESTED CANDLE DRESSINGS

- **Alum** *(Aluminum sulphate)*: has a puckering, or closing effect.
- **Adder's Tongue** *(Ophioglossum, Erythronium spp.)*: Stops enemies from mentioning your name
- **Chia Seed** *(Salvia hispanica)*: Stops gossip
- **Slippery Elm** *(Ulmus rubra)*: Put an end to both slander and gossip

SUGGESTED PRAYERS

- **Psalm 12** *(page 200)* **and Psalm 94** *(page 208)*: Both are phenomenal prayers to stop gossip

LOVERS CANDLE
To Incite a Lover or to Break Up an Affair

Symbolism

These candles are focused on passionate sexual energy between a man and a woman. It allows for magic related to sexual vitality and intimacy. With a lovers candle, the spellcaster can incite sexual lust, or even break up a sexual affair.

#1 - A Spell To Incite A Lover

YOU WILL NEED:

- A white or red lovers candle
- Six white or red small (floating) heart candles
- A petition paper
- A condition oil or olive oil
- A picture of yourself with your eyes showing
- A picture of your target, with eyes showing
- ¼ teaspoon honey

- ✅ If you are female, your vaginal secretions
- ✅ If you are male, your semen
- ✅ A pizza pan or cookie sheet (in lieu of a candle holder)

Illustration #6: Spell To Incite A Lover

Smear your vaginal or seminal secretions on both sides of the candle. If you have access to your target's secretions, then smear your secretions on the side representing you and the target's secretions on the opposite side.

The honey will act as a glue. Spread the honey over the images of both people, then set the pictures together, face-to-face. Place your petition paper in the middle of the pizza pan or cookie sheet, put the pictures over the paper, and set the candle atop the pictures.

Cleanse the six small heart candles, which are referred to as *"Helper Lights."* On the top of each one, write the words *"Make Love To Me"* (or use the *"F"* word instead to read *"F___ Me"*). Anoint the candles with the oil and lightly sprinkle the candle dressings over them. Encircle the lovers candle with the helper lights **(see illustration #6)**, but not too close to the lovers candle. To avoid getting burned, light the two wicks of the lovers candle first, followed by the helper lights.

SUGGESTED CANDLE DRESSINGS

- **Damiana** *(Turnera aphrodisiaca)*: For a better sex life
- **Cinnamon** *(Cinnamomum aromaticum)*: Heats up a love affair
- **Dittany of Crete** *(Origanum Dictamnus)*: Promotes passionate desires

SUGGESTED PRAYER

- Intimacy With Spouse Prayer *(page 189)*

> **Note:** If the target is not a spouse, do not recite the suggested prayer. Instead, verbally call the target's name and tell him or her your desire. It doesn't hurt to role play and enact your target's sexual desires toward you. Attempt to do so intermittently for a total of seven times.

#2 - A Spell to Break Up to Affair

After having researched the most common sexual *"turn-offs"* for both men and women, the predominant answer, from both genders, is offensive body odor. Because this spell complies with my research, it is not for the faint of heart. It's a little messy and quite malodorous!

YOU WILL NEED:

- A white or black lovers candle
- A petition paper
- A pair of disposable gloves
- Candle dressing
- A heated knife

Cleanse the lovers candle and inscribe your birth name and birthdate, of the man on the male portion of the candle and the woman's name on the female side. Baptize and name both images. Then, in a horizontal fashion, from the top to the bottom of the candle, inscribe the words *"Shit"* over both their names. Then, continue to inscribe that word all over both images.

Heat the blade of your knife, ensuring that the handle is heat-resistant. Insert the knife blade into the area where the vagina and penis would meet on the candle **(see illustration #7)** Do not remove the knife. Once the blade has cooled down, don your gloves, and generously distribute the dressing all over the candle. Place your petition paper in the candle holder and set the candle on it. Light the candle and pray.

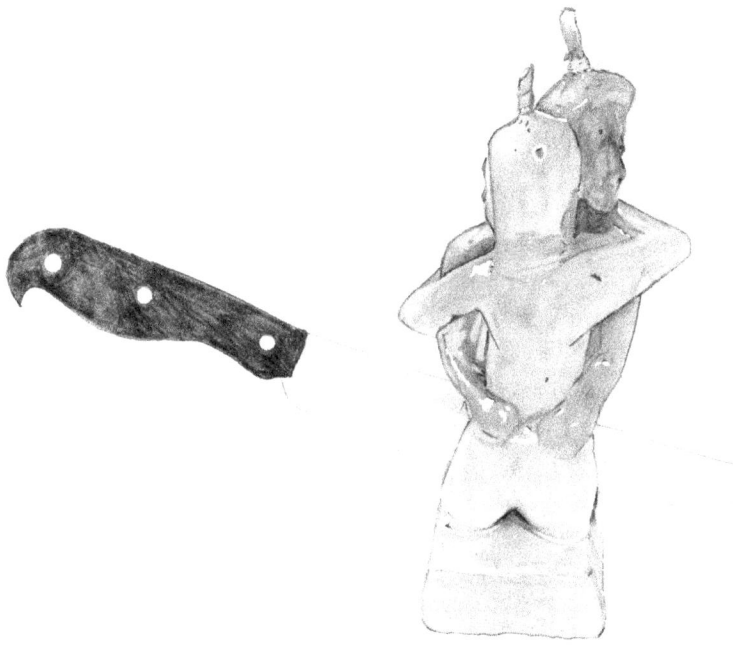

Illustration #7: Spell To Break Up An Affair

SUGGESTED CANDLE DRESSING

- Dog feces

SUGGESTED PRAYER

- Break Up Relationship Prayer *(page 185)*

Mouse Candle
To Assert Your Dominance Over Bullies

Symbolism

Throughout the world, the mouse is associated with both positive and negative connotations. In many parts of Africa, it is a symbol of undeserved arrogance. The Christian Holy Bible portrays mice as being unclean creatures. They are also symbolic of jealousy, disease, and death.

Keeping the aforementioned symbolisms in mind, mice are also unusually timid creatures. Most of us are familiar with the old expression, "*As timid as a mouse,*" which speaks to a creature who is easily frightened.

According to an article published by Psychology Today, bullies exhibit a distinctive cognitive feature, a kind of paranoia, thus imputing hostility in neutral situations. As with the African beliefs of mice possessing undeserved arrogance, bullies see themselves in a positive light.

The article also states that bullies couldn't exist without victims, and they don't pick on just anyone. Research shows that those singled out for bullying lack assertiveness even in nonthreatening situations

Bullies exist almost everywhere. They can be neighbors, co-workers, schoolmates, and even relatives. But with this spellwork, you can assert the bully's true nature into the mouse while enhancing your assertiveness, or even dominance, over the perpetrator.

A Spell for Dominance Over Bullies

YOU WILL NEED:

- A white or purple gender specific candle to represent yourself
- A small white mouse candle to represent the bully
- A petition paper stating your dominance over your target
- A petition paper for the mouse candle to run away
- A condition oil for banishing or olive oil for the mouse candle
- A condition oil for dominance or olive oil for the candle representing you
- A picture of yourself, with your eyes showing
- A picture of your target, with eyes showing
- About 3 teaspoon of your fresh urine
- Designated candle dressings for the mouse.

- Designated candle dressing for the gender candle

Cleanse both candles then, baptize and name them. On the gender candle, inscribe your birth name and birth date on both the front and back, in a horizontal direction. Then, on both sides, from the bottom of the candle to the top, cross your name over with the word *"dominant"* or *"master."* Anoint the gender candle with the oil and sprinkle the designated herbs all over it. Place your petition paper in the candle holder, followed by your picture, image facing upward. Set your candle over the picture.

The mouse candle will be prepared differently. Inscribe your target's birth name and birth date twice on the mouse candle. Then, inscribe the words *"run-away"* nine times, on random surface areas of the candle. Anoint only the back and top of it with the oil and scatter the designated herbs on the anointed areas, while avoiding its face.

Using a spoon, small syringe, or spray bottle, splash most of your urine onto its face. Place the petition paper in the candle holder. Dribble some of your urine onto it. Place your target's picture, image facing upward, over the paper and dribble your remaining urine onto it. Set the mouse candle on the picture. Both candles should be facing each other. Light your candle first, then the mouse candle, and pray.

SUGGESTED DRESSINGS FOR THE MOUSE CANDLE

- **Alum** *(Aluminum Sulphate)*: Has A Puckering or closing effect
- **Asafoetida** *(Ferula assa-foetida)*: A banishing ingredient

SUGGESTED DRESSING FOR THE GENDER CANDLE

- **Calamus/Sweet Flag, crushed** *(Acorus calamus)*: A controlling agent
- **Licorice Root, crushed** *(Glycyrrhiza spp.)*: Grants domination and control
- **Master of the Woods** *(Asperula odorata)*: A commanding and ruling herb

SUGGESTED PRAYER

- **Psalm 1:** To bind enemies *(page 199)*

Owl Candle
For Wisdom & Passing Exams

Symbolism

The symbolisms attributed to owls vary greatly across the world. From its darkest associations with bad luck, death, and evil witches, to its virtuous representations of fertility, good luck, guidance, protection, and safety, the owl embodies an array of meanings.

Here in North America, most of us associate owls with intelligence and wisdom. Various metaphysical practitioners call upon these beautiful birds to gain further knowledge into any subject matter, including academia.

A Spell for Wisdom and Passing Exams

YOU WILL NEED:

- A white or purple owl candle. However, the owl's natural colors will suffice.
- A petition paper
- A condition oil or olive oil
- A picture of yourself, with your eyes showing
- Candle dressings

Cleanse the candle, and inscribe your name, in a horizontal fashion, on random surface areas of the candle. Cross over your name with either the words *"wisdom"* or *"knowledge,"* depending on your need. Anoint the candle with the oil and scatter dressings on it.

Place the petition paper in the candle holder. Then, set the picture, image facing upward, on the paper. Hold the candle in both hands and look it in the eyes while reciting aloud: *"Great Owl Spirit, please guide me with your wisdom and show me the path that I should take. Please help me to see what is hidden in the shadows and find the truth that lies beneath. Thank you"*

Set the candle on your picture. Light the candle and pray.

SUGGESTED CANDLE DRESSINGS

- **Peach Tree Leaves** *(Prunus persica)*: Helps to pass examinations

- **Sage** *(Salvia spp.)*: Brings wisdom
- **Solomon's Seal Root, crushed** *(Polygonatum biflorum)*: Gives insight and wisdom

SUGGESTED PRAYERS

- Test-Taking Prayer *(page 196)*
- Wisdom Prayer *(page 198)*
- Wisdom In Relationships Prayer *(page 198)*

PENIS CANDLE
For Lust, Sexual Virility, Or Impotence

Symbolism

Throughout history, the phallus has represented male domination, fertility, power, and sexual potency. Some cultures design talismans in this image to protect the bearer from evil forces.

For these reasons, a phallus candle is most often used in spellwork related to sex magic, passion, and virility. Oftentimes, they're used to heal physiological difficulties related to sexual dysfunction. These candles are also employed to diminish a man's domination and sexual potency, especially when the culprit is intruding upon one's love interest.

Because sex magic predominantly involves role-playing, sometimes phallic candles are not lit. Instead, they're employed as effigies, just as with two of the three suggested spells listed in this section.

#1 - A Spell to Arouse Lust From Another

YOU WILL NEED:

- A white or red penis candle
- A small picture of your target, with eyes showing
- A small petition paper including the target's birth name and birth date
- The target's personal concerns, if available *(page 39)*
- A soldering iron

Bore a deep hole into the base of the candle, and insert the picture, personal concerns, and the paper into it. Then, restore the candle to its original form by filling the hole with melted wax of the same color.

Do not cleanse the candle with the conventional ritualistic solutions. Instead, wash it thoroughly with soap and water.

Inscribe the target's name and birthdate at the base of the candle then, name and baptize it. Perform sexual acts with the candle, as if it were the actual penis. When doing so, tell the target that he lusts for you. If and when reaching a climax, scream your command to your target.

SUGGESTED CANDLE DRESSINGS

- Your vaginal or seminal secretions

SUGGESTED PRAYER

- **Venus Prayer For Lust:** To be recited at the planetary hour of Venus or on Fridays, during the waxing moon phase, at 8:00 pm *(page 197)*

#2 - A Spell to Restore Sexual Virility

YOU WILL NEED:

- A white or light blue penis candle
- A small picture of yourself with eyes showing
- A regular-sized picture of yourself, with your eyes showing
- Your personal concerns *(page 39)*
- A petition paper
- A condition oil or olive oil
- Candle dressings
- A soldering iron

Bore a deep hole into the base of the candle and insert the picture and personal concerns into it. Then, restore the candle to its original form by filling the hole with melted wax of the same color.

Cleanse the candle, and at both the base and tip of the candle, inscribe your birth name and birthdate on it. Starting from the base of the candle, and working toward the top, inscribe the words *"Restore Virility"* nine times in a circular fashion.

Name and baptize the candle, anoint it with the oil, and sprinkle the dressings over it. Place your petition paper on the candle holder, followed by the picture, image facing upward. Set the candle on the picture. Light the candle and recite the prayer.

SUGGESTED CANDLE DRESSINGS

- **Althea** *(Hibiscus syriacus)*: A healing herb
- **Burdock Root, crushed** *(Arctium)*: Revives male nature
- **Dill** *(Anethum graveolens)*: Restores one's nature
- **Sampson Snakeroot** *(Orbexilum pedunculatum)*: Grants sexual health
- **Wintergreen** *(Gaultheria)*: Aids in sexual matters

SUGGESTED PRAYERS

- Restore Sexuality Prayer *(page 192)*
- **Psalm 41:** For Emotional or Physical Healing *(page 203)*

BONUS SPELL

If someone has either tied or cursed a man's nature, drink a cup of nettle *(Urtica)* tea while reciting Psalm 37 aloud every other day for two weeks. It contains uncrossing agents as well as antibacterial properties. Works for my clients every time!

#3 - A Spell to Induce Impotence

This is another pretty harsh spell. As always, please ensure that the spell is justified and that the punishment is equal to the crime committed against you. The candle will not be lit. Instead, it will be tortured.

YOU WILL NEED:

- A white or black penis candle
- A small picture of your target, with their eyes showing
- The target's personal concerns, if available *(page 39)*
- A condition oil or olive oil

- Candle dressings
- A soldering iron
- Thirteen rusty or coffin nails
- About ½ yard of black cloth
- A generous amount of duct tape
- A hammer

Bore deep holes on random parts of the candle. Insert the picture in the candle, and depending on the size of each hole, insert a taglock in two or three holes, a petition paper in another, candle dressings in others. Then, restore the candle to its original form by filling the holes with melted wax of the same color.

Cleanse the candle, and at both the base and tip of the candle, inscribe your target's birth name and birthdate on it. Starting from the top of the candle and working toward the bottom, inscribe the words *"Impotence"* thirteen times, in a spiral fashion. Then, name and baptize the candle.

Anoint the candle and generously roll it in the dressings. Do not light this candle because saltpeter, a candle dressing, and an agent causing impotence, are highly combustible

Heat the nails, one at a time, and drive them all the way into the candle while screaming your demands. Ensure that one nail is driven directly into the tip of the penis, and a few into the head, which are very sensitive areas.

Wrap the candle in the cloth, then use enough duct tape, about ⅓ of a roll, to completely cover the cloth. Take it outside and lay it over cement or any hard surface. Beat it with the hammer while screaming the target's name and demanding impotence. Do this for thirteen days. Then, deploy the remains.

SUGGESTED CANDLE DRESSINGS

- **Saltpeter** *(Potassium nitrate)*: Induces impotence
- Rat Poison, Pulverized *(brodifacoum, difenacoum, bromadiolone, or flocoumafen)*

SUGGESTED PRAYER

- **Psalm 109:** For cursing and crossing *(page 211)*

Praying Hands Candle
To Petition God

Symbolism

For many centuries, the Roman Empire dominated Europe by conquering numerous territories through wars. When the enemies were defeated, they clasped their hands together, giving their captors an opportunity to bind or shackle them. This posture ultimately became a universal signal of surrender, much like the waving of a white flag is today.

Although it is purely speculative, many believe that the symbolism of the clasping hands, indicating surrender, was embraced by numerous religious sects. That posture, now called *"The Praying Hands,"* was adopted to denote one's surrender and connection to a higher supernatural force. Today, it also symbolizes devotion, obedience, prayer, respect, repentance, and veneration.

Because we can appeal to our personal supreme being for virtually anything, the praying hands candle can be utilized for any request. My personal favorite use of the candle is to petition God, in a nine-day prayer.

A Spell to Petition God

YOU WILL NEED:

- A white praying hands candle
- Olive oil
- A picture of yourself, with your eyes showing
- A petition paper
- Your teardrops

Cleanse the candle and anoint it with the oil. No inscription on the candle is necessary, nor are candle dressings.

Place your petition paper on the candle holder, followed by the picture, image facing upward. Set the candle on the picture.

It is believed that crying like a baby will elicit pity from God. Do so while praying and gently blot some of your teardrops onto the candle. This may be repeated any time.

For nine consecutive days, at around the same time each day, you will light the candle for about twenty minutes and recite the prayer. Extinguish the candle using a snuffer. On the ninth day, allow the candle to burn all the way down.

SUGGESTED CANDLE DRESSINGS

- No dressing is necessary. The Holy Bible speaks solely of olive oil

SUGGESTED PRAYER

- Novena to God The Father *(page 191)*

PYRAMID CANDLE
For Money

Symbolism
It is widely believed that the Egyptian Pharaoh Khufu (AKA Cheops) ordered the Great Pyramid of Giza to be built in order to showcase his power and wealth. For this reason, pyramid-shaped objects remain a symbol of wealth. Numerous metaphysical practitioners utilize pyramid forms for several purposes, including magical spells to build wealth and manifest prosperity.

A Spell for Money
There are a variety of pyramid-shaped candles on the market. Avoid those that are molded with brick-shaped surfaces. Although they are beautiful and well crafted, they are difficult to inscribe and also produce a messy candle burn, resulting in muddled wax remains. The candles having smooth surfaces on the four sides of the pyramid are much easier to manage.

YOU WILL NEED:

- A white or green pyramid-shaped candle
- A picture of yourself, with your eyes showing
- A petition paper
- A condition oil or olive oil
- Candle dressings

Cleanse the candle and, in a horizontal direction, inscribe your birth name and birth date on each side of the candle, for a total of four times. Then, on each side of the pyramid, starting from the base of the candle and ending near the top, inscribe the words *"Prosperity Come To Me."* Anoint the candle with oil and scatter candle dressings over it.

Place the petition paper in the candle holder, followed by the picture, image facing upward. Set the candle over the picture. Light the candle and pray.

SUGGESTED CANDLE DRESSINGS

- **Alfalfa** *(Medicago sativa)*: Attracts money
- **Bayberry Root, crushed** *(Pimenta acris)*: Known for centuries to attract money
- **Blue Flag** *(Iris versicolor)*: Attracts prosperity
- **Earth Smoke/Fumitory** *(Funaria spp.)*: Brings fast money

SUGGESTED PRAYER

Money Prayer *(page 191)*

Rose Candle
(Large and Small)
To Attract Love

Symbolism

No other flower is as symbolic of love and beauty as the rose. In Greek mythology, the rose was considered sacred by Aphrodite, the goddess of love. That connection with romantic love was paralleled in Roman mythology and associated with Aphrodite's Roman counterpart, Venus. To this day, roses remain one of the most beloved flowers in the world.

While roses are bred in a large variety of colors, each with a different meaning, red roses are universally known as symbols of love and romance. For this reason, red rose-shaped candles are generally employed in spellwork for attraction, beauty, and matters of love. If embellished within the elements of this magnificent flower, you will most often radiate those very same vibrations.

#1 - A Spell For Large Rose Candles

The many ridges within this candle mold create difficulties in both anointing and inscribing it. Therefore, these two traditional steps will be excluded while working with a rose candle.

The ridges also create another nuisance by retaining the spiritual cleansing waters within the grooves. Simply cleanse the candle and turn it upside down, over a towel, until the candle is completely dry.

YOU WILL NEED:

- A white or red rose candle
- All-natural Rose Water
- A small spray bottle
- A picture of yourself, with your eyes showing
- A petition paper
- Candle Dressing

Cleanse the candle and turn it upside down to dry. When it is completely dry, fill your spray bottle with Rose Water and lightly spray the candle, picture, and petition paper with the water. Again, allow the candle to dry before proceeding with this spell.

After the candle has dried, place the petition paper in the candle holder, followed by the picture, image facing upward. Lightly scatter the candle dressing over the picture, and just a pinch on the candle. Set the candle on the picture, light it, and recite your prayer.

SUGGESTED CANDLE DRESSING

- **Dried Red Rose Petals** *(Rosa spp.)*: For luck in all love matters

SUGGESTED PRAYER

- **Psalm 45:** For love *(page 204)*

#2 - A Spell for Floating Rose Candles

YOU WILL NEED:

- Three white or red floating rose candles
- A small picture of yourself, with your eyes showing, on good photo quality paper or laminated
- A medium-sized clear or plain white bowl
- A bottle of all natural Rose Water
- A rose quartz crystal

Cleanse the candles and allow them to dry. Fill the bowl to about ⅔ its capacity, with rose water. Place your picture, image facing upward, into the bowl, and set the crystal over your picture, in order to anchor it down.

Immerse the candles, petals facing downward, into the water. Remove them and allow to completely dry. Once the candles are dry, float them, petals facing upward, on the water. Light the candles and pray.

Until the water has completely evaporated, you may float more candles on the water. However, do not, under any circumstances, refill the bowl with fresh Rose Water, which would create an undesirable mixture of stale and fresh waters.

SUGGESTED CANDLE DRESSING

- None are necessary

SUGGESTED PRAYER

- **Psalm 45:** For love *(page 204)*

SAME GENDER MARRIAGE CANDLE
(Bride/Bride, Groom/Groom)

Symbolism

These candles, shaped like a male or female couple standing together, represent the unity of two people in marriage. Oftentimes, they are employed in spellwork to magically entice a marital commitment from a reluctant mate.

In this section, individual spells to persuade a lesbian or gay marriage are offered. Please pay close attention to the candle dressings as they vary from person to person.

#1: A Spell to Inspire a Bride+Bride Marriage

YOU WILL NEED:

- A Bride and Bride candle
- A picture of your target, with her eyes showing
- A picture of yourself, with your eyes showing
- Petition paper
- A condition oil or olive oil
- ¼ teaspoon honey
- Candle dressings
- 5 real or imitation gold wedding bands
- ¼ cup uncooked rice
- White altar cloth (must be white)

Cleanse the candle. Inscribe the target's portion of the candle with her name, then name and baptize it. Inscribe your portion of the candle with your name, name and baptize it. Next, inscribe the word *"marriage"* seven times, in a circular fashion, starting from the base of the candle to the highest possible point. Anoint the candles with the oil and sprinkle the designated crushed herbs on them.

The honey will act as a glue. Spread the honey over the images of both people then set the pictures together, face-to-face. Place the cloth on the altar, followed by the candle holder. Put your petition paper and the pictures in the candle holder, then set the candle on the pictures. Surround the candle with the five rings and scatter the rice around the candle. Light the candle and recite the prayer.

SUGGESTED CANDLE DRESSINGS
FOR YOUR PORTION OF THE CANDLE

- **Vanilla Bean, crushed** *(Vanilla planifolia)*: Attracts women, used in love rituals
- **Red Rose Petals** *(Rosa spp.)*: Attracts love from others

SUGGESTED CANDLE DRESSINGS FOR YOUR TARGET'S PORTION OF THE CANDLE

- **Myrtle** *(Myrtus communis)*: Used in marital work
- **Red Clover** *(Trifolium pratense)*: Employed to encourage marriage

SUGGESTED PRAYER

- Interfaith Wedding Vows *(page 189)*

#2: A Spell to Inspire a Groom+Groom Marriage

You will basically follow the same instructions provided in **Spell #1: A Spell to Inspire a Bride+Bride Marriage** *(page 144)*, but with three exceptions:

1. Use a Groom and Groom candle

2. Put your petition paper and the pictures in the candle holder. Lightly scatter dried lavender leaves (*Lavandula spp.*) over the pictures, as it promotes same gender love and commitment. Then, set the candle on the lavender leaves.

3. On the side of the candle representing yourself, dress it instead with crushed or powdered cedar wood (*Cedrus spp.*). This is because cedar wood motivates a man to follow you.

SEVEN KNOB WISHING CANDLE
For Blessings or To Send Someone Away

Symbolism

These candles feature seven distinct sections, or *"knobs,"* each representing a step toward achieving your goal. It serves as a means to strengthen your wish *"seven-fold."* Each time a knob is lit, the petition or prayer is recited aloud. When the knob is consumed, the candle is snuffed out then, re-lit the succeeding day. This ritual is performed for a total of seven consecutive days.

Inscribing different wishes on the knobs is inadvisable because there is not enough energy output invested in the requests. It is wiser to put seven days of consistent energy output toward the same goal. To do so, inscribe each knob with your wish, in a circular fashion, all the way around the knobs. If your request only has a few words, either increase the size of the lettering or inscribe the wish more than once per knob.

When performing banishing or send away spells, just turn the candle upside down and inscribe the knobs. You will still set the candle into the holder in the traditional fashion. The only difference is that the words will be upside down.

#1 A Spell For Blessings

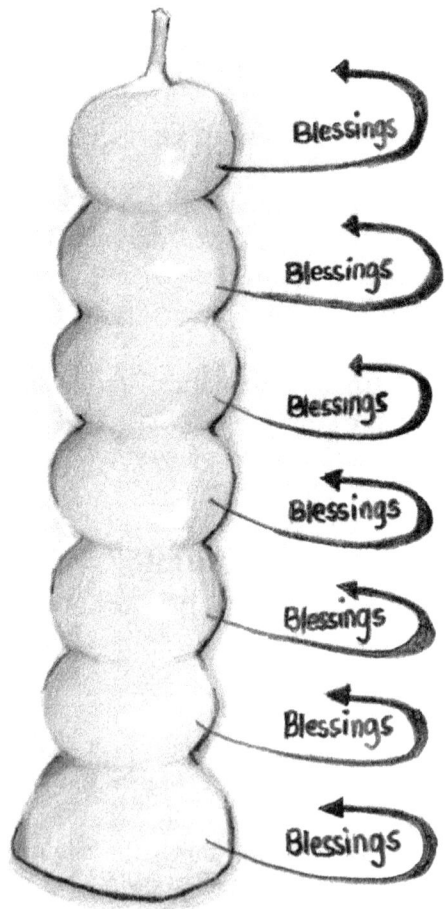

Illustration #8: Seven-Knob Candle for Blessings

YOU WILL NEED:

- A white seven knob candle
- A condition oil or olive oil
- A petition paper
- A picture of yourself, with your eyes showing
- Candle Dressings
- Candle snuffer

Cleanse the candle then, inscribe each knob with the word *"Blessings"* **(see illustration # 8)** three times. Anoint the candle and scatter the candle dressings over it. Place the petition paper in the candle holder, followed by the picture, image facing upward. Set the candle over the picture. Light the candle and pray.

SUGGESTED CANDLE DRESSINGS

- **Angelica Root, crushed** *(Angelica spp.)*: Used for blessings
- **Copal** *(Bursera sp., Protium copal)*: A Holy incense, use powdered incense for dressing a candle

SUGGESTED PRAYER

- **Psalm 145:** For Blessings *(page 213)*

#2- A Spell to Send Someone Away

YOU WILL NEED:

- A black or white seven knob candle
- A condition oil or olive oil
- A petition paper
- A picture of your target, with eyes showing
- Candle Dressings

Cleanse the candle, then turn the candle upside down. Inscribe each knob with the words "___ **[target's name]** *Go Away"* **(see illustration**

#9). Return the candle to its original posture, anoint it, and scatter the candle dressings over it.

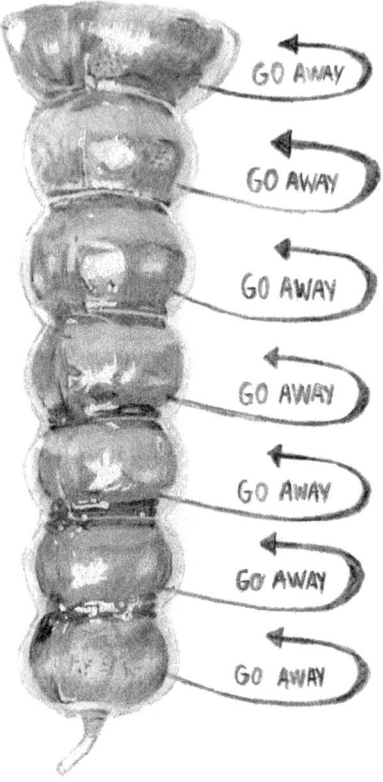

Illustration #9: Seven-Knob Candle To Send Someone Away

On the image of your target's forehead, write that person's birth name and birthdate. Place the petition paper in the candle holder, followed by the picture, image facing upward. Set the candle on the picture. Light the candle and pray.

SUGGESTED CANDLE DRESSING

🌿 **Asafoetida** *(Ferula assa-foetida)*: A banishing ingredient

SUGGESTED PRAYER

📖 **Psalm 105:** To drive enemies away *(page 209)*

Skull Candle
For Reconciliation

Symbolism

The initial appearance of a skull candle can be intimidating, but they simply represent a person's head and face, or a human brain. When these candles are approached in spellwork to represent the brain, they can be easily manipulated to change the target's attitudes or behaviors.

The human brain is divided into four main lobes **(see illustration #10)** that control the following functions.

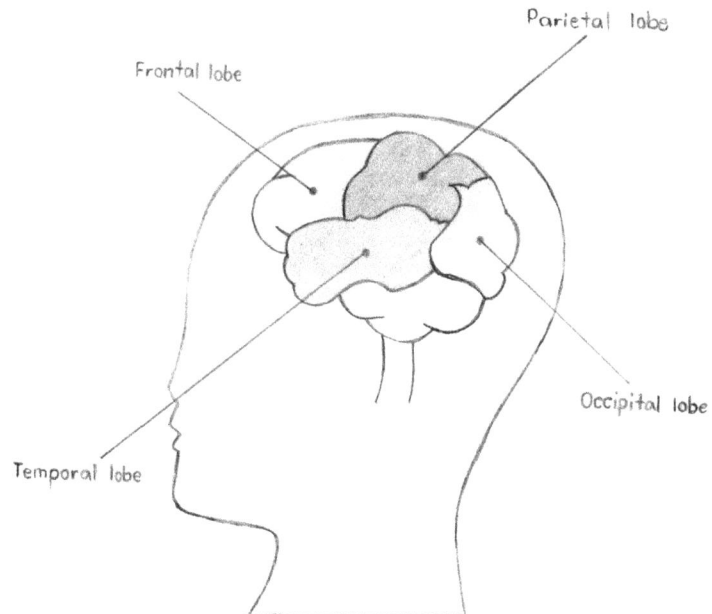

Illustration #10: Brain Lobes

FRONTAL LOBE (THE MOST UTILIZED LOBE FOR SPELLWORK

- 🕯 Personality
- 🕯 Behaviors
- 🕯 Speech
- 🕯 Speaking
- 🕯 Writing
- 🕯 Body Movements
- 🕯 Intelligence
- 🕯 Concentration
- 🕯 Self-awareness

PARIETAL LOBES (LOCATED BILATERALLY)

- 🔥 Interpretation of language and words.

- 🔥 Senses touch, pain, and temperature.

- 🔥 Interprets signals from hearing, vision, memory, motor and sensory functions.

OCCIPITAL LOBE

- 🔥 Interprets visual colors, light, and movement.

TEMPORAL LOBES (LOCATED BILATERALLY)

- 🔥 Helps to understand language, memory, and hearing.

- 🔥 Sequencing and organizational skills.

Although specific lobes can be manipulated for various purposes, my preference is to target the frontal lobe. This part of the human brain—easily found in the forehead portion of the skull candle—controls most of the behaviors which we desire to influence in spellwork.

A Spell for Reconciliation

Throughout the years, it became quite apparent to me that when a breakup of any type of long-term relationship occurs, both parties usually suffer from emotional pain. A common phenomenon, called *"Post-Breakup Guilt,"* which is a mixture of disappointment and regret, is a prevalent affliction upon both parties. Other common feelings, experienced by one or both people, include anger, sadness, confusion, loneliness, and a sense of loss.

For these reasons, when there is a request for reconciliation magic, I do not immediately cast a *"Return To Me"* spell because if it manifests, it is short-lived. This is due to the lingering effects of emotional pain, resulting in unresolved resentment toward the other person.

In an attempt to resolve these problems, my clients are first instructed to construct a honey jar **(for instructions, see the "Heart Candle" section)**. The purpose of this spell is to sweeten the target's thoughts of you and to gently nudge him or her to return. Once the jar is created, a healing and forgiveness skull candle spell is begun in order to eradicate painful memories, while only seeing and thinking of you.

YOU WILL NEED:

- A white or light blue skull candle (no smaller than 4 inches in height 7 inches in diameter)
- A metal pie pan
- Three 1-inch by 1-inch petition papers that say *"Forgive _____ [your name]"*
- Three dime-sized, or smaller, pictures of yourself
- A regular-sized petition paper to place under the candle
- A picture of your target, with their eyes showing
- Anointing oil or olive oil
- Candle dressings
- A soldering iron.

Solder a hole into the frontal region, the occipital region, the two sides of the temporal lobes, and the eye sockets. Insert a picture of yourself, facing the center of the candle, into each eye socket. Fill the holes with melted wax of the same color and allow the wax to harden before continuing. Then, insert your last picture into the occipital lobe, add a little bit of the candle dressing, refill the hole with wax, and allow it to harden.

Insert a 1-inch by 1-inch petition paper into the frontal lobe, add candle dressings, refill the hole with melted wax, and allow it to harden. Repeat the process for the two temporal lobes.

Cleanse the candle, baptize and name it. On the frontal region, inscribe the target's full name and birth date, followed by your command to forgive you. Below is an example:

John Doe
February 31, 1809
Forgive
Miss Aida

Then, on six additional random surfaces of the candle, inscribe the words *"Forgive and return to _____* **[your name]**." Anoint the candle with oil and roll it in the candle dressings or generously scatter dressings all over the candle.

Over the image of your target's forehead, write the same words as previously instructed. Place the petition paper in the pie pan, followed by the picture, image facing upward. Set the candle on the picture. Light the candle and recite a prayer. Then, walk to the front of the candle and gently tell it to forgive you. Do the same on the right side, back side, and left side of the candle. Repeat this process every hour until a viable image of the face is no longer visible.

SUGGESTED CANDLE DRESSINGS

- **Balm Of Gilead, crushed** *(Cedronella canariensis, Populus candicans, or Commiphora gileadensis)*: Soothes the pain of arguments
- **Dill** *(Anethum graveolens)*: Removes crossed conditions in love affairs
- **Forget-Me-Not** *(Myosotis spp.)*: Promotes reconciliation
- **Golden Seal** *(Hydrastis canadensis)*: A powerful healer
- **Peony** *(Paeonia lactiflora)*: Heals the person you love

SUGGESTED PRAYERS

- **Psalm 41:** For emotional and physical healing *(page 203)*
- Reconciliation Prayer *(page 192)*

SNAKE CANDLE
To Bind an Enemy

Symbolism

Snakes are one of the oldest and most widespread mythological symbols, representing both good and evil. In Judeo-Christianity, it is believed that through deception, a snake tricked the first woman on earth into violating God's orders. When she talked her partner into doing the same, God expelled them both from paradise. Thus, snakes are often representative of evil, temptation, lies, and punishment.

In literature, snakes frequently represent death and destruction, most likely because many can deliver swift, and sometimes consecutive, lethal venomous bites. Additionally, a boa constrictor's ability to fatally compress any living creature is terrifying.

For these reasons, depictions of snakes are often used to cause illness, harm, or to bind an enemy. In Palo, rubber snakes are inserted into our *"pots"* (cauldrons) in lieu of live ones, while the candles are sometimes employed for the same purposes **(see illustration #11)**.

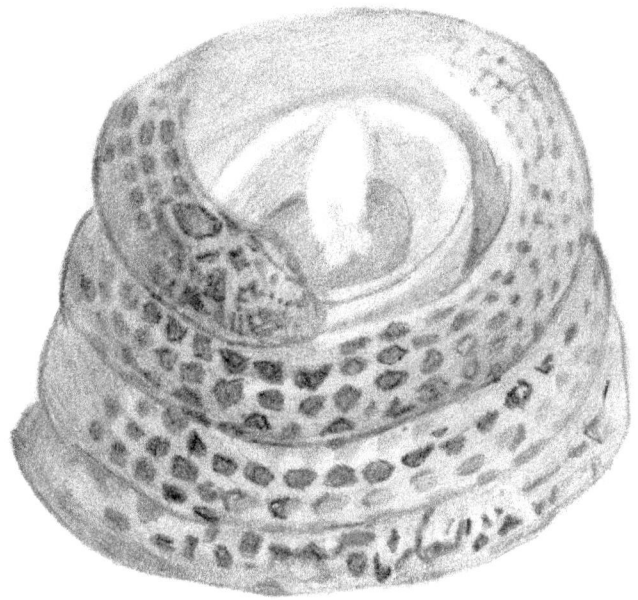

Illustration #11: Snake Candle to Bind an Enemy

A Spell to Bind an Enemy

YOU WILL NEED:

- A snake candle of any color
- A dime-sized picture of your target, with eyes showing
- A regular-sized picture or your target, with eyes showing
- An old cobweb
- A petition paper
- Candle dressings
- Anointing oil or olive oil
- A soldering iron
- A small spray bottle
- A tablespoon of your fresh urine

Hold the small picture up and state: *"This snake binds you from harming me or other."* Bore a hole into the bowl of the candle, a few inches away from the wick, and quickly insert the small picture deep into the wax. Stir the melted wax to cover the picture. Once the wax has hardened, inscribe your target's birthname and birthdate on it. Anoint the candle and lightly scatter candle dressing on the bowl of wax.

Fill your spray bottle with about two tablespoons of your fresh urine. Wrap your target's picture in the cobweb while stating aloud: *"I bind you for harming me or others."* Now, spray some of your fresh urine onto it in order to assert your dominance. Place the petition paper in the candle holder, followed by the picture with the image facing upward. Set the candle on the picture.

Due to the complexities of the snake spirit, do not call upon it for assistance. Instead, light the candle and recite the suggested prayer.

SUGGESTED CANDLE DRESSINGS

- **Devil's Shoestring** *(Viburnum alnifolium)*: Reverses harm back to the perpetrator
- **Knotweed** *(Polygonum)*: Binds and restrains the target

SUGGESTED PRAYER

- **Psalm 1:** To Bind Enemies *(page 199)*

STAR CANDLE
For Connecting to the Metaphysical

Symbolism

The celestial meaning of a star is one that has been studied for centuries by scholars, astrologers, and spiritualists alike. In addition to representing truth, guidance, enlightenment, hope, and protection, it is an ancient symbol with a long history of denoting the heavens and the presence of the divine powers who dwell within them.

It is believed that stars have a metaphysical power to lead us closer to inner peace, spiritual growth, and understanding of our true selves. A star can be seen as a reminder of our connection to the greater universe.

For these reasons, star candles are used in metaphysical practices to aid us in connecting to the astral realms, and/or to the divine powers. They are also phenomenal tools for helping those who are embarking upon spiritual quests.

It is advisable to perform this spell during the nighttime hours. While performing this magic, gazing upon the stars will enhance your powers of creative visualization, thus increasing your chances of manifestation.

A Spell to Connect to the Metaphysical

YOU WILL NEED:

- A white star candle
- ⅛ teaspoon of silver glitter
- A picture of yourself with eyes showing
- A condition oil or olive oil
- A petition paper
- Candle dressings

Cleanse the candle and horizontally inscribe your birth name and birth date in the center of both the front and back of the candle. In a vertical direction, from the lowest point of the candle to the highest possible point, cross your name over with the words *"Spiritual Enlightenment."* Continue to write these words all over the candle for a total of nine times.

Anoint the candle with the oil. Mix the candle dressings with the glitter and sprinkle the mixture all over the candle. Place your petition paper on the candle holder, followed by the picture, image facing upward. Set the candle on the picture. Light the candle and recite your petition and prayers while gazing at the night sky. If one particular star or star system catches your eye, continue to gaze upon it while envisioning your requests as having been granted.

SUGGESTED CANDLE DRESSINGS

- **Acacia** *(Acacia spp.)*: Opens the mind to visions
- **Buchu** *(Agathosma spp.)*: Enhances psychic and spiritual powers
- **Copal, crushed** *(Bursera spp., Protium copal)*: Aids in seeking divine powers
- **Mugwort** *(Artemisia vulgaris)*: Aids in psychic work

SUGGESTED PRAYER

📖 Connecting To The Metaphysical Prayer *(page 187)*

SUN CANDLE
For Empowerment and Strength

Symbolism

All planets within our galaxy, major and dwarf alike, are within the domain of the sun. For this reason, the sun is the proverbial *"rock star"* of our solar system. It is the center of all existence and a powerful symbol of life, creation, and divine energy.

Because the sun also rules *"the vital spirits,"* it has traditional associations with mental and physical soundness, vitality, and strength. We all know that a good dose of sunshine can rejuvenate our spirits. Thus, appealing to this great entity can grant us energy, confidence-building powers, and the fortitude to achieve our goals, despite any and all obstacles.

Since the sun also rules gold, try to use this color to the fullest extent with this spell. Doing so will gain favor from the mighty entity of the sun.

A Spell for Empowerment and Strength

YOU WILL NEED:

- A white or yellow sun candle
- Five metallic gold 4-inch taper (chime) candles
- Six petition papers
- A picture of yourself, with your eyes showing
- A gold or yellow altar cloth
- ⅛ teaspoon gold glitter
- ⅛ teaspoon powdered Frankincense (Boswellia sacra)
- A metal pie or pizza pan

Cleanse the candles but do not inscribe them. This is because sun candles bear a face that we do not wish to disturb. Additionally, the metallic coating on the five *"helper"* candles is fragile, and can easily fissure.

Mix the glitter and incense together, anoint just the sun candle with the oil, and lightly sprinkle the mixture over it. Place the larger petition paper in the center of the pan, followed by the picture, image facing upward, then set the sun candle on the picture. Encircle it with the five metallic candles ,setting a smaller petition paper under each, to create a total of six candles. The is because the number six belongs to the sun. To avoid risking burns, light the sun candle first, followed by the chime candles. Then, recite your prayer.

SUGGESTED CANDLE DRESSING

🌿 A mixture of glitter and Frankincense *(as previously discussed)*

SUGGESTED PRAYER

📖 **Sun Prayer:** For Empowerment And Strength *(page 196)*

VENUS CANDLE
For Beauty And Grace

Symbolism

One of the most important deities of the ancient Romans was Venus. Considered to be one of the elder gods in the Roman pantheon, Venus was recognized as the Goddess of love, beauty, grace, passion, fertility, prostitution, and victory. While more people are familiar with her Greek counterpart, Aphrodite, both hold similar attributes.

To this day, hundreds of thousands of people continue to honor, revere, and petition Venus in matters pertaining to her attributes and/or domains. The same can be said about Aphrodite. However, please avoid using their names interchangeably during spellwork because they are indeed different entities, and Venus possesses a few more attributes than does Aphrodite.

Before beginning this spell, please be aware that many vendors are erroneously selling headless and armless candles as representative of Venus. These candles actually represent the *"Winged Victory of Samothrace,"* a famous marble sculpture of the Greek goddess *Nike,* the goddess of victory.

A Spell for Beauty and Grace

Because the statue of Venus de Milo was unearthed, and rediscovered armless in 1820 A.D., most candle molds of the Goddess are also armless.

But it is my personal opinion that they misrepresent the true beauty that is Venus. Therefore, I highly recommend instead using the candle called *"The Birth of Venus"* **(see illustration # 12)**.

Illustration #12: The Birth Of Venus Candle

YOU WILL NEED:

- A *"Birth of Venus"* candle
- Seven unwrapped chocolate kisses
- A picture of yourself, with your eyes showing
- A petition paper
- A condition oil (preferably rose oil) or olive oil
- Candle dressings

Cleanse the candle, but do not inscribe it. Anoint the candle with oil and scatter the candle dressing on it. Over the image of your forehead write the words *"Beauty and Grace."* Place the petition paper in the candle holder, followed by the picture, image facing upward. Lightly scatter a little candle dressing over your picture. Set the candle on the picture. Place the candy in front of the candle as an offering to Venus, light the candle, and pray.

SUGGESTED CANDLE DRESSING

- Red Rose Petals, dried *(Rosa spp.)*: A favored flower of Venus

SUGGESTED PRAYER

- **Beauty And Grace Prayer To Venus:** To be recited during a waxing moon in the planetary hour of Venus on Fridays at 8:00 pm *(page 185)*

Vulva/Vagina Candle
For Healing, Lust in A Woman, or Cursing

Symbolism

Although the terms *"vagina"* and *"vulva"* are differentiated medically, for the purposes of spellwork, they will be used interchangeably. This is because these candle molds are sold under both labels.

Metaphysically speaking, the vulva has been a symbol of divine power and feminine potential in many ancient cultures. It has also been associated with fertility, sexual acts, and the cycles of the moon and the earth.

For these reasons, a vulva candle is most often used in spellwork related to sex magic, passion, and lust. Oftentimes, they're used to heal physiological difficulties. These candles are also employed to diminish a woman's ability to engage in sexual acts, especially when the culprit is intruding upon one's love interest.

In this section, there are three types of suggested spellwork: healing, inducing lust, and cursing the woman's vulva. In the latter spell, the candle will not be lit.

#1 - A Spell For Healing the Vagina

YOU WILL NEED

- A white or light blue vulva/vagina candle
- A picture of yourself with your eyes showing
- A petition paper
- Your personal concerns *(page 39)*
- A condition oil or olive oil
- Candle dressings
- A soldering iron

With your soldering iron, bore a hole, about two inches in diameter, into the vaginal opening. Insert your taglock into the hole along with about a half of a teaspoon of candle dressings. Seal the hole with melted wax of the same color and allow it to harden.

Cleanse the candle. On the backside, inscribe your birth name and birthdate horizontally. Then, cross it over, vertically from the lower pot to the highest, with the word *"Healing."*

Name and baptize the candle, anoint it with the oil, and sprinkle the dressings over it. Place your petition paper on the candle holder, followed by the picture, image facing upward. Set the candle on the picture. Light the candle and recite the prayer.

SUGGESTED CANDLE DRESSINGS

- **Althea** *(Hibiscus syriacus)*: A healing herb
- **All Heal/Self Heal** *(Prunella vulgaris)*: Used to improve health
- **Angelica** *(Angelica archangelica, Angelica spp.)*: A powerful healer

SUGGESTED PRAYER

- **Psalm 41:** For emotional or physical healing *(page 89)*

#2 - A Spell To Incite Lust In A Woman

YOU WILL NEED

- A white or red vulva/vagina candle
- A picture of your target, with their eyes showing
- A petition paper
- Her personal concerns, if available *(page 39)*
- Your semen, or vaginal secretions (for a same sex relationship)
- A condition oil or olive oil
- Candle dressings
- A soldering iron

With your soldering iron, bore a hole, about two inches in diameter, into the vaginal opening. Insert her taglock and your semen, or vaginal secretions, into the hole along with about a half of a teaspoon of candle dressings. Seal the hole with melted wax of the same color and allow it to harden.

Cleanse the candle. On the backside, inscribe her birth name and birthdate horizontally. Then, cross it over, vertically from the lower point to the highest, with the word *"Lust for _____* **[your birth name]**." Write these same words on random surfaces of the candle for a total of seven times.

Name and baptize the candle, anoint it with the oil, and sprinkle the dressings over it. Place your petition paper on the candle holder, followed by her picture, image facing upward. Set the candle on the picture. Light the candle and recite the prayer.

SUGGESTED CANDLE DRESSINGS

- **Cinnamon** *(Cinnamomum spp.)*: Used to heat up a love affair
- **Damiana** *(Turnera aphrodisiaca)*: Makes women willing and makes men ready
- **Dittany of Crete** *(Origanum Dictamnus)*: Creates passionate desires

SUGGESTED PRAYER

- **Venus Prayer:** For Lust *(page 197)*

#3 – A Spell to Curse a Woman's Vagina

YOU WILL NEED

- A white or black vulva/vagina candle
- A dime-sized picture of your target, with eyes showing
- A small petition paper
- Her personal concerns, if available *(page 39)*
- Aluminum foil
- A condition oil or olive oil
- Candle dressings
- A soldering iron
- A teaspoon of lemon juice

With your soldering iron, bore a hole, about two inches in diameter, into the vaginal opening. Insert her personal concerns (if available), picture, and petition paper into the hole along with about a half of a teaspoon of candle dressings. Seal the hole with melted wax of the same color and allow it to harden.

Cleanse the candle. On the backside, inscribe her birth name and birthdate horizontally. Then, cross it over, vertically from the highest point to the lowest, with the word *"Close up vagina."* Write these same words on random surfaces of the candle for a total of thirteen times.

Name and baptize the candle, anoint it with the oil, and scatter and/or spread the dressings over it. Lay out the aluminum foil, shiny side facing upward. Set the vagina candle in the middle of the foil, and scatter, and/or spread more candle dressings on it. Then, sprinkle the lemon juice on it. Recite your commands and cursing prayer aloud and wrap up the candle with the foil. Immediately place it and keep it in your freezer.

SUGGESTED CANDLE DRESSINGS

- **Alum, powdered** *(Aluminum sulphate)*: has a puckering, or closing effect.
- **Molded Cheese**: From any cheese that has a foul odor

SUGGESTED PRAYER

- **Psalm 109:** For cursing *(page 211)*

WITCH CANDLE
(Black)
To Increase Your Powers As A Magician

Symbolism

The black witch is a potent symbol of a metaphysical practitioner's authority and ability to command energies. Often seen as the *"helping hand,"* the black witch candle is used in magical spells to assert the witch's will upon another, gain esoteric knowledge, or to increase his or her own powers.

A Spell to Increase Your Powers as a Magician

YOU WILL NEED:

- A black witch candle
- A picture of yourself, with your eyes showing
- A petition paper
- Condition oil or olive oil
- ⅛ teaspoon of black or silver glitter

Cleanse the candle. Inscribe your birth name anywhere on the candle horizontally. Cross your name over, vertically, with the words *"Spiritual Power."* Repeat these inscriptions on random surfaces of the candle for a total of nine times.

Anoint the candle with the oil. Mix the candle dressings with the glitter and sprinkle the mixture all over the candle. Place your petition paper on the candle holder, followed by the picture, image facing upward. Set the candle on the picture. Light the candle and recite your petition and prayers.

SUGGESTED CANDLE DRESSINGS

- **Buchu** *(Agathosma spp.)*: Enhances psychic and spiritual powers
- **Copal, crushed** *(Protium copal)*: Aids in seeking divine powers

SUGGESTED PRAYER

- Divine Power Prayer *(page 187)*

CHAPTER SEVEN
ADDING MOTION TO THE MAGIC
Using Moving Candle Spells for Extra Power

A moving candle spell is the type of spell that involves physically moving a candle, either toward or away from another candle. The primary focus is to manifest a physical movement in your target's proximity or location. In almost all cases, the stationary candle represents the spellcaster while the ones that are moved represent the person, or people, for whom you wish to influence or control.

A moving candle spell is a form of role-playing, or the acting out of the part of a particular person or character. When doing so, it aids in enhancing the spellcaster's ability to visualize a desired outcome.

HOW LONG DOES IT TAKE TO PERFORM THIS SPELL?

Different spellcasters place diverse time frames for the continuance of these types of spells. While some people prefer to complete the spell within a day, others may choose much longer time frames. My preference is to perform moving candle spells with a five-day time period in order to provide more energy output toward achieving my goal. Determining the time frame depends on distance, regularity of the movements, and allotted candle burn time.

The distance refers to the gap that the spellcaster places between the target candle and the stationary one. For example, if the candle is only moved an inch a day, the spell would take longer to complete because it doesn't rapidly advance toward the desired location, thus prolonging the duration of the spell. Conversely, if the candle is moved around four inches daily, the spell will most likely fail because there's not enough time invested in the spellwork.

The regularity of the movements simply means that the distance chosen to separate the candles ought to be consistent each time the target candle is moved. For example, if you have chosen to move the target candle two inches on the first round, then it ought to be moved two inches each time.

The allotted candle burn time varies because, depending on the type and amount of wax used to fill the mold, candle wax is consumed at different rates. Cheaper candles are lighter and contain either less wax or more substitute fillers. This results in a much faster burn than the higher quality candles. Sadly, most consumers won't know what they have until it is burned.

Unless otherwise instructed, to overcome this enigma, my suggested is to extinguish the human figural candles, in a uniform manner, as follows:

- **First Round (or first day):** Extinguish the candles once the wax representing the head has been consumed by the fire.

- **Second Round (or second day):** Extinguish the candles when the shoulders and breast are no longer present.

- **Third Round (or third day):** Extinguish the candles when the abdomen, buttocks, and perineal areas of the candles have been consumed.

- **Fourth Round (or fourth day):** Extinguish the candles once the knees are no longer present.

- **Last round (or fifth day):** Allow both candles to complete their combustion.

Each spell requires a candle snuffer. This is because, as previously discussed, blowing out a flame is disrespectful to the element of Fire.

Come To Me
5-Day Moving Candle Spell

Casting the Spell

YOU WILL NEED:

- A white, pink, or red gender-specific candle to represent yourself
- A white gender-specific candle to represent your target
- A petition paper for the target's candle
- Three small lodestones
- A picture of yourself, with your eyes showing
- About ⅛ cup of magnetic sand (*Magnetite*)
- Red pepper flakes (*Capsicum annuum*)
- A condition oil or olive oil
- Candle dressings solely for the candle representing you
- A metal cookie sheet
- A candle snuffer

Cleanse both candles. Inscribe your name and birth date on the candle representing you. On the candle representing your target, inscribe the birth name, birthdate, and the command *"Come to* ____ **[your name]***."* Name and baptize both candles.

Anoint the target's candle with oil and sprinkle magnetic sand on it. Anoint your candle with oil and sprinkle suggested candle dressings on it. Set the candles, facing each other, on the opposite ends of the cookie sheet **(see illustration #13)**. Place the petition paper underneath your target's candle. Place the picture of yourself under your candle, image facing upward and set the three lodestones in front of it. Spread magnetic sand between the front of your target's candle and your lodestones. Set hot pepper flakes behind the target's candle.

On the first day, or first round of movement, light the candles and pray. Then, move the target's candle and petition paper approximately two inches toward your candle while gently commanding that the target come to you. Then, place more hot pepper flakes behind the target's candle to prevent him or her from turning away from you. Once the heads are no longer visible, extinguish the candles with the snuffer.

CHAPTER 7: ADDING MOTION TO THE MAGIC | 167

Repeat these steps for each round of movement. On the last day, or last round, the candles must be adjoined while completing their combustion **(see illustration #14)**.

Illustration #13: Preparing The Come To Me Spell

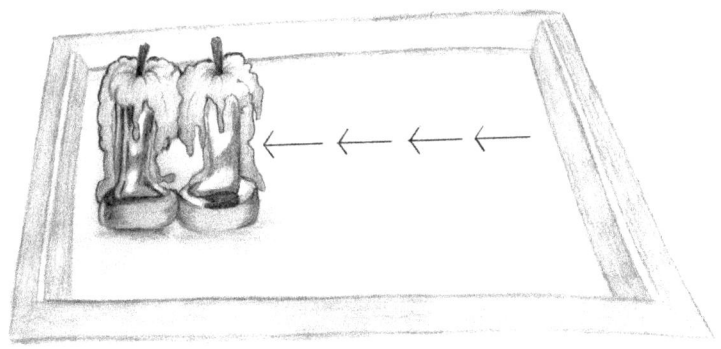

Illustration #14: Final Movement Of Come To Me Spell

SUGGESTED DRESSINGS FOR THE CANDLE REPRESENTING YOU

FOR A MAN TO ATTRACT A MAN

- **Cedar Wood, crushed** *(Cedrus spp.)*: Motivates a man to follow you
- **Lavender Leaves** *(Lavandula spp.)*: Promotes same gender love

FOR A MAN TO ATTRACT A WOMAN

- **Johnny Jump-Up** *(Viola tricolor)*: Makes a man more sexually potent and attractive to women
- **Knot Weed** *(Polygonum)*: Binds a lover to you

FOR A WOMAN TO ATTRACT A WOMAN

- **Vanilla Bean, crushed** *(Vanilla planifolia)*: Attracts women, used in love rituals
- **Red Rose Petals** *(Rosa spp.)*: Attracts love from others

FOR A WOMAN TO ATTRACT A MAN

- **Myrtle** *(Myrtus communis)*: A love herb
- **Passionflower** *(Passiflora incarnata)*: Incites a *"clingy"* type of love

SUGGESTED PRAYER

- **Psalm 45:** To obtain love *(page 204)*

SEND AWAY
(move out of town)
5-day moving candle spell

The good news is that this spell only requires the use of one candle. The bad news? If you choose to work with the repulsive ingredients, it will increase your chances of successful manifestation.

Casting the Spell

YOU WILL NEED:

- A white or black gender-specific candle to represent your target
- A map of the city or town where the target resides and a map of the desired destination

- Candy (if your target enjoys sweets)
- Money (bills and coins)
- Fresh dog feces (optional)
- Foul smelling rotting food (optional)
- Red pepper flakes (*Capsicum annuum*)
- A condition oil or olive oil
- A petition paper if a gender candle represents you
- Candle dressings for the target
- A metal cookie sheet
- A candle snuffer

Cleanse, anoint, name, and baptize the candle. Inscribe the target's birth name and birthdate, horizontally, on both sides of the candle. From the lowest to the highest portions, cross over the names with the words *"Move Away"* and continue to inscribe the command all over the candle, as many times as possible. Anoint the candle with oil and generously sprinkle candle dressing all over it.

On one side of the cookie sheet, place a map of the target's current residence. Place the candle on this side of the map, facing the desired location of residency.

On the opposite side of the cookie sheet, place a map of where you wish the target to reside. Also set the candy, money, and anything else the target is attracted to, in order to draw him or her to that location.

On the first day, or first round of movement, light the candle and recite your prayer. Next, move the candle approximately two inches toward the opposite side, while forceful commanding that the target move out of town. Once the head is no longer visible, extinguish the candle with Then, place the feces, red pepper flakes, and/or foul-smelling rotted food behind the candle to ensure that the target does not return to the current location.

Repeat these steps for each round of movement. On the last day, or last round, the candle ought to be on the opposite side of the cookie sheet, facing the pleasurable items the target may desire. Allow complete combustion of the candle.

SUGGESTED CANDLE DRESSING

Asafoetida *(Ferula assa-foetida)*: A banishing ingredient

SUGGESTED PRAYER

📖 **Psalm 105:** to drive enemies away *(page 209)*

SEPARATING A HETEROSEXUAL RELATIONSHIP
5-Day Moving Candle Spell

This spell is designed to break up a couple and lead them to better relationships. It is one of my favorite breakup spells because, in the end, everyone wins!

Casting the Spell

YOU WILL NEED:

- A black or white Back-To-Back separation candle
- A white or red female human candle
- A white or red male human candle
- Red pepper, powdered (*Capsicum annuum*)
- About ¼ cup magnetic sand (*Magnetite*)
- 6 small lodestones
- A picture of yourself, with your eyes showing (if you represent a specific candle)
- A condition oil or Olive oil
- Candle dressings (see instructions)
- A metal cookie sheet
- A heated knife blade or soldering iron
- A candle snuffer

Cleanse all the candles. On the female portion of the back-to-back candle, inscribe her birth name and birthdate but do not inscribe a command. Repeat these steps for the male portion of the candle. Name and baptize both candles. To avoid confusion with commands, just anoint them both with olive oil. With your fingers, pat the powdered red pepper on both of their back sides. Wash your hands, then pat magnetic sand on their front sides and the candle in the center of the cookie sheet.

Cleanse the other two candles. If one candle represents you, horizontally inscribe your birth name and birth date on the candle. Cross it over, from the bottom to the top, with the inscription "_____ **[target's name]** *Come To Me.*" Anoint the candle with oil, and sprinkle dressings on it.

At the far end of the cookie sheet, facing the target for whom you desire, set your petition paper on the metal sheet, followed by your picture, image facing upward. Place the candle representing you over the picture and ensure that it is facing your target. Set three small lodestones in front of your candle. Make a trail of magnetic sand from your target candle to yours.

If you do not know the name of a prospective love interest for the other person represented in the back-to-back candle, inscribe the words "*A lover for* _____ **[the name of the other person]**." With the exception of a petition paper and picture, set the candle on the opposite side of the other person, and repeat the aforementioned steps **(see set-up in illustration #15)**.

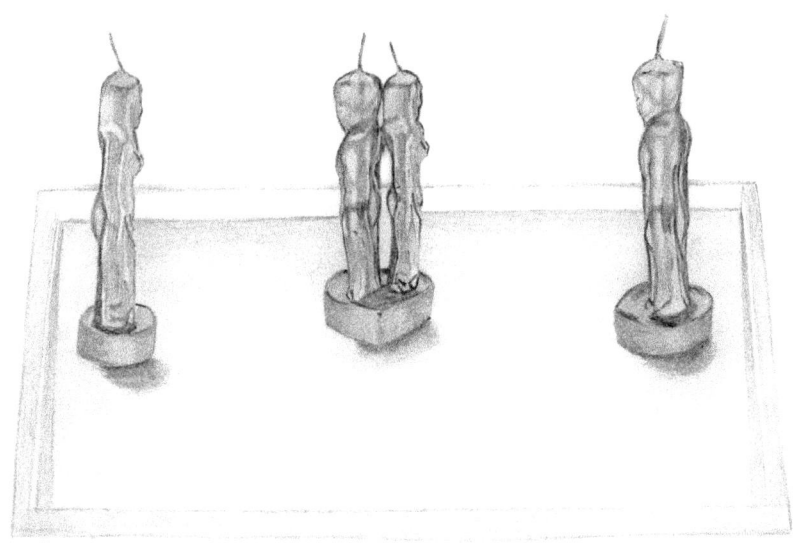

Illustration #15: Initial set-up of separating a relationship

On the first day, or first round of movement, light all the candles and recite your prayers.

Because the back-to-back separation candles are adhered together, they must be detached. So, after about 10 minutes, cut the base of the back-to-back candle with your knife or soldering iron, while demanding aloud that the couple break up **(see illustration #16 on following page)**. This is because both candles that are set on the far ends of the cookie sheet will remain stationary. Only the separated figures will move toward a love interest.

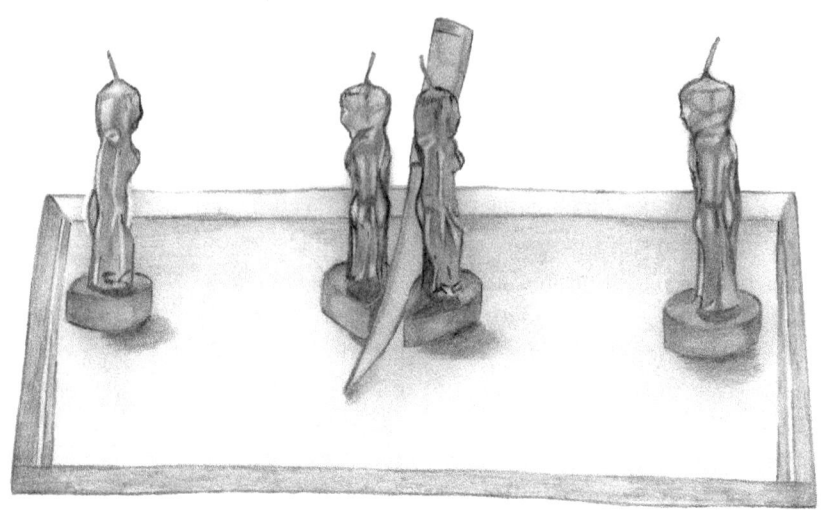

Illustration #16: Separation With Knife

Next, move the now two candles approximately two inches toward their new romances **(see illustration # 17)**. Then, place more hot pepper flakes behind the moving candles to prevent them from returning to one another. Once the heads are no longer visible, extinguish the candles with the snuffer.

Repeat these steps for each round of movement. On the last day, or last round, the moving candles will be joined with their new love interests while completing their combustions **(see illustration #18)**.

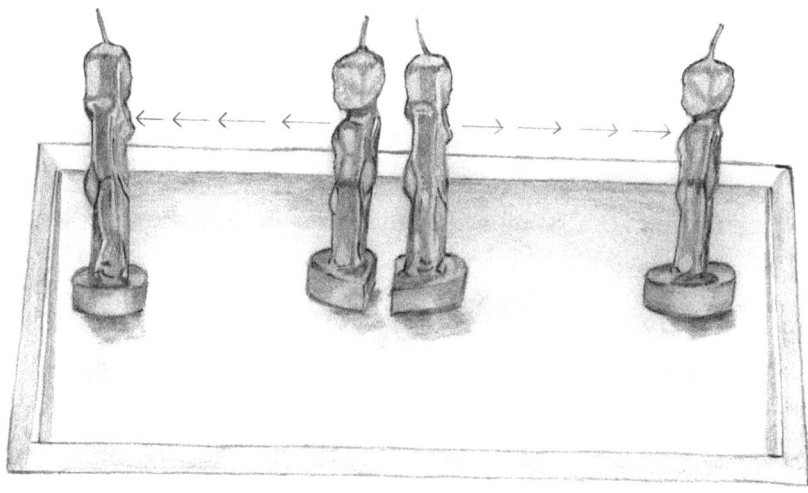

Illustration #17: Moving the Separation Candles

Illustration #18: Final Movement of Separation Spell

SUGGESTED CANDLE DRESSING

- **Myrtle** *(Myrtus communis)*: A love herb
- **Passionflower** *(Passiflora incarnata)*: Incites a *"clingy"* type of love

SUGGESTED PRAYER

- Break Up Relationship Prayer *(page 185)*

SEX WORKER'S BETTER BUSINESS
3-Day Moving Candle Spell

This spell has yielded great results for my dear clients who work in the second oldest profession in the world (the first being parenthood!). It is actually one of my very favorite spells because of its success rate. Please keep in mind that this is only a 3-day spell.

Although the presentation is of a female worker seeking male clients, you can easily change the genders of the candles. If you choose to do so, the dressings would still apply to all of the candles.

My preference for this spell is to employ the actual candle colors specified. Therefore, the neutral color of white will not be offered as a substitute.

Casting the Spell

YOU WILL NEED:

- A red female gender candle, to represent yourself
- A picture of yourself, with your eyes showing
- A petition paper
- A green male gender candle
- A red male gender candle
- A pink male gender
- Your vaginal secretions (or semen, if you are a male sex worker)
- A condition oil or olive oil
- Three small lodestones
- About ¼ cup magnetic sand
- Candle dressings (each candle will have different dressings)
- A round metal pizza pan
- A candle snuffer

Cleanse all the candles. On the candle representing you, inscribe your birth name and birth date, horizontally. Then, cross it over, from the bottom to the top of the candle, with the inscription *"Clients Come To Me."* Write the same command on any random surface available. Name and baptize your candle. Anoint the front side of your candle with your vaginal secretions (or semen) and anoint the back of the candle with oil. Then, scatter designated candle dressings on it. Set your petition paper toward the edge of the pizza pan, followed by your picture, image facing upward. Place the candle on the picture. Set the three lodestones in front of your candle.

On both the front and back sides of the green candle, horizontally inscribe the words *"Client With Money."* From the bottom to the top of the candle, cross those words with the command *"You desire _____ [your name]:. Name and baptize the candle as "A Client with Money."* Anoint the candle with oil and scatter the designated candle dressings on it.

On both the front and back sides of the red candle, horizontally inscribe the words *"Client With Lust."* From the bottom to the top of the candle, cross those words with the command *"You Lust For _____ [your name]."* Name and baptize the candle as *"A Client with Lust."* Anoint the candle with oil and scatter the designated candle dressings on it.

On both the front and back sides of the pink candle, horizontally inscribe the words *"Client Who Desires Love."* From the bottom to the top of the candle, cross those words with the command *"You desire _____ [your name]."* Name and baptize the candle as *"A Client Who Desires Love."* Anoint the candle with oil and scatter the designated candle dressings on it.

Set the three male candles toward the edge of the pie pan, side-by-side, opposite of your candle, but facing it **(see illustration #19)**. Make a trail of magnetic sand, starting from the front of each male candle and ending at the lodestones in front of your candle.

On the first day, or first round of movement, light the candles and pray. Then, move the three male candles approximately two inches toward your candle, while lustfully commanding that they come to you. Once the heads are no longer visible, extinguish the candles with the snuffer. Repeat the same process on the second day, or round of movement, and extinguish the candles when the chests are no longer visible.

On the third day, or round of movement, repeat the process but have all three male candles adjoined with your candle **(see illustration #20)**. Then, allow all of the candles to complete their combustion.

SUGGESTED CANDLE DRESSINGS

For the red female candle representing you:

- **Dittany of Crete** *(Origanum dictamnus)*: Provokes passionate desires from another
- **Jezebel Root, crushed** *(Iris foliosa, Iris spp.)*: Used by sex workers to attract paying customers
- **Mace** *(Myristica spp.)*: A money-drawing ingredient for sex workers

For the green male candle representing a man with money:

- **Lucky Bamboo Leaves** *(Dracaena sanderiana)*: Symbolizes wealth
- **Gold Glitter**: Symbolizes a prosperous person

For the red male candle representing a lustful man:

- **Blood Root, crushed** *(Sanguinaria canadensis)*: Enhances a man's sex drive
- **Ginseng** *(Panax quinquefolius L.)*: Increases male vigor
- **Johnny Jump-Up** *(Viola tricolor)*: Makes a man more sexually potent

For the pink male candle representing a man seeking love:

- **Myrtle** *(Myrtus communis)*: A love herb
- **Passionflower** *(Passiflora incarnata)*: Incites a *"clingy"* type of love

SUGGESTED PRAYER

- Sex Worker's Prayer To Venus (the Patron Goddess of prostitutes) *(page 196)*

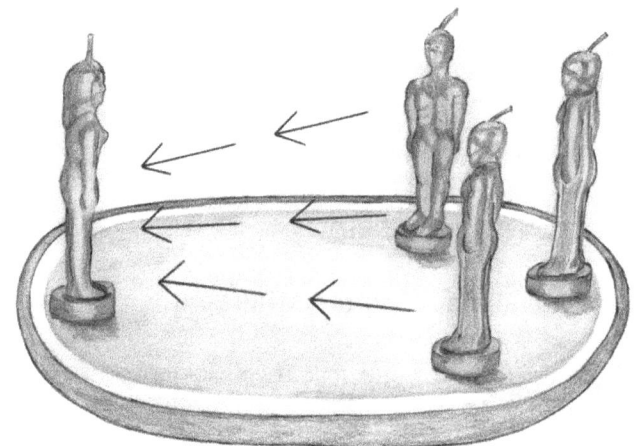

Illustration #19: Set-Up to Bring More Clients

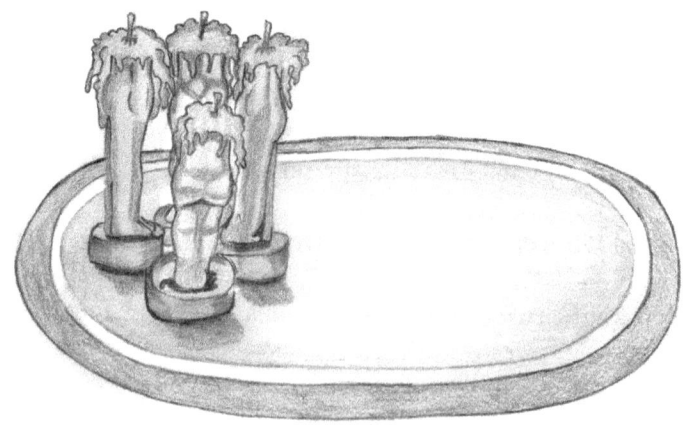

Illustration #20: Adjoining Candles to Bring More Clients

CHAPTER EIGHT
Tending to Wax & Other Remains
Deployment of the Residual Remnants

The most frequently asked questions by neophytes are: *"Is there anything I'm supposed to do with the spell remains?"* or the question that always provokes me to react in horror, while screaming at the top of my lungs, *"NO! NO! NO!"* What question could possibly be that terrifying? *"Should I just throw everything in the garbage can?"*

So, before we talk about what to do with the remains, let's discuss what not to do! Unless you're a practitioner who believes that a particular path of an entity resides in the garbage, NEVER dispose of your remains in the trash can. When doing so, the gesture implies that the spellwork was garbage, thus nullifying all of your hard labor. Rather than disposing of the remains, we instead deploy them.

The act of *deployment,* as defined in the dictionary, is to put someone or something into use or action. Examples would include positioning military troops to engage in combat or engaging spiritual forces to *"carry out"* the spellwork.

What spiritual forces exist other than revered deities or members of your spiritual court? Numerous ones! They can be found virtually everywhere including boulders, cemeteries, the crossroads, ground, grass, plants, railroad tracks, rivers, rocks, sewers, streams, trees, etc. Therefore, when we deploy our remains, we must not only politely ask these entities for their assistance, but do so with the utmost of respect.

How to Deploy Your Remains

When spiritual forces are approached for assistance, it isn't necessary to know their formal names. Simply respectfully address them by the domain for which they rule, dwell, or inhabit. Examples include: *"Spirit who rules over the river"* or *"Spirit of this beautiful tree."* Introduce yourself, explain your predicament, and ask the entity if he or she will finalize the spellwork. You will either receive a positive, neutral, or negative feeling. Proceed only after receiving positive vibrations as a response.

You will then deploy any residual wax remains, petition papers, and pictures at the site. Depending on the location, this is accomplished by either burying the remains, gently setting them down, or placing them within a containment area, such as a tree hollow or under a rock. It's that easy!

After deployment, vehemently thank the entity. Many entities, such as the spirit of a tree or of a gravesite, will require a gratuitous payment. When payment is required, it will be stipulated within the location categories.

Locations For Deployment of the Remains

Backyard of Home or Business
Burying your remains in this area is a symbolic gesture to keep something, or someone, with you. Ask permission from the spirit of the land before doing so. Express gratitude and offer a dime as payment.

Boulder or Large Rock
Placing your remains under one of these large structures is often performed to bind an enemy or to display your dominance. All stones, rocks, and crystals possess spirits, just as we do. Ask its spirit for permission prior to deployment. Express gratitude and offer a dime as payment.

Cemetery Plot
Mostly utilized in cursing spells that employ the spirits of deceased people or beloved pets. Again, explain the situation and ask if he or she will assist you. Bury the remains, express gratitude, and leave a dime for payment. But, if you are familiar with the spirit, also include something that was enjoyed in life, such as a lit cigarette, candy, flowers, libations, etc.

Church Property (Excluding The Graveyard)
Burial of the remains on church property is most often performed for the deployment of blessing and healing spells. Ask permission, bury the remains, then express gratitude. The spirit of the land will require a dime for payment.

Court House Property
Used for court case spells. Deploy the remains far from the courthouse to avoid video cameras. Ask the spirit of the land for permission, bury the remnants, express gratitude, and leave a dime for payment.

Crossroads
This is the center where two roads cross. Although almost anything can be deployed in this location, it is not recommended for any of the spells in this book. The reason is because the remains are lightweight, and the slightest of breezes can set the remnants adrift. If this happens, you will risk disclosure of your petition paper and/or photos to another person.

Decaying Dead Animals
Employed in cursing spells. Ask the spirit of the animal to take your enemy with it. Don a pair of disposable gloves and gently set your remains under the carcass. As payment, thank the spirit and recite a prayer to your God or Goddess while asking the entity to help this spirit to cross over into a world of freedom and happiness.

Fire
Burning the remains is often used in banishing spells. Respectfully ask the element of Fire for his assistance. As payment, express gratitude and feed him dried leaves or twigs.

Front Yard of Home or Business
Used in spellwork that involve attracting or bringing something, or someone, to you. Also used for protection and opening the roads. After receiving consent from the spirit of the land to accept your remains, express gratitude and bury a dime with the remnants.

Pathway, or Walkway, of the Target
Often used in cursing, crossing, and breakup spells, bury the remains in a place where the target will step on it, or pass by it. First, ask the spirit of the land for permission, bury the remnants along with a dime for payment,

and thank the spirit. The hollow of a tree is another location where these spells are deployed. Ask the tree for permission, place your remnants into the hole, thank the tree, and offer water at the base of the tree.

Potted Plant

As a last resort, used in lieu of burial in the front or back yard. Request permission from the spirit of the plant and offer a dime as payment. This is my least favorite method because people frequently forget to water their plants. If the plant dies, your spell becomes nullified.

Rivers, Sewers, Streams

These bodies of water are often employed in send-away spells, which include expelling undesired problems. The most commonly asked question regarding these waters is: *"Can I use a lake or ocean instead?"* The answer is a resounding: *"No!"* The waters of rivers, sewers, and streams move from a higher to a lower elevation thus moving away anything that is introduced into the flow. Oceans and lakes do not behave in the same manner. Respectfully ask permission from the spirit who rules over the selected domain. Gently set your remains into the water, along with a dime, and express gratitude to the spirit.

Tree

These majestic beauties represent courage, freedom, mastery, strength, power, reproduction, wisdom, and, of course, growth. Remnants can be deployed for any of these desires. Tell the spirit of the tree your situation and ask for assistance. Bury your remnants near the tree along with a dime. Thank the spirit of the tree and, as an additional payment, offer clean, fresh water at its base.

A Deployment Cheat Sheet

No, you don't have to read every single entry to figure out where to deploy your remnants. So, don't worry, I've got you covered! For almost every spell offered in this book, you are being provided with the ideal deployment location/s. Are you ready? Here we go!

🔥 **Attraction Spells:** Front yard.

🔥 **Banishing Spells:** Fire

- 🔥 **Beauty Spells:** Front yard

- 🔥 **Better Business Spells:** Front yard

- 🔥 **Binding Spells:** Boulder or large rock

- 🔥 **Blessing Spells:** Church property, front yard

- 🔥 **Break Up Spells:** Pathway, or walkway, or the target

- 🔥 **Chase Away Bad Spirits:** Front yard

- 🔥 **Come To Me Spells:** Front yard

- 🔥 **Communication Spells:** Front yard

- 🔥 **Courage Spells:** Tree

- 🔥 **Court Case Spells:** Court House property

- 🔥 **Cursing & Crossing Spells:** Cemetery

- 🔥 **Domination Spells:** Boulder or large rock

- 🔥 **Empowerment Spells:** Tree

- 🔥 **Fertility Spells:** Tree

- 🔥 **Freedom Spells:** Tree

- 🔥 **Guidance Spells:** Church property, front yard

- 🔥 **Healing/Health spells:** Church property, front Yard

- 🔥 **Honey Jar:** Do not deploy. Keep the honey jar and work it, even if spell has manifested

- 🔥 **Long Life Spells:** Backyard

- 🔥 **Love/Lust Spells:** Front yard

- 🔥 **Loyalty Spells:** Backyard

- 🔥 **Luck Spells:** Front yard, tree

- 🔥 **Mastery Spells:** Tree

- 🔥 **Marriage Spells:** Front yard or, if your mate lives with you, backyard

- 🔥 **Money Spells:** Tree

- 🔥 **Open the Roads Spells:** Front yard, crossroads

- 🔥 **Psychic Visions:** Front yard. But first allow the remains to be exposed to the rays of the full moon before burying it

- 🔥 **Power Spells:** Tree

- 🔥 **Protection Spells:** Front yard

- 🔥 **Reconciliation Spells:** Front yard

- 🔥 **Revenge Spells:** Cemetery

- 🔥 **Send Away Spells:** River, sewer, stream

- 🔥 **Stay With Me Spells:** Backyard

- 🔥 **Stop Gossip:** Boulder, large rocks

- 🔥 **Strength Spells:** Tree

- 🔥 **Uncrossing Spells:** River, sewer, stream

- 🔥 **Veneration:** Church Property; Front yard

- 🔥 **Wisdom:** Tree

- 🔥 **Wishes:** Front Yard

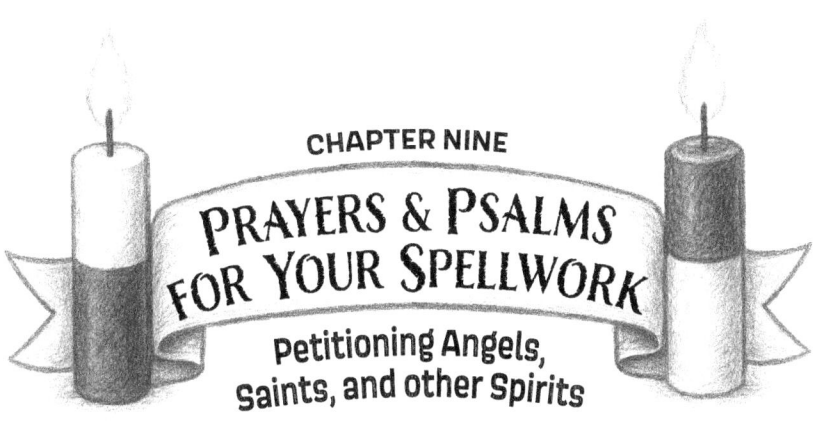

CHAPTER NINE
PRAYERS & PSALMS FOR YOUR SPELLWORK
Petitioning Angels, Saints, and other Spirits

Remember to recite your prayers aloud because sound emits energy. Besides, as my mother used to say, *"If you pray to yourself, nobody will hear you."*

Prior to closing the prayer with the word: *"Amen,"* tell your story to the entity so that he or she may have a better understanding of your predicament then plead your petition. If you are reciting a daily prayer for the same intention, keep both the story and the petition consistent each time the prayer is recited.

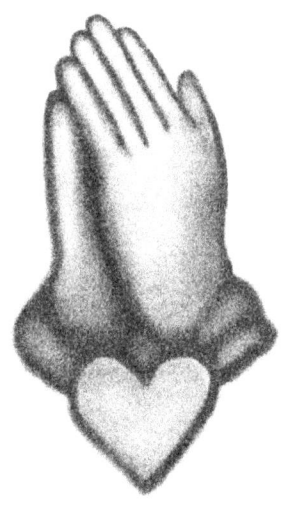

The Prayers

The power of prayer has emboldened the spells of magical practitioners throughout time. The prayers below come from a wide spectrum of spiritual traditions and make perfect companions to the spells in this book.

ARCHANGEL GABRIEL PRAYER
for Clear Communication

Archangel Gabriel, please guide me to the words, images, body language, and symbolism to use when conveying messages to others. Thank you for assisting me in connecting with others who can communicate using a shared language that we both speak, so my communications flow more easily.

Thank you for offering the symbols, gestures, and cadence needed when speaking and sharing information. Thank you for holding my energy in calming, blue lights of peace, so that the messages shared through me come out in the vibration of calm and truth. [**Explain your case and plead your petition here**]. *Amen.*

ARCHANGELS MICHAEL, GABRIEL, AND RAFAEL PRAYER
3-Day Wishing Spell

St. Michael, St. Gabriel, and St. Raphael, please be with me today. Please hear and answer my prayers with your divine intercession and kindness. Please help me so that my prayer requests come true quickly. [**plead your**

petition here]. *Heavenly Father, you have given us the Archangels to assist us during our pilgrimage on earth.*

Saint Michael is our protector, I ask that he come to my aid, fight for all of my loved ones, protect us from danger. Saitnt Gabriel is a messenger for the good news, I ask him to help me clearly hear your voice and to teach me the truth. Saint Raphael is the healing Angel. I ask him to take my need for healing and that of everyone I know, lift it up to your throne of grace and deliver back to us the gift of recovery. Help us, O lord, to realize more fully the reality of the Archangels and their desire to serve us. Holy Angels pray for us. Thank you. Amen.

BEAUTY AND GRACE PRAYER TO VENUS

O radiant Venus, goddess of beauty and love, I humbly come before you, seeking your grace to illuminate my inner and outer light. Infuse me with your divine charm, and let my presence radiate with kindness and allure. Guide my steps with elegance, my words with sweetness, and my heart with compassion. May I embody the beauty of your celestial glow, attracting harmony and love wherever I go. Thank you for your divine blessings. Amen.

BREAK UP RELATIONSHIP PRAYER

*Dear God, I come before you today with a heavy heart, acknowledging that the current relationship between __ [**his name**] and __ [**her name**] is not serving as it should. Please grant them the strength and courage to end this partnership, knowing that this decision is for their highest good. Guide them through this difficult time, help them to release any attachments with grace and compassion, and open their hearts to the possibility of finding a love that aligns with your plan. Amen.*

FERTILITY PRAYER
For Conception

O Lord of creation, Dear God, you are the giver of life, and I humbly ask for your blessing upon my body. Please grant me the gift of fertility, that I may conceive and nurture a child in your image. I pray for the health of my reproductive system. Remove any obstacles or hindrances that may be preventing conception. Help me to be physically, emotionally, and spiritually prepared for the miracle of motherhood. I trust in your wisdom and love to guide me on this journey. Amen.

COMMUNICATION PRAYER

Dear Lord, I come to You with a desperate heart and a heavy burden of emotions because I miss my lover and the object of my desires. Please grant me your favor and do what you can to help bring my lover close to me so that _____[**Name**] *might call soon. I love this person more than I can bear alone. All of the Saints know that your grace blesses our lives every day, so it is only from you that you could come to the help I need.* [**Tell God the story and plead your petition**]. *Please make this happen, Lord, if it is thy will, Amen.*

CONNECTING TO THE METAPHYSICAL PRAYER

Divine Presence, I open my heart and mind to the unseen realms, inviting a connection with the metaphysical energies that surround me. Guide me with your wisdom, illuminate my inner knowing, and allow me to perceive the subtle vibrations of the universe. Please help me in my quest to align with the flow of universal energy, to feel the interconnectedness of all things. Help me to receive this divine connection, receiving insights and guidance to navigate my life with greater clarity and purpose. Amen.

COURAGE & STRENGTH PRAYER

Heavenly Father, in this moment of need, I come before you seeking your strength and power to overcome the challenges I face. Just as you did for the mighty bear, fill me with your unwavering fortitude, so that I may stand firm against adversity and not falter. Grant me the courage to face my fears and the resilience to persevere through difficult times. May your might flow through me, enabling me to accomplish what seems impossible in my own strength. [**Plead your petition here**]. *Amen.*

DIVINE POWER PRAYER

Divine Source, I, _____ [your name] humbly open myself to the flow of universal energy, asking to be graced with the ability to access and utilize metaphysical powers. Guide me, with your divine powers, to understand these gifts and perceive beyond the physical realm. May my intentions be clear and my heart remain aligned with your will. Amen.

GARGOYLE PRAYER
For Protection

Guardians of stone, with watchful eyes, shield us from harm, ward off all lies. As you stand firm against the breeze, protect our home and bring us peace. Watch over us, silent sentinels, keep us safe from all perils. We humbly thank you for your fierce protection. Amen.

GUARDIAN ANGEL PRAYER
For Guidance and/or Protection

Angel of God, my guardian dear,
To whom God's love commits me here,
Ever this day, be at my side,
To light and guard, rule and guide
[plead your petition here]
Amen.

Holy Spirit Prayer For A Favor

O Holy Spirit, Divine Comforter, I humbly come before You today, seeking Your guidance and intervention in my life. I ask for Your grace and favor in the matter of [**Mention your specific request**], *a situation where I deeply need Your assistance. Enlighten my mind to discern the best path forward, strengthen my heart with courage and faith, and grant me the wisdom to act in accordance with Your will. If it be Your divine plan, please grant me this favor, for Your glory and my greater good. Amen.*

Interfaith Wedding Vows

"I,___, take you, ___, to be my wife/husband. I promise to be true to you in good times and in bad, in sickness and in health. I will love and honor you all the days of my life."

Intimacy With Spouse Prayer

Dear God, I come before you today seeking to deepen the intimacy in my marriage with my spouse. Help us to connect on a deeper level, not just physically, but emotionally and spiritually as well. Guide us to be vulnerable with each other, to communicate openly and honestly, and to truly see each other as you see us. May our love for one another be a true reflection of your love, and may our intimate moments be filled with joy, passion, and tenderness. Thank you for the gift of my spouse, and for the opportunity to grow closer together in your name. Amen.

Just Judge Prayer
For Court Cases

Dear Lord Jesus, You are the Just Judge, full of mercy and compassion. I come before you in this time of legal difficulty and uncertainty, seeking your divine justice. [**Explain the court case and plead your petition here**]. *I have explained the intricacies of my court case, and you see the truth that lies within. I entrust my legal matters into your hands, knowing that you are the ultimate source. Please guide my legal team, the judges, and all those involved in the legal process. May their hearts be open to the truth and to your divine will. I offer this prayer in Your Holy name and believe in Your power and authority over all things right and just. Amen.*

Loyalty and Faithfulness Prayer

Heavenly Father, I come before you today, humbly asking that you strengthen my partner's heart and mind to remain loyal and faithful in our union. Guard ___ [**target's name**] *from temptations and distractions so that ____* [**target's name**] *may always choose to be true to me, and that our bond may remain strong and unwavering. In Jesus' name, Amen.*

MONEY PRAYER

Lord Jesus, I bow to you today, knowing that only through you we can achieve salvation. I approach you because I know you are the only one who can grant me refuge and hope to keep pressing on in this life. I come before you this moment asking that you give me financial independence in this life. The Bible tells us to ask, and it shall be given to us. Today, I come to you with a request for money. Thank you for giving me what I have so far. Please do not take this request as ungrateful. I know you are always looking out for me, but recently I have been unable to provide for myself and my family. I turn to you for the wisdom to create this wealth. All things and ideas belong to you, and that is why I'm coming to you for aid. I'm tired of worry about my finances and my family's future. I would like to be financially comfortable so I can focus on other things in life besides work. Lord, I ask that you open my eyes so that I may be aware of opportunities that may be prosperous. I pray in the mighty name of Jesus Christ [**Plead your petition here**]. *Amen*

NOVENA TO GOD THE FATHER

GOD, my Heavenly Father, I adore You, and I count myself as nothing before Your Divine Majesty. You alone are Being, Life, Truth, and Goodness. Helpless and unworthy as I am, I honor You, I praise You, I thank You, and I love You in union with Jesus Christ, Your Son, our Savior and our Brother, in the merciful kindness of His Heart and through His infinite merits. I desire to serve You, to please You, to obey You, and to love You always in union with Mary Immaculate, Mother of God and our Mother. I also desire to love and serve others for the love of You. Heavenly Father, thank You for making me Your child in Baptism. With childlike confidence, I ask You for the special favor [**Plead your request here**]. *I ask that Your will may be done. Give* me what You know to be the best for my soul and for the souls of those for whom I pray. Give me Your Holy Spirit to enlighten me and to guide me in the way of Your commandments and Holiness while I strive for the happiness of heaven, where I hope to glorify You forever. Amen.

RECONCILIATION PRAYER

*Heavenly Father, with a humble heart, I come before you seeking your guidance and intervention in healing the wounds within my relationship with _____ [**target's name**]. Soften our hearts, allowing forgiveness to flow freely between us. Please help us to release any anger, resentment, or pain that may be holding us back, and guide us to let go of past hurts. Please grant us both the ability to embrace a future together that is filled with love and understanding. Grant us the strength to communicate openly and honestly, to listen with compassion, and to work together to rebuild trust.* [**Plead your petition here**]. *Amen*

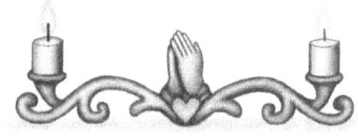

RESTORE SEXUALITY PRAYER

I invite the healing presence of Jesus to cleanse me and restore me as a sexual being in fullness of joy and wholeness. I ask you, Jesus, to fill my sexuality with your holiness, to strengthen me and restore me in your name. [**Plead your petition here**]. *Amen.*

ST. FRANCIS OF ASSISI PRAYER
For All Animals

O heavenly Saint Francis, patron of all animals, your protection for them is so great, so prompt, and so strong. Please assist (name of pet) with your powerful intercession. Through your prayer, may they obtain God's healing powers. May their suffering be taken away and their health restored. [**Plead your petition here**]. *Saint Francis, please help my pet. Amen*

ST. GERTRUDE PRAYER
For Cats

O, Holy Saint Gertrude of Nivelles, Patron Saint of cats, I ask you to pray that my cat stay free from illness and that my cat always feels safe, protected, and loved. [**Plead your petition here**]. *Saint Gertrude, please help my cat. Amen.*

ST. JOAN OF ARC PRAYER
For Victory

In the face of your enemies, in the face of harassment, ridicule, and doubt, you held firm in your faith. Even in your abandonment, alone and without friends, you held firm in your faith. Even as you faced your own mortality, you held firm in your faith. I pray that I may be as bold in my beliefs as you, St. Joan. I ask that you ride alongside me in my own battles. Help me be mindful that what is worthwhile can be won when I persist. Help me hold firm in my faith. Help me believe in my ability to act well and wisely. [**Plead your petition here**]. *Amen.*

St. Josephine Prayer
To Escape Physical or Spiritual Slavery

Saint Josephine Bakhita, as a child, you were sold as a slave and had to spend untold difficulties and suffering. Once freed from your physical slavery, you found the true redemption in your encounter with Christ and his Church. Oh, St. Bakhita, help those who are trapped in slavery; intercede on their behalf before God so that they are freed from the chains of captivity. May God free anyone who has been enslaved by man. Provide relief to those who survive slavery and allow them to see Him as a model of faith and hope. Help all survivors to find healing for their wounds. We beg you to pray and intercede for those who are enslaved among us. [**Explain your case and plead your petition here**]. *Amen.*

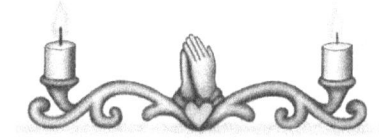

St. Michael Prayer
For Protection

St. Michael the Archangel, defend us in battle, be our protection against the wickedness and snares of the devil. May God rebuke him we humbly pray; and do thou, O Prince of the Heavenly host, by the power of God, cast into hell Satan and all the evil spirits who prowl about the world seeking the ruin of souls. [**State your petition here**]. *Amen*

ST. ROCH PRAYER
For Dogs

O Holy St. Roch, I come to you with a humble prayer for my beloved dog, who is ill. Please heal this pup who loves and comforts me so profoundly; restore its health so that it may live fully in the joy of your love. You are the patron saint of dogs, after all! Miraculously saved by your own dog to bring nourishment during your captivity and pilgrimages, you understand the great devotion between man and animal. Extend mercy to my pet through this special bond we share; revive his energy so that his tail may wag with life and happiness. [**Plead your petition here**]. *Saint Roch, please help my dog. Amen*

ST. PETER PRAYER
To Open the Roads

O Holy Apostle, because you are the Rock upon which Almighty God has built His Church, obtain for me I pray you: lively faith, firm hope, and burning love, complete detachment from myself, contempt of the world, patience in adversity, humility in prosperity, recollection in prayer, purity of heart, a right intention in all my works, diligence in fulfilling the duties of my state of life, constancy in my resolutions, resignation to the will of God, and perseverance in the grace of God even unto death; that so, by means of your intercession and your glorious merits, I may be made worthy to appear before the Chief and Eternal Shepherd of Souls, Jesus Christ, Who with the Father and the Holy Spirit, lives and reigns forever. [**Plead your petition here**]. *Amen.*

SEX WORKER'S PRAYER TO VENUS

Gracious Venus, goddess of love and beauty, I humbly beseech you. Please grant me your protection and favor in my work, so that I may be successful. Favor me with grace and allure in the eyes of all. May I be blessed with beauty and charm, that my clients may find me pleasing. I offer you this incense **[light rose incense]** *as a token of my devotion, and pray that you will grant me your blessings. Amen.*

SUN PRAYER
For Empowerment And Strength

O great radiant Sun, source of light and all life, as your golden rays bathe the earth, infuse me with your vibrant energy. Please empower me with your strength, and illuminate my path with your wisdom. Ignite within me the courage to face each day with purpose and passion. May I shine brightly, radiating warmth and positivity to all around me. Thank you for your love and boundless power. Amen

TEST-TAKING PRAYER

Loving God, be with me now as I prepare for my exams. Thank you for the many talents and gifts you have given me and for the opportunity of education. Calm my nerves and anxiety, help me to remember all that I have studied, to express it clearly, and to answer the questions the very best I can. Holy Spirit, please sit with me in my exam. [**Plead your petition here**]. Amen

TRADITIONAL IRISH BLESSING

May the road rise to meet you. May the wind be always at your back. May the sunshine warm upon your face, The rains fall soft upon your fields. And until we meet again,

May God hold you in the palm of his hand. May God be with you and bless you; May you see your children's children. May you be poor in misfortune, Rich in blessings, May you know nothing but happiness From this day forward. May the road rise to meet you. May the wind be always at your back May the warm rays of sun fall upon your home And may the hand of a friend always be near. May green be the grass you walk on. May blue be the skies above you, May pure be the joys that surround you. May true be the hearts that love you.

VENUS PRAYER
For Lust

*O radiant Venus, goddess of love and desire, I call upon your potent energy to ignite within me a passionate flame of lust. Awaken my senses, stir my heart, and draw me towards the intoxicating allure of physical pleasure. Grant me the confidence and magnetism to attract _____ [**target's name/s**], and fill our union with raw, untamed passion. As the stars dance in the night sky, let our bodies move in harmony, guided by your divine grace. May our love be fierce and consuming, a testament to your power over the realms of sensuality. Amen*

WISDOM PRAYER

*Almighty God, I humbly ask that You grant me wisdom to make sound choices and decisions. Open my eyes to see Your truth clearly. Give me spiritual discernment to distinguish right from wrong. Help me not rely solely on my own limited understanding, but trust in Your infinite wisdom to guide my steps. Grant me a heart eager to gain wisdom from Your Word and wise counselors. Let Your wisdom shape my thoughts, words, and actions each day. In Jesus' name, [**Plead your petition here**]. Amen.*

WISDOM IN RELATIONSHIPS PRAYER

*Lord, I need heavenly wisdom to navigate relationships in a way that honors You. Give me insight to discern healthy connections from ones that may prove toxic or draining. Help me see myself and others rightly, not being deceived by mere appearance or status. Teach me how and when to build closer bonds or pull away. Grant me words to speak life and encourage, yet also confront sin redemptively. Above all, help me love others unconditionally, even those who slight or oppose me. In Jesus' name, [**Plead your petition here**]. Amen.*

The Psalms

Hoodoo practitioners often fondly refer to the Holy Bible as a spellbook, for it contains many words of power that can transform our lives. The psalms below, taken from the popular King James Version, can be used to amplify many of the spells in this book.

PSALM 1
To Bind Enemies

1. Blessed is the man that walketh not in the counsel of the ungodly, nor standeth in the way of sinners, nor sitteth in the seat of the scornful.
2. But his delight is in the law of the Lord; and in his law doth he meditate day and night.
3. And he shall be like a tree planted by the rivers of water, that bringeth forth his fruit in his season; his leaf also shall not wither; and whatsoever he doeth shall prosper.
4. The ungodly are not so: but are like the chaff which the wind driveth away.
5. Therefore the ungodly shall not stand in the judgment, nor sinners in the congregation of the righteous.
6. For the Lord knoweth the way of the righteous: but the way of the ungodly shall perish.

Psalm 12
To Stop Gossip

1. Help, Lord; for the godly man ceaseth; for the faithful fail from among the children of men.
2. They speak vanity every one with his neighbour: with flattering lips and with a double heart do they speak.
3. The Lord shall cut off all flattering lips, and the tongue that speaketh proud things:
4. Who have said, With our tongue will we prevail; our lips are our own: who is lord over us?
5. For the oppression of the poor, for the sighing of the needy, now will I arise, saith the Lord; I will set him in safety from him that puffeth at him.
6. The words of the Lord are pure words: as silver tried in a furnace of earth, purified seven times.
7. Thou shalt keep them, O Lord, thou shalt preserve them from this generation for ever.
8. The wicked walk on every side, when the vilest men are exalted.

Psalm 23
To Bless An Item and For General Good Luck

1. The Lord is my shepherd; I shall not want.
2. He maketh me to lie down in green pastures: he leadeth me beside the still waters.
3. He restoreth my soul: he leadeth me in the paths of righteousness for his name's sake.
4. Yea, though I walk through the valley of the shadow of death, I will fear no evil: for thou art with me; thy rod and thy staff they comfort me.

5 | Thou preparest a table before me in the presence of mine enemies: thou anointest my head with oil; my cup runneth over.
6 | Surely goodness and mercy shall follow me all the days of my life: and I will dwell in the house of the Lord forever.

Psalm 37
For Uncrossing and To Bring Money

1 | Fret not thyself because of evildoers, neither be thou envious against the workers of iniquity.
2 | For they shall soon be cut down like the grass, and wither as the green herb.
3 | Trust in the LORD, and do good; so shalt thou dwell in the land, and verily thou shalt be fed.
4 | Delight thyself also in the LORD: and he shall give thee the desires of thine heart.
5 | Commit thy way unto the LORD; trust also in him; and he shall bring it to pass.
6 | And he shall bring forth thy righteousness as the light, and thy judgment as the noonday.
7 | Rest in the LORD, and wait patiently for him: fret not thyself because of him who prospereth in his way, because of the man who bringeth wicked devices to pass.
8 | Cease from anger, and forsake wrath: fret not thyself in any wise to do evil.
9 | For evildoers shall be cut off: but those that wait upon the LORD, they shall inherit the earth.
10 | For yet a little while, and the wicked shall not be: yea, thou shalt diligently consider his place, and it shall not be.
11 | But the meek shall inherit the earth; and shall delight themselves in the abundance of peace.
12 | The wicked plotteth against the just, and gnasheth upon him with his teeth.
13 | The LORD shall laugh at him: for he seeth that his day is coming.

14 | The wicked have drawn out the sword, and have bent their bow, to cast down the poor and needy, and to slay such as be of upright conversation.
15 | Their sword shall enter into their own heart, and their bows shall be broken.
16 | A little that a righteous man hath is better than the riches of many wicked.
17 | For the arms of the wicked shall be broken: but the LORD upholdeth the righteous.
18 | The LORD knoweth the days of the upright: and their inheritance shall be for ever.
19 | They shall not be ashamed in the evil time: and in the days of famine they shall be satisfied.
20 | But the wicked shall perish, and the enemies of the LORD shall be as the fat of lambs: they shall consume; into smoke shall they consume away.
21 | The wicked borroweth, and payeth not again: but the righteous sheweth mercy, and giveth.
22 | For such as be blessed of him shall inherit the earth; and they that be cursed of him shall be cut off.
23 | The steps of a good man are ordered by the LORD: and he delighteth in his way.
24 | Though he fall, he shall not be utterly cast down: for the LORD upholdeth him with his hand.
25 | I have been young, and now am old; yet have I not seen the righteous forsaken, nor his seed begging bread.
26 | He is ever merciful, and lendeth; and his seed is blessed.
27 | Depart from evil, and do good; and dwell for evermore.
28 | For the LORD loveth judgment, and forsaketh not his saints; they are preserved for ever: but the seed of the wicked shall be cut off.
29 | The righteous shall inherit the land, and dwell therein forever.
30 | The mouth of the righteous speaketh wisdom, and his tongue talketh of judgment.
31 | The law of his God is in his heart; none of his steps shall slide.
32 | The wicked watcheth the righteous, and seeketh to slay him.
33 | The LORD will not leave him in his hand, nor condemn him when he is judged.
34 | Wait on the LORD, and keep his way, and he shall exalt thee to inherit the land: when the wicked are cut off, thou shalt see it.
35 | I have seen the wicked in great power, and spreading himself like a green bay tree.
36 | Yet he passed away, and, lo, he was not: yea, I sought him, but he could not be found.

37 | Mark the perfect man, and behold the upright: for the end of that man is peace.
38 | But the transgressors shall be destroyed together: the end of the wicked shall be cut off.
39 | But the salvation of the righteous is of the LORD: he is their strength in the time of trouble.
40 | And the LORD shall help them, and deliver them: he shall deliver them from the wicked, and save them, because they trust in him.

PSALM 41
For Emotional and Physical Health

1 | Blessed is he that considereth the poor: the Lord will deliver him in time of trouble.
2 | The Lord will preserve him, and keep him alive; and he shall be blessed upon the earth: and thou wilt not deliver him unto the will of his enemies.
3 | The Lord will strengthen him upon the bed of languishing: thou wilt make all his bed in his sickness.
4 | I said, Lord, be merciful unto me: heal my soul; for I have sinned against thee.
5 | Mine enemies speak evil of me, When shall he die, and his name perish?
6 | And if he come to see me, he speaketh vanity: his heart gathereth iniquity to itself; when he goeth abroad, he telleth it.
7 | All that hate me whisper together against me: against me do they devise my hurt.
8 | An evil disease, say they, cleaveth fast unto him: and now that he lieth he shall rise up no more.
9 | Yea, mine own familiar friend, in whom I trusted, which did eat of my bread, hath lifted up his heel against me.
10 | But thou, O Lord, be merciful unto me, and raise me up, that I may requite them.
11 | By this I know that thou favourest me, because mine enemy doth not triumph over me.

12 And as for me, thou upholdest me in mine integrity, and settest me before thy face for ever.
13 Blessed be the Lord God of Israel from everlasting, and to everlasting. Amen, and Amen.

Psalm 45
To Obtain Love

1 My heart is inditing a good matter: I speak of the things which I have made touching the king: my tongue is the pen of a ready writer.
2 Thou art fairer than the children of men: grace is poured into thy lips: therefore God hath blessed thee for ever.
3 Gird thy sword upon thy thigh, O most mighty, with thy glory and thy majesty.
4 And in thy majesty ride prosperously because of truth and meekness and righteousness; and thy right hand shall teach thee terrible things.
5 Thine arrows are sharp in the heart of the king's enemies; whereby the people fall under thee.
6 Thy throne, O God, is for ever and ever: the sceptre of thy kingdom is a right sceptre.
7 Thou lovest righteousness, and hatest wickedness: therefore God, thy God, hath anointed thee with the oil of gladness above thy fellows.
8 All thy garments smell of myrrh, and aloes, and cassia, out of the ivory palaces, whereby they have made thee glad.
9 Kings' daughters were among thy honourable women: upon thy right hand did stand the queen in gold of Ophir.
10 Hearken, O daughter, and consider, and incline thine ear; forget also thine own people, and thy father's house;
11 So shall the king greatly desire thy beauty: for he is thy Lord; and worship thou him.
12 And the daughter of Tyre shall be there with a gift; even the rich among the people shall intreat thy favour.
13 The king's daughter is all glorious within: her clothing is of wrought gold.
14 She shall be brought unto the king in raiment of needlework: the virgins her companions that follow her shall be brought unto thee.

15 | With gladness and rejoicing shall they be brought: they shall enter into the king's palace.
16 | Instead of thy fathers shall be thy children, whom thou mayest make princes in all the earth.
17 | I will make thy name to be remembered in all generations: therefore shall the people praise thee for ever and ever.

PSALM 51
Forgiveness of Sins

1 | Have mercy upon me, O God, according to thy lovingkindness: according unto the multitude of thy tender mercies blot out my transgressions.
2 | Wash me throughly from mine iniquity, and cleanse me from my sin.
3 | For I acknowledge my transgressions: and my sin is ever before me.
4 | Against thee, thee only, have I sinned, and done this evil in thy sight: that thou mightest be justified when thou speakest, and be clear when thou judgest.
5 | Behold, I was shapen in iniquity; and in sin did my mother conceive me.
6 | Behold, thou desirest truth in the inward parts: and in the hidden part thou shalt make me to know wisdom.
7 | Purge me with hyssop, and I shall be clean: wash me, and I shall be whiter than snow.
8 | Make me to hear joy and gladness; that the bones which thou hast broken may rejoice.
9 | Hide thy face from my sins, and blot out all mine iniquities.
10 | Create in me a clean heart, O God; and renew a right spirit within me.
11 | Cast me not away from thy presence; and take not thy holy spirit from me.
12 | Restore unto me the joy of thy salvation; and uphold me with thy free spirit.
13 | Then will I teach transgressors thy ways; and sinners shall be converted unto thee.
14 | Deliver me from bloodguiltiness, O God, thou God of my salvation: and my tongue shall sing aloud of thy righteousness.
15 | O Lord, open thou my lips; and my mouth shall shew forth thy praise.

16. For thou desirest not sacrifice; else would I give it: thou delightest not in burnt offering.
17. The sacrifices of God are a broken spirit: a broken and a contrite heart, O God, thou wilt not despise.
18. Do good in thy good pleasure unto Zion: build thou the walls of Jerusalem.
19. Then shalt thou be pleased with the sacrifices of righteousness, with burnt offering and whole burnt offering: then shall they offer bullocks upon thine altar.

Psalm 61
For A Long Life

1. Hear my cry, O God; attend unto my prayer.
2. From the end of the earth will I cry unto thee, when my heart is overwhelmed: lead me to the rock that is higher than I.
3. For thou hast been a shelter for me, and a strong tower from the enemy.
4. I will abide in thy tabernacle forever: I will trust in the covert of thy wings. Selah.
5. For thou, O God, hast heard my vows: thou hast given me the heritage of those that fear thy name.
6. Thou wilt prolong the king's life: and his years as many generations.
7. He shall abide before God for ever: O prepare mercy and truth, which may preserve him.
8. So will I sing praise unto thy name for ever, that I may daily perform my vows.

PSALM 91
For Protection

1. He that dwelleth in the secret place of the most High shall abide under the shadow of the Almighty.
2. I will say of the Lord, He is my refuge and my fortress: my God; in him will I trust.
3. Surely he shall deliver thee from the snare of the fowler, and from the noisome pestilence.
4. He shall cover thee with his feathers, and under his wings shalt thou trust: his truth shall be thy shield and buckler.
5. Thou shalt not be afraid for the terror by night; nor for the arrow that flieth by day;
6. Nor for the pestilence that walketh in darkness; nor for the destruction that wasteth at noonday.
7. A thousand shall fall at thy side, and ten thousand at thy right hand; but it shall not come nigh thee.
8. Only with thine eyes shalt thou behold and see the reward of the wicked.
9. Because thou hast made the Lord, which is my refuge, even the most High, thy habitation;
10. There shall no evil befall thee, neither shall any plague come nigh thy dwelling.
11. For he shall give his angels charge over thee, to keep thee in all thy ways.
12. They shall bear thee up in their hands, lest thou dash thy foot against a stone.
13. Thou shalt tread upon the lion and adder: the young lion and the dragon shalt thou trample under feet.
14. Because he hath set his love upon me, therefore will I deliver him: I will set him on high, because he hath known my name.
15. He shall call upon me, and I will answer him: I will be with him in trouble; I will deliver him, and honour him.
16. With long life will I satisfy him, and shew him my salvation.

Psalm 94
To Stop Gossip

1. O Lord God, to whom vengeance belongeth; O God, to whom vengeance belongeth, shew thyself.
2. Lift up thyself, thou judge of the earth: render a reward to the proud.
3. Lord, how long shall the wicked, how long shall the wicked triumph?
4. How long shall they utter and speak hard things? and all the workers of iniquity boast themselves?
5. They break in pieces thy people, O Lord, and afflict thine heritage.
6. They slay the widow and the stranger, and murder the fatherless.
7. Yet they say, The Lord shall not see, neither shall the God of Jacob regard it.
8. Understand, ye brutish among the people: and ye fools, when will ye be wise?
9. He that planted the ear, shall he not hear? he that formed the eye, shall he not see?
10. He that chastiseth the heathen, shall not he correct? he that teacheth man knowledge, shall not he know?
11. The Lord knoweth the thoughts of man, that they are vanity.
12. Blessed is the man whom thou chastenest, O Lord, and teachest him out of thy law;
13. That thou mayest give him rest from the days of adversity, until the pit be digged for the wicked.
14. For the Lord will not cast off his people, neither will he forsake his inheritance.
15. But judgment shall return unto righteousness: and all the upright in heart shall follow it.
16. Who will rise up for me against the evildoers? or who will stand up for me against the workers of iniquity?
17. Unless the Lord had been my help, my soul had almost dwelt in silence.
18. When I said, My foot slippeth; thy mercy, O Lord, held me up.
19. In the multitude of my thoughts within me thy comforts delight my soul.
20. Shall the throne of iniquity have fellowship with thee, which frameth mischief by a law?

21 | They gather themselves together against the soul of the righteous, and condemn the innocent blood.
22 | But the Lord is my defence; and my God is the rock of my refuge.
23 | And he shall bring upon them their own iniquity, and shall cut them off in their own wickedness; yea, the Lord our God shall cut them off.

PSALM 105
To Drive Enemies Away

1 | O give thanks unto the Lord; call upon his name: make known his deeds among the people.
2 | Sing unto him, sing psalms unto him: talk ye of all his wondrous works.
3 | Glory ye in his holy name: let the heart of them rejoice that seek the Lord.
4 | Seek the Lord, and his strength: seek his face evermore.
5 | Remember his marvellous works that he hath done; his wonders, and the judgments of his mouth;
6 | O ye seed of Abraham his servant, ye children of Jacob his chosen.
7 | He is the Lord our God: his judgments are in all the earth.
8 | He hath remembered his covenant for ever, the word which he commanded to a thousand generations.
9 | Which covenant he made with Abraham, and his oath unto Isaac;
10 | And confirmed the same unto Jacob for a law, and to Israel for an everlasting covenant:
11 | Saying, Unto thee will I give the land of Canaan, the lot of your inheritance:
12 | When they were but a few men in number; yea, very few, and strangers in it.
13 | When they went from one nation to another, from one kingdom to another people;
14 | He suffered no man to do them wrong: yea, he reproved kings for their sakes;
15 | Saying, Touch not mine anointed, and do my prophets no harm.
16 | Moreover he called for a famine upon the land: he brake the whole staff of bread.
17 | He sent a man before them, even Joseph, who was sold for a servant:

18 | Whose feet they hurt with fetters: he was laid in iron:
19 | Until the time that his word came: the word of the Lord tried him.
20 | The king sent and loosed him; even the ruler of the people, and let him go free.
21 | He made him lord of his house, and ruler of all his substance:
22 | To bind his princes at his pleasure; and teach his senators wisdom.
23 | Israel also came into Egypt; and Jacob sojourned in the land of Ham.
24 | And he increased his people greatly; and made them stronger than their enemies.
25 | He turned their heart to hate his people, to deal subtilly with his servants.
26 | He sent Moses his servant; and Aaron whom he had chosen.
27 | They shewed his signs among them, and wonders in the land of Ham.
28 | He sent darkness, and made it dark; and they rebelled not against his word.
29 | He turned their waters into blood, and slew their fish.
30 | Their land brought forth frogs in abundance, in the chambers of their kings.
31 | He spake, and there came divers sorts of flies, and lice in all their coasts.
32 | He gave them hail for rain, and flaming fire in their land.
33 | He smote their vines also and their fig trees; and brake the trees of their coasts.
34 | He spake, and the locusts came, and caterpillers, and that without number,
35 | And did eat up all the herbs in their land, and devoured the fruit of their ground.
36 | He smote also all the firstborn in their land, the chief of all their strength.
37 | He brought them forth also with silver and gold: and there was not one feeble person among their tribes.
38 | Egypt was glad when they departed: for the fear of them fell upon them.
39 | He spread a cloud for a covering; and fire to give light in the night.
40 | The people asked, and he brought quails, and satisfied them with the bread of heaven.
41 | He opened the rock, and the waters gushed out; they ran in the dry places like a river.
42 | For he remembered his holy promise, and Abraham his servant.
43 | And he brought forth his people with joy, and his chosen with gladness:
44 | And gave them the lands of the heathen: and they inherited the labour of the people;
45 | That they might observe his statutes, and keep his laws. Praise ye the Lord.

PSALM 109
For Cursing and Crossing

1 | Hold not thy peace, O God of my praise;
2 | For the mouth of the wicked and the mouth of the deceitful are opened against me: they have spoken against me with a lying tongue.
3 | They compassed me about also with words of hatred; and fought against me without a cause.
4 | For my love they are my adversaries: but I give myself unto prayer.
5 | And they have rewarded me evil for good, and hatred for my love.
6 | Set thou a wicked man over him: and let Satan stand at his right hand.
7 | When he shall be judged, let him be condemned: and let his prayer become sin.
8 | Let his days be few; and let another take his office.
9 | Let his children be fatherless, and his wife a widow.
10 | Let his children be continually vagabonds, and beg: let them seek their bread also out of their desolate places.
11 | Let the extortioner catch all that he hath; and let the strangers spoil his labour.
12 | Let there be none to extend mercy unto him: neither let there be any to favour his fatherless children.
13 | Let his posterity be cut off; and in the generation following let their name be blotted out.
14 | Let the iniquity of his fathers be remembered with the Lord; and let not the sin of his mother be blotted out.
15 | Let them be before the Lord continually, that he may cut off the memory of them from the earth.
16 | Because that he remembered not to shew mercy, but persecuted the poor and needy man, that he might even slay the broken in heart.
17 | As he loved cursing, so let it come unto him: as he delighted not in blessing, so let it be far from him.
18 | As he clothed himself with cursing like as with his garment, so let it come into his bowels like water, and like oil into his bones.
19 | Let it be unto him as the garment which covereth him, and for a girdle wherewith he is girded continually.

20 | Let this be the reward of mine adversaries from the Lord, and of them that speak evil against my soul.
21 | But do thou for me, O God the Lord, for thy name's sake: because thy mercy is good, deliver thou me.
22 | For I am poor and needy, and my heart is wounded within me.
23 | I am gone like the shadow when it declineth: I am tossed up and down as the locust.
24 | My knees are weak through fasting; and my flesh faileth of fatness.
25 | I became also a reproach unto them: when they looked upon me they shaked their heads.
26 | Help me, O Lord my God: O save me according to thy mercy:
27 | That they may know that this is thy hand; that thou, Lord, hast done it.
28 | Let them curse, but bless thou: when they arise, let them be ashamed; but let thy servant rejoice.
29 | Let mine adversaries be clothed with shame, and let them cover themselves with their own confusion, as with a mantle.
30 | I will greatly praise the Lord with my mouth; yea, I will praise him among the multitude.
31 | For he shall stand at the right hand of the poor, to save him from those that condemn his soul.

PSALM 121
To Repel Evil Entities

1 | I will lift up mine eyes unto the hills, from whence cometh my help.
2 | My help cometh from the LORD, which made heaven and earth.
3 | He will not suffer thy foot to be moved: he that keepeth thee will not slumber.
4 | Behold, he that keepeth Israel shall neither slumber nor sleep.
5 | The LORD is thy keeper: the LORD is thy shade upon thy right hand.
6 | The sun shall not smite thee by day, nor the moon by night.
7 | The LORD shall preserve thee from all evil: he shall preserve thy soul.
8 | The LORD shall preserve thy going out and thy coming in from this time forth, and even for evermore.

PSALM 133
For Friendship

1 | Behold, how good and how pleasant it is for brethren to dwell together in unity!
2 | It is like the precious ointment upon the head, that ran down upon the beard, even Aaron's beard: that went down to the skirts of his garments;
3 | As the dew of Hermon, and as the dew that descended upon the mountains of Zion: for there the Lord commanded the blessing, even life for evermore.

PSALM 145
For Blessings

1 | I will extol thee, my God, O king; and I will bless thy name for ever and ever.
2 | Every day will I bless thee; and I will praise thy name for ever and ever.
3 | Great is the Lord, and greatly to be praised; and his greatness is unsearchable.
4 | One generation shall praise thy works to another, and shall declare thy mighty acts.
5 | I will speak of the glorious honour of thy majesty, and of thy wondrous works.
6 | And men shall speak of the might of thy terrible acts: and I will declare thy greatness.
7 | They shall abundantly utter the memory of thy great goodness, and shall sing of thy righteousness.
8 | The Lord is gracious, and full of compassion; slow to anger, and of great mercy.
9 | The Lord is good to all: and his tender mercies are over all his works.

10	All thy works shall praise thee, O Lord; and thy saints shall bless thee.
11	They shall speak of the glory of thy kingdom, and talk of thy power;
12	To make known to the sons of men his mighty acts, and the glorious majesty of his kingdom.
13	Thy kingdom is an everlasting kingdom, and thy dominion endureth throughout all generations.
14	The Lord upholdeth all that fall, and raiseth up all those that be bowed down.
15	The eyes of all wait upon thee; and thou givest them their meat in due season.
16	Thou openest thine hand, and satisfiest the desire of every living thing.
17	The Lord is righteous in all his ways, and holy in all his works.
18	The Lord is nigh unto all them that call upon him, to all that call upon him in truth.
19	He will fulfil the desire of them that fear him: he also will hear their cry, and will save them.
20	The Lord preserveth all them that love him: but all the wicked will he destroy.
21	My mouth shall speak the praise of the Lord: and let all flesh bless his holy name for ever and ever. Amen.

Conclusion

It seems as if writing a book is similar to parenthood. The author has a book idea and gives it birth through the introduction. As the chapters progress, the book grows from infancy to its late years. Finally, once the book is completed, the author is then left solely with memories of a sentimental journey, joined by all of you.

But, what a journey it has been! Together, we have time-travelled from the days of the Stone Age periods, and proceeded forward throughout the centuries, while learning how our ancestors struggled to create a flawless portable lamp. From torches and oil lamps, to disgusting types of candle wax, and finally to perfection, it was not an easy task!

While following our ancestors, we were introduced to the spirit of fire. Together, we learned all about the nature of this phenomenal entity. We now have a deeper understanding of his endless role in our lives, his language, and his willingness to help all of us.

Once we became aware of the metaphysical intricacies within the union between fire and candles, we proceeded to examine almost every aspect of candle magic. In doing so, we have enlightened ourselves in the quest toward becoming formidable spellcasters.

Finally, we explored numerous figural candle types. The complimentary spellwork, fitting to their images, helped us to optimally utilize these candles. Also, with the help of both the spirit of Fire, and members of our spiritual court, we are now able to heighten our chances of successful spell manifestation.

So, together, we have engaged in a wealth of exploration. Whew! I hope you've enjoyed reading this book as much as I've enjoyed researching the history and sharing my decades of knowledge with you. Thank you for joining me in this incredible journey. May God/Goddess bless all of you.

- Miss Aida

APPENDIX A
Recommended Shops

If you're looking to purchase figural candles for the spells in this book, here are a list of shops I can personally recommend!

3 CROWS CONJURE
7210 Madison Avenue, Indianapolis, Indiana
(317) 992-7606
3crowsconjure.com

CROW HAVEN CORNER
125 Essex Street, Salem, Massachusetts
(978) 745-8763
CrowHavenCorner.com

HEX: OLD WORLD WITCHERY
184 Essex Street, Salem, Massachusetts
(978) 666-0765

1219 Decatur Street, New Orleans, Lousiana
(504) 613-0558

HexWitch.com

WHITERAVEN & WITCH'S LAIR
WhiteRavenandWitchsLair.com

BIBLIOGRAPHY.

Aida, Miss. *Cursing and Crossing: Hoodoo Spells to Torment, Jinx, and Take Revenge on Your Enemies.* Forestville, California: Lucky Mojo Curio Company, 2017.

———. *Destroying Relationships: Hoodoo Spells to Break Up, Separate, Hot Foot, and Drive Off Your Foes and Rivals.* Forestville, California: Lucky Mojo Curio Company, 2018.

———. *Hoodoo Cleansing and Protection Magic: Banish Negative Energies and Ward off Unpleasant People.* Newburyport, Massachusetts: Weiser Books, 2020.

———. *Hoodoo Justice Magic: Spells for Power, Protection and Righteous Vindication.* Newburyport, Massachusetts: Weiser Books, 2021.

———. *Traditional Hoodoo & Conjure: A Handbook of Spirits, Spells, & Rootwork.* Chicago, Illinois: Crossed Crow Books, 2025.

———. MissAida.Com.

"The 1997 Fire." Shroud.Com.

Annus, Amar, et al. *Divination and Interpretation of Signs in the Ancient World.* Chicago, Illinois: The University of Chicago, 2010.

BibleGateway.Com.

Braun, Amy LCPC. "50 Prayers To Conceive: Powerful Prayers For Getting Pregnant." AmyBraunLCPC.Com.

"Bullying." PsychologyToday.Com.

"Candle Fire Statistics." NFPA.Org.

"Carromancy." Wikipedia.Org.

"Ceroscopy." Encyclopedia.Com.

"Chartres Burned But Relic Survived." Christianity.Org.

"Clarke's Fairy Lamp Candles." Collector'sWeekly.Com.

"Conflicting Crystals: Bad Combos To Avoid." MarouthJewels.Com.

Conklin, Edward, PhD. *In The Beginning: A New Theory Of The First Religion.* Independently Published, 2014.

Cunningham, Scott. *Cunningham's Encyclopedia of Magical Herbs.* Woodbury, Minnesota: Llewellyn Publications, 2009.

"Description and History of Oil Lamps." *MilwaukeePublicMuseum.Edu.*

DirectFromLourdes.Com (source of holy water).

"Exploring The Celestial Meaning Of The Stars: Uncovering The Symbolism Of A Star." StarRegistry.Com.

"Fairy Lamp." *Wikipedia.Org.*

Fenton, Sasha. *Tea Cup Reading: A Quick and Easy Guide to Tasseography.* York Beach, Maine: Red Wheel/Weiser, LLC, 2002.

Forlong, J.G.R. *Fire Worship*. Whitefish, Montana: Kessinger Publishing, (Reprint 2005).

"History of Candle Use." *Candles.Org*.

"The History of Candle-Making." BottleStore.Com.

The Holy Bible, King James Version, Rev. Edition, Thomas Nelson, Inc., 1976.

Jackson, Michael. "Beat it." *Thriller*. Epic Records, 1982.

Gimbutas, Marija. *The Language of the Goddess: Unearthing the Hidden Symbols of Western Civilization*. San Francisco: Harper & Row, 1989.

Lauper, Cyndi. "Girls Just Want to Have Fun." Portrait Records, 1983.

"The Magic Of Candle Wax Divination." WitchesLore.Com.

"The Magic of Fairy Lamps." Glanmore.ca.

Mahmud, Zeeshan. *Fire Worship Throughout History*. Independently Published, 2024.

Melody. *Love is in The Earth: A Kaleidoscope Of Crystals Updated*. Wheat Ridge, Colorado: Earth-Love Publishing House, 2002.

Morgan, John H., PhD. *In The Beginning: The Paleolithic Origins of Religious Consciousness*. N. Fort Myers, Florida: Wyndham Hall Press, 2021.

"Mouse Symbolism." WorldBirds.Com.

"Oil Lamp." Wikipedia.Org.

"Powerful Prayers For Wisdom." DivineDisclosure.com.

"Prayers For Abundance, Prosperity, Money, and Wealth." OurFatherPrayer.Org.

"Prayers For Studying And Exams." Xavier.Edu.

"Prayer To St Roche for a Sick Dog." YourPrayersNow.Com.

Rodgers, Ann. *Fire Captain Makes Way Through Ruins of Incinerated Church to Find Tabernacle Intact*: Cathstan.Org.

Ryan, The Reverend Edwin, D.D. *Candles In The Roman Rite*. Faribault, Minnesota: A. Gross Candle Co., Inc., 1933.

"Saint's Relics Survive Fire That Destroyed Village Church." OrthoChristian.Com.

Smithsonian Books. *Do All Indians Live in Tipis?* Washington, D.C. Smithsonian Books for The National Museum Of The American Indian Smithsonian Institution, 2019.

Stephens, D.R.T. *Sacred Flames: Fire Worship in Various Pagan Traditions*. Independently Published, 2023.

Wightman, Gregory J., PhD. *The Origins of Religion in The Paleolithic*. Lanham, Maryland: The Rowman & Littlefield Publishing Group, Inc., 2015.

Yronwode, Catherine. *Hoodoo Herb and Root Magic: A Materia Magica of African-American Conjure*. Forestville, California: Lucky Mojo Curio Company, 2002.

INDEX

A
abusive relationships: 91
altars: 37-38
angel candle: 79, 82
angels: 80-81
Anglin, Captain Robert: 51-52, 54
animal candle: 84
ankh candle: 85
anointing a candle: 35
Archangels
 ▸ Gabriel: 80, 184
 ▸ Michael: 80, 97-98, 184, 194
 ▸ Rafael: 80
archangels: 80, 82-83, 185
aura: 13, 20, 23

B
bear candle: 92
beeswax (see: wax)
Bible: 109-110
blessing and baptizing a candle: 34
brain, human
 ▸ frontal lobe: 149
 ▸ occipital lobe: 150
 ▸ parietal lobes: 150
 ▸ temporal lobes: 150
bride & groom candle: 86
butterfly candle: 93

C
candle colors: 30-31
 ▸ black: 31
 ▸ blue: 31
 ▸ brown: 31
 ▸ gold: 31, 210
 ▸ green: 31
 ▸ orange: 31
 ▸ purple: 31
 ▸ red: 31
 ▸ silver: 31
 ▸ white: 31
 ▸ yellow: 31

candle dressings
 ▸ abre camino: 109
 ▸ acacia: 155
 ▸ agrimony: 23, 98, 102
 ▸ alfalfa: 108, 123, 141
 ▸ all heal/self heal: 85, 107, 122, 160
 ▸ althaea leaves: 106
 ▸ althea: 85, 122, 137, 160
 ▸ alum: 128, 133, 162
 ▸ angelic root powder: 106
 ▸ angelica: 85, 106, 122, 147, 160
 ▸ angelica root: 147
 ▸ asafoetida: 101, 115, 133, 148, 169
 ▸ balm of gilead: 152
 ▸ basil: 89
 ▸ bay laurel: 104, 122, 127
 ▸ bayberry root: 108, 123, 141
 ▸ benzoin: 113
 ▸ black cohosh: 113
 ▸ black or brown mustard seeds: 96, 121
 ▸ black snake root: 91
 ▸ blood root: 175
 ▸ blue flag: 108, 123, 141
 ▸ blueberries: 96, 121
 ▸ boneset leaves: 106
 ▸ borage: 89
 ▸ buchu: 155, 163
 ▸ burdock root: 137
 ▸ cactus spines: 96, 121
 ▸ calamus/sweet flag: 133
 ▸ caraway seeds: 88
 ▸ cascara sagrada: 106
 ▸ cedar wood: 145, 167
 ▸ celandine: 106
 ▸ chia seed: 128
 ▸ chickweed: 89
 ▸ chicory root: 96, 121
 ▸ cinnamon: 89, 107, 130, 161
 ▸ cinquefoil: 113

- cloves: 120
- copal: 147, 155, 163
- coriander seeds: 100
- couch grass: 91
- cubeb berries: 117
- damiana: 88, 107, 130, 161
- dill: 103, 137, 152
- dittany of crete: 89, 100, 107, 130, 161, 175
- dried pink or red rose petals: 100, 103
- dried red rose petals: 142
- earth smoke/fumitory: 108, 123, 141
- eucalyptus: 23, 25, 95, 98, 102, 114, 125
- forget-me-not: 89, 120, 152
- ginseng: 175
- glitter and frankincense: 157
- golden seal: 152
- jezebel root: 175
- johnny jump-up: 168, 175
- knot weed: 168
- knotweed: 154
- lavender leaves: 145, 167
- lemon grass: 109
- lemon verbena: 91
- licorice root: 133
- life everlasting: 86
- lovage root: 117
- lucky bamboo leaves: 175
- mace: 175
- marjoram: 88
- master of the woods: 94, 123, 133
- master root: 94, 104, 122, 127
- mugwort: 155
- mullein: 93, 105
- myrtle: 87-88, 117, 145, 168, 173, 176
- passionflower: 88, 117, 168, 173, 176
- peach tree leaves: 134
- peony: 152
- pink rose pedals: 120
- poppy seeds: 91
- rat poison: 138
- rattlesnake grass: 123
- red clover: 87, 145
- red pepper: 96, 121, 166, 169-170
- red rose petals: 100, 103, 142, 144, 159, 168
- rose petals: 100, 103, 117, 142, 144, 159, 168
- rosemary: 23, 25, 98, 102
- rue: 23, 25, 94-95, 98, 102, 114, 125
- sage: 135
- salt peter: 138
- sampson snake root: 93, 105
- sampson snakeroot: 137
- self-heal/all heal: 85, 107, 122, 160
- shame brier: 106
- slippery elm: 128
- snake weed: 113
- squaw vine: 112
- vanilla bean: 144, 168
- verbena/vervain: 91, 103
- wintergreen: 137
- yarrow: 93, 105

candle holders: 55, 87-88, 90, 100, 112, 133, 144
capnomancy: 59, 70-71
cardinal directions: 59-61
- east: 60, 62
- north: 60-61
- south: 60
- west: 60-61

cat candle: 94
Catholic Church: 21, 50
ceromancy: 73-74
ceroscopy: 73
citrine: 19
cleansing a candle: 33
coffin candle: 95
color (see: candle colors)
condition oil: 84, 103, 119, 132, 147
Cro-Magnon: 4-6

cross candle: 97
crystals: 19

D
days of the week
- 1_Sunday: 42
- 2_Monday: 42
- 3_Tuesday: 43
- 4_Wednesday: 43
- 5_Thursday: 43
- 6_Friday: 44
- 7_Saturday: 44

deployment: 177-178, 180
diaspora practices, African: 6, 36
divination: 65, 67, 73-74
dog candle: 99
dogs/cats: 16
domination: 132, 135
double-action candle: 100
dove candle: 109
dressing a candle: 35
dressings (see: candle dressings)
Druids: 47, 112

E
eclipse (solar or lunar): 40
egg candle: 111
eggs: 111
energy output: 16-17
entities: 6, 15, 17, 42, 64, 67, 124

F
fairy lamps: 10
fire extinguisher: 55, 57
fire safety: 32, 49, 53, 55
fire statistics: 54
Fire, formidable nature of: 50
Fire, fostering nature of: 47
Fire, the element of: 3, 5, 8, 46-51, 54-55, 65-66, 69, 179
Fire, the language of: 3-6, 37, 46-49, 51-57, 59, 70-71, 210, 215
firefighter: 50-51, 57-58
flame, the behavior of: 65-67
Florida Water: 20-22

four-leaf clover candle: 112

G
Gabriel, Saint (see: archangels)
gargoyle candle: 113
ghost candle: 114
gods, goddesses, and deities: 3, 18-19, 21, 23, 31, 34, 42-45, 49-50, 58, 60, 79, 109, 139, 152, 157, 179, 185-186, 188, 191, 194-197, 204-206, 208-209, 212, 215
golden Rules: 12-15
good luck: 31, 77, 112-113, 134, 200

H
heart candle: 116
heat, convective: 52
heat, radiant: 52
herbal waters: 22
herbs (see: dressings)
Holy Water: 21-22, 97
human candle: 119

I
incense: 147, 196
inscribing a candle: 33

J
jack-o'-lantern candle: 124

K
knife: 91, 131

L
legal matters: 31, 106, 190
lip candle: 125
lodestone: 166, 170-171, 174-175
lovers candle: 117, 128

M
magnetic sand: 166, 170-171, 174-175
male candle: 175
Mercury in retrograde: 40
Michael, Saint (see: archangels)
moon phases

- full moon: 41-42
  - full moon closest to Halloween: 42
  - full moon in your moon sign: 42
- waning moon: 41
- waxing moon: 41

mouse candle: 132-133
moving candle spells: 164

N
naming a candle: 32, 34, 84, 119
negative spellwork: 26, 38

O
oil lamps: 6-7
olive oil: 24, 35, 81-82, 84, 97, 103, 110-111, 119, 126, 132, 140, 147, 170
owl candle: 134

P
Paleolithic era: 4
paraffin (see: wax)
pareidolia: 74-75
penis candle: 135
personal concerns: 26, 39, 84, 92, 96, 99, 136, 162
- blood: 39, 175, 209-210
- dandruff: 39
- earwax: 39
- feces: 39, 131, 169
- fingernails: 39
- hair: 26, 39, 48
- mucus: 39
- saliva: 39
- scabs: 39
- semen: 39, 129, 161, 174
- skin cells: 39
- sweat: 39
- tears: 39, 76
- teeth: 39, 201
- toenails: 39
- urine: 39, 132-133, 153-154
- vaginal secretions: 39, 111, 129, 161, 174

petition paper: 37, 90, 111, 115, 142, 147, 166
- preparing: 36

planets
- 1_Sun: 42
- 2_Moon: 42
- 3_Mars: 43
- 4_Mercury: 43
- 5_Jupiter: 43
- 6_Venus: 44
- 7_Saturn: 44

plants (see: dressings)
popping sounds: 64
prayer: 183
prayers
- for a favor: 110, 189
- for all animals: 85, 193
- for beauty and grace: 185
- for cats: 85, 193
- for clear communication: 104, 127, 184
- for communication: 126, 186
- for connecting to the metaphysical: 187
- for courage and strength: 93, 105, 187
- for court cases: 106, 190
- for divine power: 163, 187
- for dogs: 85, 195
- for empowerment and strength: 157, 196
- for fertility and conception: 112, 186
- for guidance and/or protection: 81-82, 188
- for interfaith wedding vows: 87, 145, 189
- for intimacy with spouse: 89, 130, 189
- for loyalty and faithfulness: 100, 190
- for lust: 136, 161, 197
- for money: 123, 141, 191

- for novena to god the father: 191
- for protection by gargoyle: 114, 188
- for protection of St. Michael: 194
- for reconciliation: 152, 192
- for sex workers: 176, 196
- for test-taking: 135, 196
- for traditional Irish blessing: 113, 197
- for victory: 193
- for wisdom: 135, 198
- for wisdom in relationships: 135, 198
- for wishing: 83
- to break up a relationship: 91, 131, 173, 185
- to escape physical or spiritual slavery: 194
- to open the roads: 195
- to restore sexuality: 107, 137, 192

praying hands candle: 139
priming a candle: 32
Psalms
- for a long life: 86, 206
- for blessings: 147, 213
- for cursing and crossing: 96, 121, 138, 162, 211
- for emotional and physical health: 89, 107, 115, 122, 137, 152, 160, 203
- for friendship: 120, 213
- for protection: 25, 207
- for uncrossing and to bring money: 24, 102, 108, 137, 201
- forgiveness of sins: 24, 205
- to bind enemies: 25, 95-96, 120-121, 125, 128, 133, 138, 147-148, 154, 162, 170, 199-200, 209, 211-213
- to bless an item and for general good luck: 22, 200
- to drive enemies away: 148, 170, 209
- to obtain love: 88, 103, 117, 119, 142-143, 168, 204
- to repel evil entities: 25, 95, 125, 212
- to stop gossip: 25, 95, 125, 128, 200, 208, 212

pyramid candle: 140
pyromancy: 59, 65

R
Rafael, Saint (see: archangels)
roots (see: dressings)
rose candle: 141

S
Saints: 45
same gender marriage candle: 143
Santería: 7, 25-28, 50
seven knob wishing candle: 145
skull candle: 149
smoke, the behavior of (see: capnomancy)
snake candle: 152-153
soap: 23
soldering iron: 96, 160-162
sound: 17
spell
- for a honey jar: 118
- for a man to attract a man: 167
- for a man to attract a woman: 168
- for a woman to attract a man: 168
- for a woman to attract a woman: 168
- for attraction: 103
- for beauty and grace: 157
- for blessings: 146
- for courage: 104
- for courage and emotional strength: 92
- for court case obstacles: 105
- for cursing and crossing: 120
- for dominance over bullies: 132

- for empowerment and strength: 156
- for fertility: 111
- for freedom: 93
- for general attraction: 119
- for good luck: 113
- for healing: 84, 121, 160
- for healing the vagina: 160
- for health matters: 106
- for home protection: 114
- for justifiable revenge: 95
- for long life: 85
- for love with a floating heart candle: 118
- for love with a large heart candle: 117
- for loyalty: 99
- for mastery and power: 122
- for money: 108, 123, 140
- for protection with a cross candle: 97
- for reconciliation: 150
- for separating a heterosexual relationship: 170
- for sex worker's better business: 173
- for uncrossing: 101, 103-109
- for wisdom and passing exams: 134
- for wishing upon the archangels: 82-83
- spell for guardian angel veneration: 80
- spell for guidance from guardian angels: 81
- to arouse lust from another: 135
- to attract love with floating rose candles: 143
- to attract love with large rose candles: 142
- to banish haunting memories: 115
- to bind an enemy: 153
- to break up a marriage: 89
- to break up to affair: 130
- to connect to the metaphysical: 155
- to curse a woman's vagina: 162
- to enhance love in a marriage: 87-89
- to enhance lust in a marriage: 88
- to improve your communication: 103
- to incite a lover: 128
- to incite lust in a woman: 161
- to increase your powers as a magician: 163
- to induce impotence: 137
- to inspire marital commitment: 86
- to invoke the holy spirit for favors: 110
- to mend a broken marriage: 89
- to obtain eloquent speech: 126
- to open the roads: 108
- to petition god: 139
- to protect from negative forces: 94
- to receive communication: 125
- to restore lust: 107
- to restore sexual virility: 136
- to scare away malicious spirits: 124
- to send someone away: 147
- to stop gossip: 127

spirits: 124, 156, 178
spiritual cleansing: 24
spiritual court, getting assistance from: 44
spiritual protection: 24
- protection amulets for: 25
- protection oils for: 25
- protection waters for: 25

star candle: 154
statistics, candle fire: 54
strategy for spellwork: 40
sun candle: 156
symbolism: 78, 111, 114, 139

T
taglocks (see: personal concerns)
tallow (see: wax)
test-taking: 135, 196
tools, basic: 32

V
venus candle: 157-158
vulva/vagina candle: 159

W
wax: 7, 9-10, 32-33, 55, 59, 61, 63-64, 73-77, 126, 136, 151, 154, 165
- ▸ beeswax: 7-9
- ▸ paraffin: 6-7, 10
- ▸ tallow: 7-10
- ▸ the shape of: 73-74

wick, trimming: 33
wind: 197
witch candle: 163

About Miss Aida

Witch, author, and teacher of the metaphysical, Miss Aida was born into a Cuban family that practiced Brujería, Santería, and Palo. An initiate of these traditions herself, she is also a natural-born psychic medium and a renowned Hoodoo practitioner, specializing in spirit eradications, spiritual cleansings, and protection.

Miss Aida has appeared on Warner Bros. Discovery and Discover+, The Travel Channel, HBO MAX, Court TV (as an expert metaphysical practitioner), and independent hit films such as *"A Haunting On Adams Street."* She has been a guest on numerous radio shows, including Coast to Coast AM and The Best of Coast to Coast AM.

She is also a Registered Nurse, a proud United States Air Force Veteran, and holds a Master's of Science degree.

You can find Miss Aida on her website MissAida.com and on Facebook at Facebook.com/MissAidaPsychic

Warlock Press™

WarlockPress.com

Warlock Press is an independent occult publisher that is driven to provide unequalled content written by a diverse roster of today's magical adepts. Our authors hail from a spectrum of magical traditions, but share crucial things in common: authentic practice, established credentials, thorough research, and genuine devotion. This means that you can trust that you are getting the very capstone of the pyramid of occult wisdom.

THE RELIGION OF WITCHCRAFT
Brian Cain
Foreword by Jimahl DiFiosa
Witchcraft is both a religion and a myth. It is a secret society, a fertility cult, a mystery cult, and a Priesthood. The Initiatory culture of Witchcraft spans generations, representing the lives of thousands of our forebears. After thousands of years of suppression, the Witch, the Priestess, reclaims her role, returning that lost power and holy presence to Western civilization once again.

INITIATION INTO WITCHCRAFT
Brian Cain
Foreword by Maxine Sanders
This is a book about the religion of Witchcraft. It honors the old Gods, the ancient mysteries, and the secrets of magic. It is an exploration of the timeless traditions, essential ethics, and the awe-inspiring power of our Craft and provides basic practices that will help the reader to embrace the deeper ways of the Witch. It is a signpost for those seeking the path that begins the journey of initiation into Witchcraft and primer of occult techniques and rituals to prepare for that journey.

THE WITCHES' BOOK OF THE DEAD
Christian Day
Foreword by Laurie Cabot

The revised and expanded tenth-anniversary edition of this genre changing classic is available August, 2021. Readers will learn to summon and honor the spirits of the dead to bring blessings in their everyday lives, discover Witches of legend who raised the dead, and explore methods of spirit contact, necromancy, potent rituals, recipes, and exercises, and features two new chapters, new foreword, and a new preface!

MOTHER: ECSTASY, TRANSFORMATION, AND THE GREAT GODDESS
Levi Rowland
Foreword by H. Byron Ballard

The Great Goddess is reclaiming her place as the preeminent force of life and creation. Devotion to Mother is a transformative experience. No matter what incarnation we invoke, she comes. She breathes into life, echoing the prayers and incantations of every initiator, Witch, believer, and devotee that has ever stood at her shrine and felt her presence, as real as anything under the sun (or beyond it). In her worship, in her magic, in her dance, is a living spiritual tradition, drawing from many sources but still focused on one multifaceted absolute. This book is a guide to the seeker who wishes to live a life turned towards the altar of the Great Goddess. Drawing from history but firmly rooted in the modern search for God the Mother, readers will be taken on an exploration of Goddess religion as a lived experience, an endless source of transformation and growth.

LIVING THE ELEMENTS: EXTREME ADVENTURES FOR WITCHES
Fiona Horne

Join world traveling rockstar Witch, Fiona Horne and experience the sacred elements of Witchcraft in an action-packed, dynamic way that enlivens every fiber of your being and supercharges your spell casting. Air, Earth, Fire, Water, and Spirit are at the core of magickal work and in this unique book, Fiona gives you the advice you need to invoke your most empowered self. Fiona's personal stories entertain, enchant, and educate. She gives you the tools to get out of your comfort zones, stretch your boundaries and let go of limitations. Fiona offers three activity levels, Transcendent, Potent and Passionate—choose one or work through all three—from visiting waterfalls to freediving, kite flying to skydiving, firedancing to volcano climbing, dark retreats to stargazing. Whatever your physical or financial conditions, Living the Elements will change your life!

VOODOO AND AFRICAN TRADITIONAL RELIGION
Lilith Dorsey

Journey beyond the basic tenets of the faiths of the African diaspora to the vibrant, living spirit world of their peoples. This seminal guide to African spirituality has been revised and expanded to include tools for activists to empower their work for social change with the wisdom of their ancestors, as well as never-before-published recipes, personal spells and charms, such as root magick for protection and protest, and devotional rituals readers can perform themselves.

THE ART COSMIC: THE MAGIC OF TRADITIONAL ASTROLOGY
Levi Rowland
Foreword by Sorita d'Este

A detailed guide to the fundamentals of planetary magic using the seven sacred spheres of the ancients, including a system of celestial correspondences to use as a basis for meaningful spells, rituals, and workings. Readers will learn how to interpret natal charts using timeless methods of traditional astrology, use horary astrology for divination, incorporate the planetary hours for more successful spell work, and perform potent magical rites for each planet.

www.ingramcontent.com/pod-product-compliance
Lightning Source LLC
Chambersburg PA
CBHW072152070526
44585CB00015B/1111